Records of the Closeburn Kirkpatricks

Closeburn Castle

Records of the Closeburn Kirkpatricks

by
Major-General
Charles Kirkpatrick, C.B., C.B.E.

Glasgow
The Grimsay Press
2003

The Grimsay Press
an imprint of
Zeticula
57 St Vincent Crescent
Glasgow
G3 8NQ

http://www.thegrimsaypress.co.uk
admin@thegrimsaypress.co.uk

First published 2004

Copyright © Mrs. May Butler, Ivone, Roger, Susan, John,
Charles and Grizelda Kirkpatrick 2004

Previously printed for private distribution
in Great Britain in 1954

ISBN 0 902664 05 0 Hardback
ISBN 0 902664 78 6 Paperback

Contents

List of illustrations, 7
Foreword, 9
Preface, 11

1. Traditional origin of the Closeburn family, 19

2. The Closeburn family records, 27

3. First Charter of Closeburn, 35

4. Earliest recorded history of Closeburn, 37

5. Early history of the Torthorwald branch, 45

6. The Period of King Robert the Bruce, 51

7. Some family relationships after Bannockburn, 59

8. Caerlaverock, 67

9. The Succession continued, 75

10. Closeburn Castle, 105

11. The last of the Torthorwald and Ross Kirkpatricks, 117

12. The Baronetcy of Closeburn, 127

Appendices

Appendix I. Genealogical tables of the Kirkpatricks of Closeburn, 143

Appendix II. Our own family story, 149

Appendix II a. Captain A.W. Beauchamp Proctor, V.C., D.S.O., M.C., D.F.C., 153

Appendix III. Heraldry, 157.

Appendix IV. Coat of Arms of Kirkpatrick of Closeburn (Nisbet's Heraldic Plates), 161

Appendix V. Collateral branches of Closeburn, 163

Appendix VI. Closeburn and the Empress Eugenie of France, 169

Appendix VI a. Copy of Patent, 181

Appendix VI b. The Conheath connection according to Dr. Clapperton, 185

Appendix VI c. Extract from a Letter addressed to Sir Thos. Kirkpatrick, 187

Appendix VI d. Table Giving Births and Deaths of William Escott Kirkpatrick's children, 189

Appendix VI e. Extract from a Letter of William Escott Kirkpatrick, 191

Appendix VI f. Copy of Extracts of a letter to the Editor ... , 193

Appendix VI g. The Irish Kirkpatricks' History, 195

Appendix VII. In the days of "John Company", 197

Appendix VIII. Addendum, with Table of Early Ancestors, 201

Appendix IX. Paper read to the Dumfriesshire and Galloway Antiquarian Society on 18th December, 1953, 205

Index of Place Names, 229

List of Illustrations, Charts, Tables, etc

Closeburn Castle, *opposite Title Page*

First Charter, *34*

Family Tree around the time of Bannockburn, *61*

Facsimile Charter, *81*

Sir Thomas Kirkpatrick, 3rd Baronet, *97*

Wrought Iron Gate at Closeburn Castle, *104*

Sir James Kirkpatrick, 4th Baronet, *130*

Sir Thomas Kirkpatrick, 5th Baronet, *132*

Kirkpatrick Coat of Arms, *156*

Table of Connections between Closeburn,
Isle of Wight and Conheath Kirkpatricks, *182.*

Table of Possible Early Birth Dates, *203*

Foreword

I have written this book for two reasons.

The first, the obvious one, mentioned in the preface, is to leave some coherent record of our history for my descendants.

The second reason is the need to correct some erroneous statements concerning the Closeburn family history made by writers who obviously have not had access to family records which I refer to in these pages.

I had written the major portion of this book and included an early chapter dealing with this matter, when I found a long article entitled "The Early Kirkpatricks" published in July, 1953, which demanded a much fuller reply.

I then decided it was best to allow this history to stand as already reproduced; to complete it and to reserve a fuller comment and criticism for the end of this book, as an Addendum, Appendix VIII.

The history left without the above introductory notes, thus contains some allusions to matters, which later form the subject of comment, so requiring some mention here.

Briefly these are:-

1. The fundamental errors made in the report of the Historical M.S.S. Commission for Scotland, 1881, Vol. XV regarding the Closeburn Kirkpatricks, where it was stated that:-

(a) The Kirkpatrick traditions have connected this family with Nithsdale at an earlier date than is warranted by Charter evidence.

(b) All the Closeburn Charters were lost in the fire of 1748.

2. Articles written thereafter have stated that the claim of the Closeburn Kirkpatricks to be the main line of the family is wrong.

That there was a senior branch of Kirkpatricks in Annandale, which died out at the close of the 15th Century, whereupon the Closeburn Kirkpatricks adopted the traditions and motto which rightly belonged to the extinct senior stem of the Kirkpatrick family.

These statements, amounting to a negation of the traditions and history of the Kirkpatricks of Closeburn as maintained by the family, and set forth in this book, cannot be left unchallenged or unexplained and I have been at some pains to discover the origin of these misrepresentations.

Bearing this in mind, the reader will, I think, read, with the more interest, the story as it unfolds, and make his own judgement thereon.

Preface

I have always been much interested in our family history, but, until I retired from the army in 1935, I had not the leisure to devote to its study.

I now find myself left as the sole male representative of my generation of the branch of the Closeburn family descended from my great grandfather Sir James Kirkpatrick, the 4th Baronet of Closeburn, Dumfriesshire.

Consequently I have come into possession of, or have had access to, a considerable number of important family documents which have remained uncollated, while the history of Closeburn has not been written up in this family since 1858. The present head of the family is Sir James Kirkpatrick, the 10th Baronet, who is resident in Kenya.

I have felt it my duty therefore to try and bring the history up to date, by referring to these and other available records in this country, for the benefit of my children and grandchildren, who have a long line of ancestors to be proud of, because of their unfailing loyalty to King and Country through the centuries.

That story needs to be told, and to do so, I must first explain the relationships of our branch of Closeburn.

My great grandfather, Sir James Kirkpatrick, the 4th Baronet, who died in 1804 had two sons. The oldest, Thomas, succeeded his father as 5th Baronet, becoming Sheriff of Dumfries.

The second son, Roger, Collector of Cess for the county of Dumfries, was my grandfather.

He married Lilias, daughter of Robert Anderson of Stroquham. By her he had four sons and two daughters.

The eldest son, James, my father, became Deputy Surgeon General in the Honourable East India Company's Service, and he died in 1890.

My mother was Margaret Proctor, daughter of William Proctor of Co. Kilkenny, Ireland and Drooge Vlei, South Africa; Formerly Lietenant in H.M. 21st Light Dragoons.

My parents had five sons and five daughters. I alone survive, as youngest of that family.

Only one of my father's three brothers married, Roger, whose wife was Isabella Kirkpatrick of the Isle of Wight branch.

They had three sons and two daughters and all of these died unmarried.

Isabella Kirkpatrick's father and mother were curiously enough, both Kirkpatricks.

Her father, Joseph Kirkpatrick of St. Cross, Isle of Wight, was descended from a younger son of the 1st Baronet.

Her mother, Maria Manuela Kirkpatrick of the Conheath branch of Kirkpatricks. The latter married the Conte de Teba and Montijo, and was mother of the Empress Eugenie of France, married to Napoleon III. (This is the second, and later, connection of the Empress with our family.)

I am neither an antiquarian nor a historian, and to read the secrets of the distant past, such scientists, while looking to tradition, must have expert knowledge to decipher the old Latin charters and records, besides the crabbed English writing of even the fourteenth and fifteenth centuries. They must be able to evaluate Heraldic signs, and have access to family records, as well as to public documents.

There are many traps for the unwary.

Lacking all qualifications therefore as a historical writer, I count myself lucky in my task of collating these notes, to have some extraneous and expert support for the history I shall tell of my ancestors.

Of tradition, Lord Hailes, an eminent historian of the late eighteenth century wrote:-

"There are some facts which may be termed the land marks of history, by which men have been wont to conduct themselves.

He who removes them, or endeavours to place them in a different point of view, is considered by all parties as a pragmatic and dangerous innovator"

Elsewhere someone has written:-

"Tradition is a term for the kind of fact most easily dismissed in argument, and yet has the most decisive influence in the affairs of men".

The Kirkpatricks have strong traditions handed down through the centuries.

With regard to heraldic signs. I have been privileged to be able to consult Sir Frances Grant K.C.V.O. as regards our family. His forty seven years distinguished service at the Lyon Court, as Keeper of the Records, and later as Lord Lyon King of Arms for Scotland from 1929 to 1945, have gained for him the reputation of being the greatest living authority on Scottish Heraldry.

As producer, with Andrew Ross, of "Nisbets' Heraldic Plates", in 1892, he wrote the account therein, of the Kirkpatricks of Closeburn. These plates were prepared by Alexander Nisbet in 1696, for incorporation in his great work "The System of Heraldry", But expense of production at that time prevented their then being used. It was only in 1722 that the book's first edition was published, without the plates, which were later produced, as related.

Sir James Fergusson in "Lowland Lairds" has this to say of Nisbet, who lived in 1657 - 1725.

"Nisbet has been authoritively described as the ablest and most scientific writer on heraldry in the English language.

In his preface to 'The System of Heraldry', he writes:-

'The original design of heraldry is not merely to show pageantry - but to distinguish persons and families - to represent heroic achievements of our ancestors - to trace the origin of noble and ancient families, and to perpetuate their memory - to distinguish the different branches descended from the same families, etc'.

"This is a testimony to Nisbet's earnestness in his work.

He writes intimately, like a man talking, and his frequent endorsements of a blazon with - 'I have seen....' when citing a particular carving or seal as evidence, carries all the conviction of the first hand witness".

These remarks, which so clearly so clearly establish Nisbet's position as a historian, are particularly apt with regards to our family, as seen below.

The following remarks on the Kirkpatricks of Closeburn are given in Nisbet's System of Heraldry -

(i) "This principal family has been in use to carry supporters since 1435, as by their evidents and seals which I have seen by the favour of the late Sir Thomas Kirkpatrick of Closeburn, a few of which I may mention:

Bridburgh 1319

Ayr 14th October 1409.

1435. To the writ of service of Roger, (who was one of the Barons of inquest on Lord Somerville's estate; and retour which I have seen in the custody of Somerville of Drum, Closeburn's seal is appended, upon which are the aforesaid memorial figures, viz. A saltier and chief, the last charged with three cushions - For crest, a hand holding a dagger and for supporters, two lions guardant, holding up a helmet in the chief point of the shield - (from the old bearing of the Bruce "esto ferox ut Leo")"

Elsewhere Nisbet writes:-

(ii) Stephen de Kirkpatrick is the ancestor of a very ancient family, the Kirkpatricks of Closeburn in Nithsdale. They have very good vouchers for their antiquity.

Chartulary of Kelso and Bridburgh.

There is an exact and complete series of the family from this time down to Sir Thomas Kirkpatrick of Closeburn baronet".

These tributes to our ancestry by so great an authority as Nisbet, are valuable, in view of the serious loss, by fire in 1748, of many important Closeburn records, and of subsequent attempts some writers, in much later years, have made to discredit the antiquity of our family.

The relationship of our kinsman Charles Kirkpatrick Sharpe to Closeburn now needs to be given, for we are indeed fortunate to have had this famous Scottish antiquarian to act as historian of the family, in the early nineteenth century.

Born in 1781, he was a great grandson of Sir Thomas Kirkpatrick, 2nd Baronet of Closeburn, and the third son of Charles Sharpe of Hoddam, who had changed his name from Kirkpatrick to Sharpe, when his mother's grand uncle, Matthew Sharpe, bequeathed his estate of Hoddam to him.

Charles Sharpe's father was William Kirkpatrick of Alisland, M.P. for Dumfries Burgh for years, who was third son of the 2nd Baronet - Charles Sharpe's mother was Jean, daughter of Sir Charles Erskine of Alva, Lord Chief Justice Clerk of Scotland, who was descended from John, Earl of Mar, Treasurer of Scotland, whose wife Lady Maria Steuart was daughter of the 1st Duke of Lennox.

Charles Sharpe himself married Eleanora Renton, daughter of John Renton of Lammerton and Lady Susan Montgomery, a famous beauty, daughter of the Earl of Eglinton.

14

Charles Kirkpatrick Sharpe's sister, Jane, was married to her cousin Sir Thomas Kirkpatrick, (the Sheriff), the 5th Baronet of Closeburn.

Sharpe lived in Edinburgh as a bachelor, with many social contacts. Thus he had a wonderful knowledge of the ancestral history of many of the old Scottish families - He was very well qualified to write the history of his family.

This he left in manuscript when he died in 1851, in possession of his Sharpe relations, and this history has never been published - Needless to say, it forms the foundation for the story I shall tell, as my many references to it will show. Mine is however an abbreviated version of the original Manuscript. Charles Kirkpatrick Sharpe's genealogy is wonderfully complete through the centuries, though naturally, in two or three places there is some doubt. I have commented on such, in the appropriate place.

Unfortunately, after his death, other antiquarians, in ignorance of his work, have produced pedigrees differing in varying degrees from his. Certain writers who could not have had access to the family papers have caused much confusion.

It is presumptuous for anyone who has not seen the private records of a family, like these I quote from hereafter, to present a quite different picture, as the history of that family! Yet this has been done in the twentieth century, and I venture therefore to hope I may be excused if I appear to labour small points unduly.

To judge a story aright both public and private papers need to be consulted.

As to our oldest Scottish records. It is well known that they suffered sad and irreparable loss, when Edward I, in 1296, carried away to England, or destroyed, many priceless Scottish papers.

It is not so well known that the old Heraldic and other records prior to 1650, in the office of the Lyon King of Arms in Edinburgh, were at that time carried off by the then Lord Lyon for security, to his castle, where he died in 1656.

No one knew where these records were in 1660, and it was stated they had been carried off by Oliver Cromwell.

In 1661, when certain other records were being returned to Scotland, a large number were lost from the vessel carrying them back.

In 1672, when no trace had yet been found of the missing records, an Act of Parliament was passed, probably to rectify confusion which had resulted from their absence. This Act ordained that every person who wished to bear arms in future must be registered at the Lyon King's Officer. Those who already had arms had also to register, after verification. The old lost records were only recovered in 1696; and amongst them was Sir David Lindsay of the Mount's (Lord Lyons) Register of 1542.

This is now in the National Library of Scotland, and, in it, the Closeburn arms are given.

"This is the oldest official Register of Arms in Scotland now existing, and is the predecessor of the present register. This gives the Closeburn arms as re-registered in 1673".[1]

In collecting data for this history, Charles Kirkpatrick Sharpe had many difficulties to overcome, for, in 1570, the Earl of Sussex's army "destroyed with poulder Cleisburne and divers utheris houss, and carried away great spulzie".

In 1646, it was sacked by the Douglas, who took away "quhat was amy wayis transportabill".

In 1672, when the re-registration took place, the national Heraldic historical records were temporarily missing, as shown above; and Seton, in "Scottish Heraldry", has described what dis-satisfaction this caused among the old Scottish barons re-registering at that time.

Finally, in 1748, fire gutted Closeburn mansion house, as related in the following pages.

In these circumstances, as Charles Kirkpatrick Sharpe declares, his task was no easy one.

Where ever it is necessary and possible, I have quoted from other authorities in support of the narrative.

Moreover, without some general knowledge of old Scottish history, it is impossible to picture the conditions in which our early ancestors existed.

Charles Kirkpatrick Sharpe had no need to repeat, in his family history, the oft told tales of the Scottish struggle for freedom. Such classics as "Tales of my grandfather", upon which I was brought up, are now out of print, or, generally, out of mind; so, for those of the next generation, I must give a very brief account of what then occurred.

For fuller knowledge, reference can be made to Lord Hailes' three volumes, "Annals of Scotland", and to Miss Agnes Mure MacKenzie's

"Robert Bruce King of Scots", which so clearly gives the antecedents to his struggle, as does Barron's "Scottish War of Independence", and McDowell's History of Dumfries. The history is, that from the 12th century, for close on a hundred years, there had been peace and friendship between Scotland and England.

After the death of Alexander III in 1286, a failure of direct succession to the throne of Scotland occurred. Commissions of regency and a full dozen of claimants for the throne bred jealousies and intrigues of every sort, which led to bitter quarrels between the old Scottish barons.

There emerged the two great rival factions, the powerful Baliol-Comyn faction, and that of the Bruces, Lords of Annandale, with their much earlier claim to the throne, dating back from the time of Alexander II. All of these had lands in England as well as Scotland, and had long had connection with the English court.

Edward I of England, an ambitious and ruthless King, when asked to arbitrate in 1292 on the unsettled Scottish succession, eagerly agreed to do so; in his own interests.

He established John Baliol as King of Scotland, who proved himself a puppet of Edward's - being a weak man, he only lasted four years.

Then Edward turned on him, invading Scotland, routed and took Baliol prisoner, making him abdicate.

By then, years of civil strife had divided Scottish loyalties, and, with English troops quartered though half the country, the situation must have been something between the present Allied occupation of Germany, (with some barons helping to maintain order) and that of Russian domination as in East Germany or Poland today.

A great many of the Scottish barons and land owners, much against their will, had to swear allegiance to Edward, since active resistance, in their misery and disorder, was hopeless.

A long list of their names forms "the Ragman's Roll".

But when Edward himself moved South, the Scots rose in anger, and with Wallace as their leader, fought gallantly for freedom. Because of their jealousies, very few of the Scottish nobility joined him.

At first, he was successful, but later, he suffered defeat at Falkirk.

He was soon afterwards treacherously betrayed to Edward, imprisoned by him in the Tower of London, and barbarously put to death.

Duncan Kirkpatrick's assistance to Wallace in battle is sung of in verse by "Blind Harry" the Minstrel, as quoted later.

Nine years of English domination of strong points and castles in Scotland were to follow, until, by a stroke of fate, our great national hero, Robert the Bruce, emerged into prominence as leader in revolt. Of his subsequent eight years, Fordun writes:-

"His frequent perils - his retreats - the cares and weariness by which he was beset - the hunger and thirst he had to suffer - the cold and nakedness to which he was exposed - the exile into which he was driven - the snares and ambushes from which he escaped - the seizure, the imprisonment and the execution of his nearest and dearest. And then - after emerging from the furnace - what a King he made! - the greatest by far that ever occupied a Scottish throne!"

With him is associated, in the words of Charles Kirkpatrick Sharpe "by unanimous tradition", the name of one of our ancestors, "Sir Roger Kirkpatrick of Closeburn, who Buchanan refers to as "vetus amicus" of Robert the Bruce, and Abercrombie calls "the constant friend of Sir William Wallace."

10th February 1953

Note:
1. Sir Francis Grant K.C.V.O.

Chapter 1

Traditional origin of the Closeburn family

"There are few families that can be traced further back into the obscurities of Caledonian history than that of "Kirkpatrick", for the surname primarily a place name, indicates their Celtic origin."[1]

After the Romans withdrew from Britain, anarchy ruled for some centuries, till gradually two Kingdoms emerged; Northumbria in the east, largely Teutonic, and Cumbria or Strathclyde, in the west, peopled by the Britons or Celts. The later Kingdom stretched from Dumbarton in the north to the Derwent in Cumberland.[2]

The name of Kirkpatrick or Kilpatrick, seems to be associated with the early Brito-Celtic churches which were founded in the fifth century by St. Patrick in the south west of Scotland, from the Clyde to the Solway Firth.[3]

Antiquarians explain that the word "Kil" or "Ceall" first meant a missioners cell, then a chapel with its consecrated ceinture, increasing afterwards to mean a small community; and the term "Cella Patricii" was applied to the religious communities thus formed by St. Patrick.

The Gaelic "Gilla" or "Gilli", meaning servant, came to indicate the officials or lay holders in these churches, and we early find the name Gilpatrick, more particularly in Galloway.

It has been suggested that "Kil" began to change to "Kirk" after the original church of St. Ninian at Whithorn became subordinate to York and English officials, some time after the eighth century, but variations of the name range from its northern limit Dumbarton, with the churches of Kirkpatrick, or Kilpatrick on the Clyde, to Kirkpatrick Durham and Kirkpatrick Irongray in Galloway. Then, in Nithsdale there are the old farms of Kilpatrick and the lands of Kirkpatrick in Closeburn.

Again in Annandale, are the parishes of Kirkpatrick-Juxta (originally Kilpatrick) and Kirkpatrick Fleming, with Roinnpatrick, (now Redkirk), an old ecclesiastical center on the shores of the Solway. With these, went "church lands", which were self supporting.

In Cumberland, (the southern part of Cumbria, the land of the Britons), a further variation perhaps of the name, Gospatrick, existed. Gradually, the original Britons were overrun by outside elements; and especially in Nithsdale, according to McDowell, the Scoto-Irish immigration through Galloway established itself firmly on the left bank of the Nith, which had been previously stoutly held by the British tribe of Selgovae in support of the Romans in occupation there, against all attacks by the Pictish invaders from the north.

Much intermarriage must have taken place, but, until David I came north from Yorkshire with his Anglo Norman followers, Nithsdale was generally Celtic, and authoritative antiquarians therefore consider that the Kirkpatricks were probably of the original Scoto-Irish stock of Nithsdale.

It was Dunegal, the Galloway Chief, who was Lord of Nithsdale, (Stranid), before David I came to Scotland as King in 1124, and then granted to Robert Brus, (whom he had brought with him as a close friend from Yorkshire), the Lordship of Annandale.

Dunegal lived in feudal state in the castle of Morton, only four miles up the Nith from Closeburn. His sons inherited his extensive lands. One of these appears to have been called Gillipatrick, which may indicate a Closeburn connection of some sort.[4]

A descendant, (perhaps a grandson), Richard Edgar, later possessed the castle of Morton and half the Barony of Sanchar, with lands on the Nith, which included part of the lands of Kilpatrick, for which he held charters from Robert Brus.

(Incidentally, I now possess a silver cup, presented to my grandfather, Roger Kirkpatrick, as Captain of the Morton Company of Volunteers, raised in 1807, when Napoleon Bonaparte threatened to invade Britain.   The inscription on this cup shows it was presented to him by the non-commissioned officers and men of his company).

"Tradition says that the ancestor of the Barons of Closeburn possessed land in Nithsdale in the year 800, but the first of this principal family "(as Nisbet styles it), on record, is Ivone Kirkpatrick, who flourished before 1141." [5]

As is shown more fully later, "he was a witness to a charter by Robert Brus, the elder or first Lord of Annandale and his wife Eufemia, heiress of Annan, granting the fishing of Torduff to the monks of

20

Abbeyholm". This Robert Brus died in 1141.

This is a long way back; but in an old family paper, it is written that Malcolm III, soon after his accession, A.D. 1056, held a Parliament at Forfar, where he ordained that, after the custom of other nations, the Scots should take their surnames from their lands.

At this time, it was added, many new surnames were given.

This information is attributed to Boece, an historian whose veracity is often questioned, but in this case, the above is stated to have been confirmed by Buchanan.

In support also of our traditional background, Cosmo Innes, in his "Scotland in the middle ages," describes how the church lands of that time, were in some districts of very large extent, and that two thirds of the parish churches and lands were in the hands of the monks, who were skilled agriculturalists, besides being the only scribes. These "church lands" were cultivated by "villeins" from several "granges". The granges of each abbacy, "spacious farm steadings", had attached to them, "pertinents", mills, etc., with hamlets occupied by "cottars", sometimes accommodating thirty or forty families; "the situation of these being far above the class now known of that name". (These were obviously developments of the earlier "religious communities", previously referred to).

Under the great Kelso Abbacy, (to which Kelosburn was subordinate), each cottar occupied from one to nine acres of land, along with his cottage.

The tenants of twenty one cottages of Clarilaw were bound to shear the whole corn of the Abbey "grange" and "Newton". (The latter property formed part of the Barony of Closeburn later), and as will be seen, our ancestor, Adam, "Lord of Kelosburn" in 1264, had a lawsuit with the Abbot of Kelso over Kelosburn Church.

The first Ivone was a witness to a charter of fishings granted by Robert de Bruce, the elder, and his wife Euphemia. The first of several Robert Bruses. The first charter of Closeburn in 1232, (full text given later), is a "charter of confirmation" of land held.

When Affrica, the natural daughter of King William the Lion, married Roger de Mandeville, she received as her dowry from him, the Barony of Tynwald and the "temple lands of Dalgarnock and Closeburn.[6]

At her death in 1232, the Closeburn lands reverted to the

Crown, and were granted to Ivon de Kyrkpatric by Alexander II on 15th August 1232, in these words:- "We have given, granted and in this our charter, confirmed, to Ivone de Kyrkpatric, in return for his homage and service, all the land of Kylosbern by the same boundaries by which we held it, and Affrica before us, except the land which lies next to Auchenleck on the northern side of the underwritten boundaries etc. etc".[7]

Legal opinion has pointed out that the word "confirm" in a grant was used, either a) to feudalize land where the grantee previously had no such title, or b) to further regularize the situation towards the "superior", if the grantee held no such feudal title.

In Ivon's case, the first alternative applies. It would appear that Ivon was in informal possession of the Closeburn lands, (part of Affrica's dowry) before her death, and that Alexander's charter of 1232 was probably the first time that the lands of Closeburn became a properly feudalized holding of the crown in the Closeburn Kirkpatricks. The grant containing the word "confirming" was necessary as an original "writ", issued to give Ivon a feudal title to lands he had held previously without one, and which, in this charter had their boundaries most specifically defined.

The Kirkpatricks were also known to have been early settled in Annandale, for the Bruses took over Kirkpatrick lands on their coming from Yorkshire, for shortly afterwards, there is recorded, "the munificent grant by Robert, son of Robert de Brus, Lord of Annandale, to the canons of Guisborn (in Yorkshire) of the church of Annan and five other churches in Annandale, including that of Kirkpatrick". This is another indication that the Kirkpatricks were firmly established as early inhabitants in Dumfriesshire, long before the advent of David I and his Anglo Norman knights.[8]

A Roger de Kyrkpatric was witness to the above charter, apparently of date between 1141-1171 the period of the second Robert Brus.[9]

Cosmo Innes in commenting upon our system of "conveyancing", in that "all property flows from the crown", refers to the feudal character of some of the most ancient charters of William the Lion and Malcolm IV of the 12th century.[10]

Cosmo Innes quoted a charter of Malcolm IV King of Scots "to Walter Fitzalan my steward", granting him the lands of Birchside and Loggarwode, "and to aforesaid Walter, Molle, for service of one knight".

The witnesses were Arnold, Bishop of St. Andrews, Abbots of Kelso, Melrose and Osbert, etc. The date of this charter must be 1153 - 1169, and it is possible to deduce that Abbot Osbert (or Osbern) flourished at "Cella osberni" - the chapel of Osbern at that time - later termed "Kylosbern" - the local name for the parish church of the ecclesiastical cult of St. Patrick - "Cella Patricii - (Kilpatric).

From a reasonable probability of the traditional story of those times, as we have it from monastic sources, and tradition, we pass through a long period of charters making grants of land, (frequently undated) which is a realm of antiquarian speculation, until we reach a much later period, when sufficient documentary and other evidence of current events, or eye witnesses accounts, existed.

But, even in the sixteenth Century, Charles Kirkpatrick Sharpe observed:- "from the public bonds of that date, it appears that very many gentlemen could not write their own names".[11]

In such circumstances, family records were likely to have been meagre.

In the seventeenth century, we find our local traditional story put into writing by the Rev. W. Black, minister in Closeburn, in his history of the Presbytery of Penpont (Sibbald's Mss.).

The 18th, 19th and 20th centuries produced a large number of historians and other writers, some of whom sought to repair gaps in family histories. One, especially, a prolific writer, has brought upon himself criticism for frequent inaccuracies in his published works.

Like other mortals, antiquarians sometimes make mistakes, but some writers are more worthy of credence than others, as the difficulty in securing accuracy of detail in ancient Scottish history and of giving such detail its proper significance, is seen to be very real. This is the case with regard to our family history, as will be seen in the following pages.

Long established tradition, the testimony of early accepted authorities, with our recorded history and papers, have provided me with material for this family record down to 1858. Without access to this material, writers subsequent to this date are seriously handicapped in painting the picture of eight centuries of our family's history, and I would say they would be somewhat rash to do so.

Finally, a theological authority has pointed out to me that the big Oxford dictionary has a long article on the derivation of the word "Kirk";

and it decides that it must come from the Greek word 'Kyriakon', meaning "the Lord's (house)". Jameson's Scottish dictionary states this is generally accepted.

In our earliest charters the name is often spelt 'Kyrkepatric'.

It has been told that the original celtic 'kil', meaning 'missioner's cell' began to change to 'Kirk' when, about the 8th century, the ancient Whithorn in Galloway came under the jurisdiction of York. What would be more likely than that the Scottish monks of the border resistant to the assumption of English authority, searched for an alternative designation for their own distinctive St. Patrick's "missioner's cells", and adopted the Greek term modified, 'Kyriakon - 'the Lord's (house)', in place of the 'Kil' of still earlier days - the name becoming "Kyrkepatic".

The surname was spelt in a number of different ways. Kilpatrick and Kirkpatrick are seen to be used as one and the same name, e.g. "Chappel of Kilpatrick", (Hume of Godscroft); "little farm of Kilpatrick near Closeburn" (Hewison).

The Nithsdale "lands of Kilpatrick" in Edgar Randolph's time, appear as "the lands of Kirkpatrick" of Closeburn in the sasine records for the parish of Dalgarnock in 1753; and these "lands of Kirkpatrick" are shown in the sale of the Barony in 1783.

In the report of the Historical Mss. Commission, an Annandale Kirkpatrick is termed 'Lord of that ilk'. It appears quite wrong to translate the Latin 'dominus' as 'Lord'. The minor Scottish barons were 'lairds'.

No Kirkpatrick was ever raised to the Peerage. Neither was there a Lord of Kirkmichael, nor of Tortherwald; until the first Lord Carlyle circa 1475 was made a peer and took the title of Lord Carlyle of Tortherwald.

I have not yet found the Latin equivalent for the term, "of that ilk", but it is unlikely that any particular family of Kirkpatricks in Dumfriesshire in these early days would seek to distinguish themselves from their cousins by adopting that designation, as certain historians would now have us believe, when there were "lands of Kilpatrick" or "Kirkpatrick" in Nithsdale as well as Annadale at that time.

It will thus be seen that the whole trend of historical "tradition" is towards the family being of the early Celtic stock of Dumfriesshire.

But in 1925/26, the following statement is found in the pages of the Dumfriesshire and Galloway Antiquarian journal:-

"We know that the originator of the family was a Norman or

Anglo Norman named "Ivo", who possessed no surname". The charter, this refers to, is without a date.

That is bald statement devoid of any qualification, for which no proof is, or can be, offered.

It appears to be based on a suggestion to that effect made in the report of the Historical Mss. Commission for Scotland Vol. XV published in 1881; where likewise no proof of this theory is given.

Such dipping into the mists of the past might be termed a "guess"; and a "guess" cannot form a "foundation" for a history.

Moreover, while the name in the report is first mentioned in English as "Ivo", it is seen later, in the original Latin given there, to be spelt "Iuoni". (The charter deals with fishing rights).

Mr. L.G. Pine, F.R.S.A. Editor of Burke's Peerage, writing of whether ancient families of Britain are of Saxon or Norman origin, states: - "At an early period after the Norman Conquest it became the fashion for all families with any social pretensions to use French and Norman Christian names. It is much more likely that such families had lived on in the north, where the ravages committed by William the Conqueror had made the land a far less attractive proposition than in the South, or Normans married local inhabitants."

In the first Edition of Nisbet, 1722 our early pedigree is given. He refers to the first of the principal family to obtain a charter of the lands of Kilosbern as 'John Kirkpatrick'.

The name 'John' in Breton is "Yánn", and in Gaelic, it is the Scottish 'Ian'.

Dr. Clapperton transcribes the first name he found in the earliest charters as "Ivon" or "Yvon", perhaps the same as we call and pronounce "Ewen" - and the "I's" and the "Y's" of the Latin text, are very similar to "J's".

I think the above is a very reasonable explanation for the origin of this first Christian name recorded of our family.

It is observed that the Historical Report fails to mention the first of the two grants of fishing rights on the Solway known to us.

This one is a charter of the fishing rights of Torduff, given to the monks of Holmcultram Abbey by Robert Brus, the Elder, or first Lord of Annandale and his wife Euphemia, heiress of Annan. This Robert Brus is shown as having died in 1141, and Ivon is witness to this charter.[12]

The Latin text is given hereafter, with a fuller note on these charters.

It is the second charter of Blawode which has been mistakenly alluded to as "the foundation charter of the family of Kirkpatrick".

Blawode has never been alluded to as such in any Kirkpatrick records; and these fishing charters are mentioned here as they verge on the "traditional" period; when information about such things is more often speculative than definite.

Dr. Ramage mentions both these charters, and in the preface to his historical record of upper Nithsdale states:- "I have not failed to examine all the chartularies of monasteries that contain references to these parishes".[13]

Notes:
1. C.K.S. Mss. Written circa 1811
2. McDowell's "History of Dumfries"; "Story of the Church in Scotland", Bishop Mitchell.
3. Articles by the Rev. J. W. Hewison D.D.
4. McDowell' "History of Dumfries".
5. C.K.S. Mss.
6. McDowell's "History of Dumfries".
7. Ramage "Drumlanrig and the Douglases."; C.K.S. Mss.
8. Ramage; McDowell's "History of Dumfries"; C.K.S. Mss.
9. Ramage "Drumlanrig and the Douglases"; Ref. Harl Charters Br. Museum App. No. II Reg. Glasg.
10. "Scotland in the Middle Ages"
11. C.K.S. Mss.; Ruff's History; and Crawford's Peerage.
12. McDowell's "History of Dumfries" page 29
13. "Drumlanrig and the Douglases" page 190

Chapter 2

The Closeburn Family Records

The tragedy of the Closeburn family is that "the new mansion" of Closeburn built by the first Baronet, Sir Thomas Kirkpatrick, at the end of the 17th century, was, on the night of 29th August 1748, burned to the ground by the carelessness of a drunken servant of a guest.

The first Baronet, finding the old castle falling into decay, had "pulled down everything except the "keep", (tower) which he also then repaired; and, with the stones of the old castle, built this new mansion". (This, I will write of later).

"In the dolorous fire", wrote Charles Kirkpatrick Sharpe in his Mss. history, written shortly before 1811, "were consumed (*hei mihi*), all the curale honours, the portraits of the family, all the furniture; and, with the exception of those few charters quoted above* - the whole papers and writs - documents which would have changed into an easy task, the irksome and frequently unavailing labour of this imperfect compilation". (His Mss. history of Closeburn 1141-1808).[1]

*Note. Ten of these, including the first charter of 1232, are noted in his history, as being in possession of Sir Thomas Kirkpatrick 5th Bt. Of Closeburn (the Sheriff of Dumfries), at the time of his writing. He quotes charters from other sources to support the narrative.

There was stated to have been sufficient documents, public and private in existence then, to prove the pedigree as set forth later.

There is still in our branch of the family, an old pedigree, which must have been in successive family possession before the fire in 1748, because the signatures of the 2nd, 3rd and 4th Baronets, recognisable as such from other documents, are entered in their own handwriting in their individual positions on the chart.

This pedigree was not complete, but it is valuable as evidence, as the second and third baronets lived before the fire, and Charles Kirkpatrick Sharpe's genealogy, written sixty years later, corresponds very nearly to it.

One box of records is now known to have escaped the fire. This was surprisingly deposited at Register House, Edinburgh, only in 1952, by a firm of Glasgow law agents, who I think, acted for the Menteth family that bought Closeburn in 1783. This box contains many papers not yet fully examined by the Register House staff, but an inventory book shows dates of Closeburn land and other transactions, from date 1552 to 1672; and there is also a record of the contract of sale to Jas. Stewart Menteth dated 1783.

As Charles Kirkpatrick Sharpe was only born in 1781, he probably never saw these papers, which might have been in the hands of that firm, in his boyhood. It may be a long time before the small staff of Register House experts can examine and transcribe these. A few however are referred to in these notes.

After the fire, a local antiquarian, Dr. Clapperton of Lochmaben, near Torthorwald, wrote a paper in 1784, entitled "Anecdotes relating to the surname of Kirkpatrick". Dr. Clapperton is reported to have then had access to many Charter chests, particularly to that of the Lords of Carliel of Torthorwald, so Dr. Clapperton besides quoting from their "writs" the history of Torthorwald and Ross Kirkpatricks, was able to give some account of their descent from the main line of Closeburn, as will be seen. No doubt he then conferred with my great grandfather at Closeburn.[2]

Charles Kirkpatrick Sharpe was only three years old, when Dr. Clapperton wrote his paper, but after the latter's death at the end of that century, Charles Kirkpatrick Sharpe, as a young man from Oxford, gathered together all available material and undertook the task of writing up the Closeburn history.

From this it is seen that he worked in conjunction with his brother-in-law, Sir Thomas Kirkpatrick the 5th Baronet of Closeburn and Sheriff of Dumfries, who presumably could refer to many Burgh records.

By 1811, after much research, Charles Kirkpatrick Sharpe produced an authoritative, annotated history of the family from 1141 to 1808, which has also much of Scottish historical interest in it.

In order to preserve evidence for posterity, he had lithographed copies made of a few early charters saved from the fire, previously referred to; in each case adding a note stating in whose possession the originals were at the time of writing. Some of these lithographs are in family possession. Copies are with others. (I have eight, lithographs or photographed copies of these lithographs.)

It is important to note that the original first charter of 1232 is recorded as having been produced by my great grandfather Sir James Kirkpatrick 4th Baronet, before an arbitration court held at Dumfries to prove his case for ownership of his property of Thriepmuir, to which, Charles, Duke of Queensberry laid claim, in 1773. The case was settled by arbitration in my great grandfather's favour before Mr. James Ewart of Mullock, who gave judgement on 24th July 1773, that having heard all the evidences, "together with a plan or eyesketch of said Thriepmuir, and the charter granted by King Alexander upon 15th day of August and eighteenth year of his reign" (1232), he declared that the Duke "had no right or interest in the said Thriepmuir".

Sir James had written that the boundaries "are very accurately marked upon my old charter". "It is impossible for anyone who is upon the spot and has the charter in his hand, to mistake them".

Ramage, who wrote in 1876, very fully, as regards the Closeburn family in "Drumlanrig and the Douglases", gave these boundaries, referring them to Charles Kirkpatrick Sharpe's lithograph of this charter.

After Charles Kirkpatrick Sharpe's death in 1851, his valuable Mss. record and other papers passed into the hands of his executor and nephew, the Rev. W.R. Bedford of Sutton Coldfield, Warwickshire.

This Mss. remained in the hands of the latters descendants until I discovered it, in 1952, in Wiltshire. Two volumes of his letters were published in 1888, "from a mass of correspondence". It was remarked in the preface that "several hundred letters from gentlemen engaged in historical and antiquarian work had been examined and passed over, with the exception of a few illustrative specimens". It is tragic to think that such correspondence was so mishandled; and this accounts for the ignorance in Scotland of the whereabouts, or existence of this Mss.

By the great kindness of the present Mrs. Bedford, I have been granted the loan of this work, so that I can proceed with my present task.

I hope to be able, at the end of this book, to include a few of his letters which are of family interest.

Charles Kirkpatrick Sharpe was regarded as a very distinguished antiquarian in Scotland, being consulted by many people on such subjects, but his mordant wit made him some enemies. His eccentricities of dress were likewise remarkable.

It is unfortunate that most of his antiquarian "treasures", and certainly other valuable records, disappeared from public ken after the auction of his effects at his death.

A continuation of the family history was published privately in 1858, as "Kirkpatrick of Closeburn".

Unfortunately, this can hardly have an official status. For one thing, the author's identity is not disclosed, although I have every reason to believe it was written by Richard Godman Kirkpatrick of Barham Court, Maidstone, Kent. I find he had this property on lease in 1855, and correspondence from there in 1857 shows that he was about to publish a history of the family. He was, I believe, an Isle of Wight Kirkpatrick. This book was useful in corroboration of other evidence, and he clearly drew much of his information from the Mss. of Charles Kirkpatrick Sharpe, which probably he had gained access to in England; but he also is seen to have made considerable personal research.

Very few copies of this book are known to exist, as it was published for distribution within the family.

This book thus has remained the only printed volume of Closeburn records until now. Since then, the Closeburn Kirkpatricks have published no further record of their past, which is easily understandable, as, with the sale of their last estate in 1844, the Closeburn family became widely scattered throughout the world.

I find that assertions or assumptions founded on inaccurate information, wrong dates, or even guesses, present the amateur historical writer with many difficulties, and Doctor A.M. Mackenzie gives a warning about even such a classic reference work as Joseph Bain's "Collection of Documents relating to Scotland" - "which is a collection, not of actual texts, but abridgements of English - a useful guide, but to be handled with care, as some conjectural dates are very uncertain". She cites a good example of this in her "Robert the Bruce, King of Scots" App. II, where she shows that a guessed date, made by Bain in 1881 despite contrary evidence, can be held responsible for the calumny that Robert Bruce showed base treachery to Wallace by being present at Falkirk, on the English side; whereas evidence shows he was elsewhere! (Two much discussed undated letters were the subject of argument). Hill Burton is quoted, ""who, as a lawyer, knew something of evidence and juries", - 'Historians seem to have found....in the charge of treachery, a sort of revenge for the perplexities they have had to endure from the indistinct and unaccountable movements of many of these barons.' [3]

30

Perplexity as to the history of the ruins of Auchencas Castle, caused a later writer to refer to Bain for enlightenment, in a effort to establish the complicity of an unknown and apparently innocent Kirkpatrick in another crime. Here, Bain's evidence bears no relation to that case.

Amongst the Kirkpatricks, from earliest times, "Roger" and "Ivone" were favourite and common names. In our family, there were only two "Johns"; one lost amidst the mists of the past, though figuring in the Ragman's Roll.

In later generations, few of the eldest sons escaped being called "Thomas", thereby causing confusion amongst their descendants when trying to distinguish them.

These ancestors of ours not only married two or three times, but in those days of large families, there were often two of a name, where one child having died, the parents christened a later arrival with the same name.

In Charles Kirkpatrick Sharpe's family, there were two Isabellas, one John William and one William John!

He has pointed out that a 'nephew' was frequently alluded to as a 'grandson'.

All these complications seem designed to tease antiquarians.

It can be seen that anyone who, in the twentieth century evolves theories of his own as to the distant past is on very tricky ground.

I can only hope, that, basing my story on Charles Kirkpatrick Sharpe's history and by quoting from accepted authorities, I may, with recent family papers, be able to bring our family history up to date, avoiding the worst traps.

Having regard to the many vicissitudes through which our family has passed in its long history, some mistakes can hardly fail to be found. If so, I crave the readers indulgence.

In 1783, as will be related, all the Closeburn estates had to be sold, with the exception of Capenoch and Thriepmuir; and on the death of my grand uncle, Sir Thomas Kirkpatrick, the 5th Baronet, in 1844, Capenoch was also sold. Thriepmuir was "bought in" by my father, so that the Closeburn family might still retain a small portion of the lands which were, for so many centuries, in possession of our ancestors.

This property is now held by my nephew Ivone Kirkpatrick.

Active participation of the family in the affairs of Dumfriesshire thus ceased with the death of the Sheriff, (more than a century ago), and since then, with the exception of Crawford Tait Ramage, it may be said that other writers have arison "which knew not Joseph!"

I hope this account of the family records, will correct the impression sometimes given by the erroneous statement that all the Closeburn records were irretrievably lost in the fire. As you see this was not the case.

"Closeburn! I love thine ancient towers.
The proud abode of many a Baron brave
And many a stately dame.
Heroes, who erst dear Caledon did save
From southern tyrants.
Piercing the Saxon breast plates with their glaive.
Long sunk in dust. Ah! Nevermore to rise,
Till the last trumpet calls them trembling to the skies."
From the original Mss. of Charles Kirkpatrick Sharpe.

Notes:
1. C.K.S.Mss.
2. C.K.S.Mss.
3. Dr. Agnes Mure Mackenzie C.B.E., M.A.

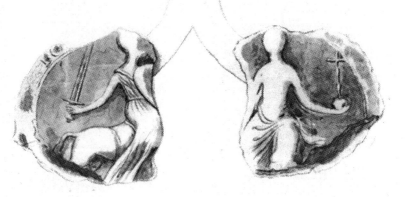

Facsimile of Charter of Lands of Closeburn granted to Ivone Kirkpatrick by King Alexander, 15th August, 1232

Chapter 3

The First Charter of Closeburn

15th AUGUST, 1232.

There are two facsimile lithographs of the first Charter as illustrated here, in family possession.

Charles Kirkpatrick Sharpe produced these lithographs in the early nineteenth century, from the original Charter, then in possession of Sir Thomas Kirkpatrick, 5th Baronet of Closeburn. (Charles Kirkpatrick Sharpe is stated to have started working in copper plate in 1813.)

Here the seal of King Alexander II can be seen drawn in below the Charter, in two portions - to show both the front and the reverse of the seal.

A portion of the seal was missing but sufficient is there to identify it as that illustrated in Seton's Scottish Heraldry as one of the earliest Scottish Royal Seals, appertaining to King Alexander II. The transcription of this Charter, recorded by Dr. Maitland Thomson, is registered in the Register House, Edinburgh.

There is another lithograph of the Charter where a single medallion seal shows the front of the seal only, with King Alexander II's figure as above. A photograph copy of this Charter shows the seal blotted, black, but if comparison is made with the above seals, the horse's rump, its tail and the sword arm with sword, can just be made out.

The reason for the black-out is that a photographic plate is not sensitive to the yellow or reddish colour of a wax seal, and is more sensitive to other colours.

Chapter 4

Earliest Recorded History of the Closeburn Family

The Kirkpatricks were seen to be a powerful family in the early times, having considerable possessions in different parts of the south of Scotland, but although settled for many years, both in Nithsdale and Annandale, the family names of Ivone and Roger do not appear in documentary form till the reign of David I and Alexander II. [1]

Charles Kirkpatrick Sharpe[2] writes:- "The first of the principal family". (as Nisbet styles it), is:-

1. IVONE KIRKPATRICK, who flourished before the year 1141. Ivone, or, as his name of frequently written Yvone Kirkpatrick, lived in the reign of David I, King of Scotland.

He is a witness to a charter of Robert Brus, the elder, or first Lord of Annandale, together with his wife Eufemia, heiress of Annan, granting the fishing of Torduff to the monks of Abbeyholm, which runs thus:- "Robertis de Brus tam absentibus quam presentibus omnibus amicis suit salutem. Sciatus me et mulierem meam Eufemiam et heredes meas dedisse piscatorium illam de Torduff in perpetuam eleemosinam abbati Everardo et conventus et Fratribus de Holm pro animabis nostris et animabis parentum nostrorum. Testibus - Yvone - etc". This Robert died A.D. 1141. This charter is undated. Both local antiquarians, Dr. Clapperton (1784), and Ramage testify to its being found in extracts from the register of Holmcultram Abbey. This charter was confirmed by Robert, son of the above Robert Brus, who was Lord of Annandale 1141-1171 - It will be remembered that Ramage stated he had not failed to examine all chartularies pertinent to the parish. (Everard the eldest, Abbot of Holm, is to be found a witness also to a confirmation charter to Jedburgh by King William the Lion in 1165, the first year of his reign.) Charles Kirkpatrick Sharpe, after quoting the first fishing charter, wrote:- "Again, Robert the Brus, Lord of Annandale grants a charter of the fishing of Blawode and Eister to Ivone Kirkpatrick". This charter is seen in the writs of Carliel. The Latin text given in the Report of the Historical Mss. Commission shows the name spelt as "Iuoni", but in the English, the Report spells this "Ivo". "Both fishings charters are without Surname or Date." [3]

The brief statement there, is as follows:- "The earliest known ancestor was Ivo, c. 1190, who afterwards, c. 1194-1214, became Ivo de Kirkpatrick". [4]

It is to be noted that the first and earliest fishing charter to which Ivon was a witness, is not mentioned; and that c. 1190 in the report is just a guess at the date of the second charter.

The man who got the grant of land c. 1194-1214 appears obviously to be he, whom Ramage quotes from the Drumlanrig charters as Yvone de Kirkpatrick, who received a grant of 20.lib land of Pennirsax (in Middlebie, Annandale) called Thorbeck or Williambie from William de Brus, who died 1214.

No proof is offered for a statement that this man got a grant of land in Kirkpatrick Juxta and that thereafter, the family there called themselves "of that ilk".

The next on the list is William, and Charles Kirkpatrick Sharpe writes that he was this Ivone's son or brother. [5]

2. WILLIAM KIRKPATRICK, "of the honourable family of Kirkpatrick in Nithsdale", (Sir David Dalyrmple's Annals Vol. 2. P. 242)" who assisted Gilbert, son of Fergus, in his wars against Rolland, for the Lordship of Galloway about 1187. After Gilbert's death, Rolland declared himself Lord of Galloway and slew Gilpatrick, who headed the faction of his, (Rolland's), cousin Duncan". [6]

Henry II and William the Lion "settled the affairs of Galloway, forcing Rolland to give Duncan the part of Galloway called 'Carrick'."

"Then of July the second day
Betwene this Rolland of Galloway
and Gyllpatryk a batell fell
wes dune baith sare and scharpe and snell
And this Gyllpatryk slaine was then.
And mony that with that day were".
Wynton, who dates this event 1183.

3. IVONE KIRKPATRICK. [7] The above Ivone's son, (later, C.K.S. makes him a grandson), received from King Alexander II a grant of confirmation[8] of the lands of Closeburn dated 15th August 1232. This charter in Latin, is translated by Ramage:- "Alexander, by the grace of God,

King of Scots, to all good men of the whole Kingdom, whether clergy or Laity, greeting. Be it known to all men in the present and all succeeding ages, that we have given, granted and, by this charter, confirmed, to Yvoni de Kyrkepatric for his homage and service, all the lands of Kelosbern, bounded in the same manner as we held them, and Affrica[9] before us, excepting the land near Auchinleck on the north side of the under written boundaries. viz. By the course of the rivulet called Poldunelarg (Crichope Linn) near where it falls into another rivulet called Potuisse, (Cample Burn) up to the dry dyke which goes through the middle of the moss, and then falling down, on the north side of a cairn of stones towards Auchinleck, all the way to the river called Poldovy, (Polidivan), which divides Kelosbern from Glengarrock, to be holden by the said Yvone and all his heirs, from us and our heirs, in fee and heritage by their just marches and with all their lawful pertinents, in hill and dale, in land and water, in meadow and pasture, in muir and moss, in lakes and milldams, with power of pit and gallows, with seck and scythe, with "thol," (the right to exact custom), and "infang thef", (right to punish thief caught within the boundaries), and with all other lawful pertinents of the said lands; freely, quietly, fully, and honourably, for the service of a fourth part of one knight, in name of Alba firma, (the annual rent paid to the lord). Before these witnesses - W. Bondington Cancellario, Rogero de Queney, Waltero filio Alani Senescallo Justiciario Scotie, Johanne de mauns, Will Cameravic, Rogero Avenal, David Marscallo, Thoma filio Ranulf, David de Lindeseya, Rogero filio Glaii, Roberto de Meyners, Apud Edinburg quinto decimo die Augusti Anno Regno Dmini Regis Octavo decimo." (All men of high office).

This Yvone[10] appears to have married a daughter of Robert Brus Lord of Annandale and Cleveland, ancestor of King Robert Bruce; and it is probable that her name was Eufemia, for I find that, among the writings carried away from Edinburgh Castle by Edward I in 1296 in "memorandum quod omnia subscripta inventa fuerunt in castro de Edinburgh et liberato fuerunt domino Hugoni de Crepingham Thesauvarie Scotiae, apud Berwyk super Twedam, anno regni regis Edwardi Vicessimo quarto 1296" was:- "una litera patens de ..... .ad firmam domino Galtero Moubray per Eufemiam de Kirkpatrick. The Moubrays possessed the estate of Kirkmichael in Nithsdale.

In the index of charters granted by Robert I is one:- "To Will. Lindsay, Chanoun in Glasgow, of the Barony of Kirkmichael, in Walle de

Neth, whilk, Roger Moubray tint by forfaulture."

The inference may be drawn that Ivone had a previous connection with Closeburn, and was in favour with the King , for, the previous year, on 6th April 1231, he was witness to a charter of King Alexander II, whereby he confirms a grant by Maldouen Earl of Lennox to Absalom, "filius Maxhid", the original ancestor of Buchanan of that ilk, "de ilo insule que vocatur Clarnis", in Loch Lomond, (the island of Clarines). "Charter penes Ducem de Montrose". [11]

In the reign of Alexander II also, "Humphrey de Kirkpatrick" got the lands of Colquoun from Maldouen Earl of Lennox, and his son Ingram took his surname from these lands. [12, 13]

In a list by Nisbet of Scottish families of ancient lineage which are linked by family connections, that of Kirkpatrick - Colquhoun is cited.

Ingram's son was Robert, and the father of another Robert who had three sons, the eldest of whom, Humphrey, married the heiress of Luss in 1394, and the youngest son kept the name of Colquhoun; but the second son, Patrick, who seems to be the ancestor of the family of Corstoun in Fife, transmitted the name of Cowan to his posterity and retained the saltier of Colquhoun with a chief for difference in his armorial bearings.

In "Kirkpatrick of Closeburn", its author amplified Charles Kirkpatrick Sharpe's information by stating that Humphrey was the second son of No. 2 William Kirkpatrick of Closeburn, and that of the Colquhouns of Luss still claim to belong to the family of Kirkpatrick.

In trying to verify these statements, I find they come from Colquhoun sources, and so have a claim to credence, in view of the clear chain of succession with change of name produced from Humphrey Kirkpatrick's descendants.

I find that Richard Godman Kirkpatrick wrote a private letter from Barham Court, Kent, dated 21st November 1857, addressed to "Dear Maria", who was, from the context, Maria Isabella Kirkpatrick of the Isle of Wight, first cousin to the Conheath branch of the family.

In this letter he stated, that he was about to publish a history of the Closeburn Kirkpatricks, written by himself.

He asked for replies on certain family interests, and mentioned that "Mr. Colquhoun, an English barrister descended from a Kirkpatrick,

40

was giving him assistance in his work."

It is obvious that Mr. Colquhoun was not only interested in his own family connection with the Closeburn Kirkpatricks, but that he had Colquhoun records to quote from in support of it, and was probably responsible for the statement that Humphrey was the second son of William Kirkpatrick. (No. 2 in our pedigree).

There was a Humphrey Kirkpatrick, just about that time, who acted as Steward of Annandale. He is shown as witness to several charters of land there, between 1218 and 1245. He is shown as having "a meadow" but is not shown as having received any grant of land. It is possible this was the same man referred to above.

Ivone Kirkpatrick of Closeburn's son, Adam Kirkpatrick, succeeded. Adam Kirkpatrick is shown in Chalmers "Caledonia" as possessing the manor of Kirkpatrick in N. W. Annandale.[14]

It is possible that when the above Humphrey died and his son Ingram went off to Colquhoun lands, his father's, (Humphrey's), 'meadow' may have passed to Adam.

4. Adam, styled 'Lord of Closeburn' had a lawsuit in 1264 with the monks of Kelso about the advowson of the church of Kylosbern. The Bishop of Glasgow appointed the addot of Jedburgh to act as arbiter, and the case was decided against Adam in a deed signed at Roxburgh that year.[15]

The Closeburn church lands (called Templands), were the rich holms lying along the banks of the Nith, which later brought in a considerable income to the monks.

5. Stephen, son of Adam succeeded and in the chantulary of Kelso "Stephanus Dominus villae de Kylosbern, filius et haeres Domine Ade de Kyrkepatric militis." [16] He entered into an agreement with the Abbot concerning the convent's right to Closeburn Church, thus settling a long dispute. "Die mercurii proximo post festum purificacianis Beate Marie Virginis". 1278. Three years afterwards, the convent entered into an agreement with the native of Kylosbern, Adam de Kulenhat, to whom they let large tithes and offerings. [17]

Nisbet wrote "Stephen de Kirkpatrick is the ancestor of a very ancient family, the Kirkpatricks of Closeburn in Nithsdale. They have very good vouchers for their antiquity. Chartulary of Kelso and Bridburgh."[18]

"There is an extract and complete series of the family from this time down to Sir Thomas Kirkpatrick of Closeburn." [19] With regards to Nisbet's "System of Heraldry", Sir James Fergusson has pointed out that the first edition, published in 1722, "has been injured by an unscrupulous republication of it, several times reprinted, 1742, when he was dead"[20.] Stephen was probably a man about fifty years of age, when he signed the Ragman's Roll in 1296, no doubt much against his will, as so many Scottish landowners were then forced to do; and in his position as Lord of Closeburn, he is likely to have played his part in those troublous times keeping order in the district.

Stephen had two sons; Roger, who was his heir, and Duncan, who gained the Barony of Torthorwald by his marriage with Isobel, heiress and daughter of Sir David Thorald of Torthorwald.[21] 6. Roger "is well known from our history, to have assisted King Robert Bruce in killing Red John Cuming at Dumfries 10th February 1306" [22]

Buchanan alludes to Roger as "vetus amicus" of Robert the Bruce.

According to Abercrombie, he was the constant friend of Sir William Wallace, "a circumstance from their relationship very probable". (This will be explained later). Bruce was 32 when crowned King and Roger and Duncan might have been a few years younger. [23]

Roger is said to have been one of those who, at the assembly in the Forest Kirk, elected Wallace Warden of all Scotland, and perhaps was that Kirkpatrick mentioned by "Blind Harry" as a partizan of the same hero, when he relieved Sir William Douglas, who was besieged in Sanquhar Castle by the English and the routed foe was driven in disorder down Nithsdale, swept past Closeburn and the lands of Kirkpatrick [24]

Charles Kirkpatrick Sharpe remarks that historians seem sometimes to confuse Sir Roger with his brother Duncan, who is so frequently mentioned in the book of Wallace.

Chronololologically, it is best to deal first with Duncan's story, bound up as it is with the beginning of the Scottish War of Independence.

Notes:
1.References:Ramage, "Drumlanrig and the Douglases."
2. Charles Kirkpatrick Sharpe's Mss.; Dr Clapperton's Mss (1784)
3. C.K.S. Mss.; Dr. Clapperton; Ramage.

4. Further note reference the report of the Historical Mss. Commission

5. C.K.S. Mss.

6. Genealogy of the house of Maxwell. History of the Lords of Galloway, on the Archaeologia - Gilbert was uncle to Rolland, killing him after the death of their father Fergus - On Gilbert's death, his nephew Rolland recovered the lordship. Gilbert died in 1165, his son becoming 1st Earl of Carrick.

7. C.K.S. Mss.

8. Charter penes Thos Kirkpatrick of Closeburn 5th Baronet

9. McDowell's History Of Dumfries. Affrica was the natural daughter of William the Lion, married to a Norman Knight, Roger de Manderville. Note from the wording of this charter, Affrica must have predeceased King Alex. And this is the indication that Ivone was already in possession of the lands of Closeburn before he received this charter of confirnation, which is the family tradition.

10. C.K.S. Mss.; Family tree of the Bruces of Clackmannan in the possession of the Earl of Elgin; Statistical account of the parish of Clackmannan

11. C.K.S. Mss.; Dr. Clapperton

12. Dr. Clapperton Mss.; C.K.S. Mss; A.D. 1225 vide cart: of Lennox, Baronage etc.

13.. The change of surname of Humphrey's son Ingram to Colquhoun is a good example of the custom of those early days, previously mentioned, whereby surnames were adopted from aquired lands.

14 C. K. S. Mss..

15. Chart. Kelso 342.

16. C.K.S. Mss..

17. Chart. Kelso 343.

18. Nisbet "System of Heraldry".

19. Nisbet.

20."Lowland Lairds". Sir James Fergusson, Bart..

21.C.K.S. Mss.

22. Mr. Clapperton Mss. 1784.

23. C.K.S. Mss..

24. Preface to the Book of Wallace; C.K.S. Mss.; Wallace Book 9.

Chapter 5

The early history of the Torthorwald Branch of Kirkpatricks

Duncan Kirkpatrick's marriage to Elizabeth, daughter of Sir David Thorald of Torthorwald probably took place in the days before the war of Independence, when the Scots rallied to Sir William Wallace's call to arms, to overthrow the English domination and when Duncan responded gallantly as "Baron of Torthorwald".

"This Duncan as a strenuous patriot, and would by no means yield to the haughty usurpations of the English Edward - assisting Sir William Wallace with all his might, and that more especially at the fight near Lochmaben, when Wallace was pursued by the English garrison there, for the slaughter of Lord Clifford's son and two others, who he had killed, (according to the Blind minstrel) for cutting off the trails of his horses. Sir John Graham with the Baron of Torthorwald and their followers came opportunely to his aid." [1]

"Blind Harry", is not regarded as an authentic historian, but he sang of the traditions and great deeds of those times, and is often quoted as recording the early incidents of Wallace's struggle, in conjunction with the chief authorities of that time, Wyntoun, Fordun and Hemingburgh. Blind Harry's story of the fight at Lochmaben emerges from the somewhat uncouth English used.

> *"Kyrkpatrick yat cruell was and keyne*
> *In Esdaill wode yat half zer he had beyne.*
> *With Inglismen he couth nocht weill accord,*
> *Of Torthorwald he Baron was, and Lord;*
> *Off Kyn he was to Wallace modyr[2] ner*
> *Off Crawford syd yat mydward had to ster".* [3]

The Scots won the battle, in which, sings the bard, "Kyrkpatric's douchty deid was nobill fer to ken".

> *"Kyrkpatryk als, with worthi men in wer,*
> *Fifty in front, at anys doun(?) thai ber,*

Through the thikkest off thre hundreth' thai raid,
Of Southeron men full gret slauchter thai maid.
Thain to reskew, that was in fallone thrang.
The Southeron fled, and left them in that place".

Duncan received the thanks of Wallace.
"Kyrkpatric syne that was his cusin der.
He thankyt hym rycht in gud maner".

They chased after the English commander, Greyston, and slew
him, "at the Knockheid".

After further fightings and retreats. Duncan again issued forth to
join his cousin Wallace at the Battle of Biggar

"Yar, came intill his company, Kyrkpatric befor in Esdaill war"[4].

Charles Kirkpatrick Sharpe remarks that "Duncan seems to have
outlived these troublesome times, for King Robert grants him and his
spouse Isobel the lands of Torthorwald, dated the 10th August, the year of
God being omitted"[5].

It is to be noticed that there is no traditional early history of
Torthorwald like that of Closeburn; nor is there any record of an 'Ivo'
being at any time connected with it.

There is a mention of John de Soulis, a Norman knight, receiving
the Torthorwald lands from Robert Bruce, but the first holder with whom
we are concerned is Sir David Thorald of Torthorwald, and he is shown as
being among a number of Scottish land owners who in 1296, held lands
in England as well as Scotland[6].

Edward I at that time issued two edicts against all such, who had
not sworn fealty to him, directing that their lands and possessions were to
be forfeited and that they be evicted back to Scotland. Amongst names
mentioned in this edict are the Baliols and Comyns; and in Cumberland,
the Carliels and Sir David Thorald, The latter shown as holding lands at
Gunrow (Greenrow), worth £6 a year.

Sir David de Thorald (Torthorwald) had signed the Ragman's
Roll at Berwick on 4th December 1291.

Long before that however, his family had crossed to the best side
of the border, and he was established there as "Sir David Torthorwald" for
we find him in 1287-1288, receiving payment of his fees as such from the

Chamberlain of Scotland[7].

Again, in approximately 1289, the name of Sir David Torthorwald is found in the Chartulary of Holmcultram (Abbeyholm), "a witness amongst a great many gentlemen of Galloway to the donation of one mark to the monks of that Abbey[8].

He is referred to as "of that ilk", meaning he was of the stock of the Dumfriesshire Torthorwalds. After Bannockburn, those Scots who had possessed lands in England, in turn, lost their Scottish lands, and were driven across the border, whence some fought against their fellow Scots. Amongst these, were certain "de Torthorwalds". Between Bain and Nicolas Carlyle, there are very confusing accounts of their activities, as seen later; and this must account in large measure, for absence of early Torthorwald history.

Dr. Clapperton, wrote in his "Anecdotes":- "Upon Duncan and his spouse Isabel's resignation, King Robert Bruce grants them a charter of the lands of Torthorwald, dated 10th August". The year is not given, as is frequently the case in early charters. He continues:- "Their son Humphray, gets another charter of the same lands from the same King, dated 16th July the 16th of his reign, which was in year 1322, vide writs of Carliel". (Elsewhere the date is given as 1321).

"Umphray Kirkpatrick's son seems to be Sir Robert Kirkpatrick, who was taken prisoner at the battle of Dupplin, 1333. (Umphray is later given an "H" to his name, and much confusion is seen in records as between Humphrey, Umfred and Winifredus. These names were nearly as common as the as the Rogers).

"Roger Kirkpatrick, Laird of Torthorwald got a charter from John the Graham, son of son of John Graham of Mosskesson, of an annual rent of 40/- out of the lands of over Dryff dated 1355".

(A continuance of the story of the Kirkpatricks of Torthorwald and of Ross, had better be told later).

Duncan and Isabel's charter is not in Robertson's revised edition of King Robert I's charters, which was published in 1709, "to show as complete as possible the contents of the Register of the Great Seal of Scotland for 1306-1424" of which a number of portions were known to be missing, including Rotulus C, of King Robert I, which was reported lost. It is stated that twelve rolls and one book only remain of the original 1306-1424 register.

47

I have referred in the preface to the loss of early Scottish records; and Seton quotes from Robertson's report of "Proceedings relating to the Peerage of Scotland ", that it appears from the records of Parliament, 8th January 1661, that amongst the registers which had earlier been carried off to England by Cromwell, 85 hogsheads of them were lost at sea, when they were being brought back to Scotland from London after the Restoration[9].

In a storm, these 85 hogsheads of registers were shifted out of the frigate which was carrying them into another vessel, "the Eagle", which sank with these records on board in the storm. This may account for the early charter of Duncan Kirkpatrick and his wife Isobel being missing, or it may have been amongst those burnt at Closeburn in 1748.

It would appear from Grierson records that it was customary for our ancestors to keep their records in hogsheads; not, it would seem, the best method of preserving them for posterity. A Barjarg Grierson, (his relative), suggested to Charles Kirkpatrick Sharp that he might send him over a "hogshead" of their old family papers that Sharpe might look over in his antiquarian researches; but he was doubtful about the condition they would be in!

I fancy that even fewer of our ancestors could read Latin charters than their present day descendants, and so found their empty hogsheads convenient receptacles into which to dump such documents!

Writing of this Duncan Kirkpatrick, Charles Kirkpatrick Sharpe summarizes the subsequent changes in Torthorwald as follows:-

His family, which had acquired by marriage the Barony of Torthorwald, subsequently merged by marriage in the Lords Carliel, who thereby became Barons of Torthorwald; and the Barony not long afterwards passed to Douglas of Drumlanrig, by the marriage of Margaret, daughter of William Douglas, third Baron of Drumlanrig, who died in 1464, whose descendent William 3rd Earl of Queensberry was in 1682 created Marquis and in 1684, Duke of Queensberry, Marquis of Dumfriesshire, Earl of Drumlanrig, Viscount of Nith, Torthorwald and Ross.

Charles Kirkpatrick Sharpe has pointed out that in those early days, there was no other Baronial family of the name of Kirkpatrick in Dumfriesshire save that of Closeburn.

It will be later shown how the Torthorwald Kirkpatricks exchanged their lands of Torthorwald for those of the Carliels of Ross.

The last of the Kirkpatricks to be a Laird of Torthorwald was

Sir Duncan Kirkpatrick, who, with his wife Isabel Stewart of Castlemilk, received a grant of the Barony of Torthorwald for their life time, from King Robert III in 1398. This Sir Duncan had three daughters. The eldest married Sir Wm. Carliel of Kinmount, and, on Duncan's death, Sir Wm. Carliel took the title of Laird of Torthorwald.

The first Lord is shown as Sir John Carlyle. Up till then, the Scottish branch, appear to have spelt their name (as possibly pronounced), "Carliel".

These Scottish 'Carlyles' lost their lands and patrimony later, and only a fragment remains of the old ruined tower of Torthorwald, last inhabited by the Douglases of Dornock in 1687.

The exchange of lands and intermarriage has led to much speculation regarding the cousinly relationships as between Torthorwald, Ross and Closeburn. This had better be left for the present.

Notes:
1.C.K.S. Mss.
2.It is explained that the mother of Wallace was daughter of Sir Reginald Crawford, Sheriff of Ayr and Aunt of Kirkpatrick; perhaps two sisters marrying.
3. A.D. 1297 Wallace Book 5.
4.Wallace Book 6.(There are several editions of this book).
5. C.K.S. Mss.
6.McDowell "History of Dumfries" p. 54.
 7.Historical Documents Vol I. p 39-51.
8.Dr. Clapperton Mss..
9.Seton "Scottish Heraldry".

Chapter 6

The period of Robert the Bruce

To revert now to Roger, eldest son of Stephen Kirkpatrick.

By 1304, Scotland had been ruthlessly ravaged and oppressed by Edward I, and he then parcelled out the Kingdom into four divisions and constituted two justiciaries in each, (one English, one Scot). Among these, Roger Kirkpatrick and Walter Boughton were appointed justiciaries of Galloway in 1305[1,2]. The two great remaining rivals for the throne at that time were Bruce and Comyn, and circumstances had made them bitter enemies.

The cause and course of the quarrel which later occurred have been variously narrated, owing to lack of first hand contemporary evidence as already explained.

This young Robert Bruce, (grandson of the old claimant to the throne), being then in the power of Edward, had taken no active part in the struggle, though he secretly encouraged the opposition, but Baliol's abdication and the death of Bruce's father, cleared his path. Both Bruce and Comyn had been involved in intrigues in their own interests, but now Bruce had a conference with the Red Comyn, at which, after representing the miserable effects of civil discord, he is said to have proposed they should henceforth act as friends.

"Support" said Bruce "my title to the crown, and I will give you all my lands - or give me all your lands, and I will support your claim". Comyn, knowing the weakness of his own claim, accepted the former alternative, and an agreement was drawn up, accordingly, sealed and confirmed by mutual oaths of fidelity and secrecy.

Comyn, however, (perhaps frightened by the step he had taken), later revealed the matter to Edward who unguardedly expressed himself determined on revenge.

Our traditional story is that Bruce flying from England and Edward's treachery, found this Roger Kirkpatrick of Closeburn, his "ancient friend", with his own brother Edward Bruce, Robert Fleming, ancestor of the Earls of Wigtown, James Lindsay, and Sir Thomas

Charteris, commonly called Thomas of Longueville, at the Castle of Lochmaben[3].

Accompanied by these barons, Bruce repaired to Dumfries, where, meeting with the traitor Red John Comyn, in the Greyfriers church, he became so enraged by the insolence and perfidy of this man, who had been elected Regent of Scotland and had acted a part of monstrous dissimulation, that he stabbed him before the high altar[4]. Issuing forth to take horse, all pale and in confusion, his friends who waited for him in the churchyard, demanded the cause.

"I doubt" said he "that I have slain the Comyn". "Doubtest though" said Kirkpatrick "I mak sicker", and, together with James Lindsay, hastening into the church, he despatched the wounded Regent with his dagger, hence came the crest and motto of the family, adopted from an action which however sanguinary and shocking it may appear, was highly admired and applauded in those ferocious times[5].

For centuries this story remained the general tradition of the countryside, but, as the importance of this incident in Scottish history became recognized, some writers, especially in the 18th and 19th centuries, introduced variations.

They had however little new material to cause them to add to the story of the early authentic historians.

Lord Hailes' comment in 1797 was:- "From Fordun's account of this deed, it is uncertain whether Lindsay or Kirkpatrick struck the decisive blow. In this uncertainty I follow the common tradition. See Hume Vol. ii p. 120". There can be no dought that the murder was unpremeditated and done in a moment of hot anger, under intense provocation. But with it, in an instant, the whole situation was changed, and an un-imagined development had brought the hour and the man to Scotland.

The murderous affair in the church soon raised a general alarm. The followers of Comyn rallied round their fallen chief, and after a short struggle, the Bruce party overcame the Comyns; the uncle of Comyn, Robert Comyn, being killed in the fight.

The "History of Dumfries" tells how the English judges, then holding court in the castle hall, having been sent news of the action, hastily barricaded the doors[6].

Bruce assembling his followers, then threatened to force an entrance, by setting fire to the building; and compelled those within to surrender.

The castle of Dumfries was captured, and by dawn the next day, the small English garrison had either been killed, or had fled, spreading the alarm to Carlisle. Dumfries, triumphant, found itself freed after ten years of English domination.

The glad news spread like wild fire through Scotland.

After, it is thought, some days in the Castle of Dumfries, Bruce sought safety in flight.

Charles Kirkpatrick Sharpe quotes the local tradition as given in the Rev. Black's history of the Presbytery of Penpont[7].

There is described:- "The steep hill called the Dune of Tyrone, near Closeburn, upon the top of which, there hath been some habitation or fort - on all hands of it very thick woods, into which King Robert Bruce is said to have been conducted by Roger Kirkpatrick of Closeburn, after they had killed the Comyn at Dumfries. It is reported that, during his abode there, he did often divert to a poor man's cottage later known as Cairneys Croft.

The poor man's wife, being advised to petition the King for somewhat, was so modest in her desires, that she sought no more but security of the croft and liberty of pasturage, of which that ancient family, by the injury of time, hath a long time been, and is, deprived; but the croft continues in the possession of the heirs and successors lineally descended of this Brownrigg and his wife, so that this family being more ancient than rich, doth yet continue in the name, and, as they say, retains the old charter."

In the country around, place names by tradition, as we have it, show that this may well be true e.g. King's well on the farm of Glencorse, Bruce's well - King's Quarry - Rob's Corse (cross) - Kingsland Burn. These on Auchencairn - King's stone across the border Auchengeith.

Meanwhile Edward, when the news of the revolt reached him, swore, in fury, with uplifted arm, to avenge the murder of Comyn, and to visit all rebel Scots with dire punishment[8].   He prepared a great army under the Earl of Pembroke to march on Perth.

Retaking the castle of Dumfries and others in the vicinity, the English, within that year, perpetrated many barbarous cruelties and executions. For their services in this campaign, Henry de Percy received the Earldom of Carrick, (the lands of Bruce), and the Earl of Hereford was rewarded with the lordship of Annandale.

That summer, "Nithsdale lay once more beneath the proud foot of the conqueror".

Stephen Kirkpatrick, his son away with Bruce, alone in Closeburn, must have seen his home occupied by the English. What happened to him then we do not know, but he appears to have got his reward later by a grant of church land in Pennirsax. The charter is by Robert King of Scots to Stephano de kyrkepatrike, Knight of all the land which belonged to the Preste of Pennirsax within the tenement of Pennirsax, together with the mill of Pennirsax; to be held by the said Stepheno and his heirs, in feu and heredity, rendering the same Lord service due. Witness - Bernard, Abbot of Abirbrothok, Walter Steward of Scotland, William de Soulis, Robert de Keth our Marshal, and Alexander de Seton Knight[9].

The charter is undated, but is placed as 1309-1320. Bernard became chancellor in 1309.

Edward I is said to have asked the Pope to excommunicate Bruce for the crime committed before the high Alter in Greyfriars Church, Dumfries.

This was later done, but in the bull of excommunication issued by the pope, (which is quoted in Rymer Foed Vol. iii p. 810,) the name of Bruce's companion is given as "Robert".

Dr. Ramage writes of this:- "We hear of no such individual of this name except in this bull, and it is by no means unlikely in the confusion in which the monks would be thrown, that they might have got hold of a wrong name, and Roger had no interest in undeceiving them, as he would only be bringing himself under the direct fan of the church".

"This seems more likely, as even the names of Comyn and Dumfries, where the murder took place, are so changed in the bull of Pope John, (Avignon 6th January 1326), that we would have had difficulty in recognising them, if we had not other sources of information. The murder is said to have been "in eccelsia fratrum minor de Dynifis, and Comyn's brother, is called Robertus de Caymins;" and that "Robert" was killed in the struggle.

Robert Bruce was crowned King of Scots at Scone on 27th March 1306. Thereafter he and his follower became fugitives; but in February 1307, with about 180 trusty knights and followers King Robert Bruce landed in Carrick.

54

McDowell, of all historians is alone in giving the names of those Barons then with him, and Lord Hailes quotes Landtoft for account of the fight. McDowell, the Galloway Chief, hostile to Bruce, routed the party, which included Edward, (Bruce's brother), Lennox, Lindsay, Kirkpatrick of Closeburn, and "the good" Sir James Douglas and a few others[10]. Bruce and Kirkpatrick must have escaped, but Hailes relates that Bruce's two brothers and Sir Reginald Crawford, (relation to Kirkpatrick), fell wounded. They were carried to Carlisle to be brutally murdered; but, before they died, torture may have caused them to disclose the names of their leaders.

"The Chronicum of 'Lanercost' was written by the Friars minor of Lanercost near Carlisle, who moved freely about the border at that time". These were likely to know details of this incident. (Landtoft and Lanercost are clearly the same name)[11].

It is remarkable that Wm. McDowell who wrote his classic "History of Dumfries" in 1867, and who, I think, had reason to claim descent from the Galloway Chief McDowell, should provide the names of the Scottish participants in this fight, then Landtoft only mentioned the names of those brought to Carlisle. I can only think that local and family tradition provides fuller information at times.

After the Battle of Bannockburn, sir Roger Kirkpatrick of Closeburn was sent by the King as one of four Commissioners to treat for peace with Edward II in person, at Berwick[12].

Their safe conducts, in old French, are given by Charles Kirkpatrick Sharpe dated for 18th September 1314, which include the name of Roger de Kirkpatrick.

Edward's letter of safe conduct contains the following passage: - "Et meismes celi frere Rauf nous eit prie, de par le dit Sire Robert, qui nous un vousissions donner nos lettres de sauf conduit a Neel Campbell, Roger de Kirkpatrick, Robert de Keth, et Gilbert de la Haye Chivaliers, de venir vers nous, etc. Don a Everwyk le 18 jour de Septembre, l'an de nostre regne vasme".

Some years after this embassy, Sir Roger was employed in a similar transaction which is proved by an article published by Rymer. "De salve conductu, pre gentibus Roberti de Brus, durante treuga". (This was in 1320). The safe conduct is again in old French, and the names of the peace commissioners were: Sirs William de Soulis, Robert de Keth, Roger de Kirkpatrick, Alexander de Seton, William de Mont Fichet, Chivaliers, with four assistants and three Vadlets[13].

In the family records, it is stated that "the adopted motto appeared in old seals and documents in various forms sometimes 'I'll mak sicker', or 'sickar', which were probably the words originally uttered. This appears to have been considered inconsistent with the crest, the drops of blood intimating a deed done, and we find it written, 'I hae made sicker' or 'sickar'.

This however is evidently a bad form of motto, which ought to be a rallying cry, or the expression of a family habit.

For this purpose, 'I mak sicker', or as it has for centuries been used by the head of the family, 'I make sure', is decidedly the proper form.

When a Kirkpatrick finds himself in circumstances of doubt or difficulty, his motto is his trumpet call to duty. 'I make sure' is the form registered at the Lyon King of Arms Office upon the grant of the baronetcy in 1685.

Some branches of the family however, settled outside Scotland, have reverted to 'I mak sicker' as a reminiscence of their Scottish descent.

I must add that those modern writers, who, from whatever motive, six centuries after the event, wrangle as to what were the actual words used at the church of Greyfriars on 10th February 1306, are merely indulging in speculation.

No one knows for certain, for there were no microphones then installed to register the hasty ejaculations emitted during that grim struggle!

No one can say whether Bruce said, 'I doubt that I have slain the Comyn'; or possibly in his agitation exclaimed in his Anglo Norman French, Je me doute' - 'I fear'. There is no reason to think that Roger Kirkpatrick responded otherwise than as tradition has it - for the term 'sickar' appears to be of ancient origin. In fact it was possibly then more commonly used than now; from King to Commoner.

In James II's time, when he was dealing with dangerous feuds and oppressions within his kingdom, circa 1450, "the King's peace was proclaimed," we are told, " over all the country, under which 'all men mycht trauel sikkerly', without needing to pay mail for private protection"[14].
The traditional story has, I feel the ring of truth about it.

I now add a further note to that overleaf, where comment is made on the suggestion of some modern historians, who have declared that Roger probably spoke Norman French when he killed Comyn, "and certainly did not speak lowland Scots".

Because of this perversion of the traditional story, it has been even suggested, that the phrase "I mak sicker" was a modern invention of Charles Kirkpatrick Sharpe.

If you look up the big Oxford dictionary, (so necessary a precaution when quoting old time words) you will see that this gives no less than five meanings to the word "sicker", which was so commonly used then.

Dr. Agnes Mure Mackenzie points out that it was a word of Danish origin; thus more frequently used in Scotland. It occurs in an English poem of c. 1170 - The Poema Morale - Barbour, born c. 1320, used it in his book "The Bruce", Brunne's Chronicles in 1338 gave "Edward sikkered him welle". Chaucer used it in 1384. I find that the more light that is thrown on our history, the clearer it becomes that our traditions, (with an S), are corrected.

Notes:
1. C.K.S.Mss; Lord Hailes "Annals of Scotland"
2. C.K.S. questions whether this was Roger Kirkpatrick of Closeburn.
3. C.K.S. Mss; Buchanan; "Marvellous achievements" Abercrombie.
4. Nisbet 1722 Edition; C.K.S.: Fordun, see p. 28.
5. Hume's History of England, Henry's History Of Britain, C.K.S. Mss., Playfair.
6. McDowell.
7. The Rev. Mr. Black ministered in Closeburn in 1647.
8. History of Dumfries. McDowell.
9. Robertson's Index. R.M.S. 1306-1424 App II p. 96 Facsimile in family possession.
10. Lord Hailes' Annals Vol II p. 23-24-28; McDowell's History of Dumfries p. 104.
11. Dr. A.M. Mackenzie - Robert Bruce King of Scots.
12. C.K.S. Mss.; Lord Hailes - Annals Vol. II p.69;Rymer (tom 3rd p. 495); Dr. A.M. Mackenzie - Robert Bruce King of Scots. C.K.S. Mss..
13. C.K.S. Mss.; Lord Hailes Annals Vol II p. 114; Dr. A.M. Mackenzie's Robert the Bruce, King of Scots; C.K.S.
14 Dr. A.M. Mackenzie C.B.E., M.A., D. Litt. The Kingdom of Scotland.

Chapter 7

Some family relationships after Bannockburn

"Sir Roger Kirkpatrick of Closeburn dying, appears to have left two sons, Sir Thomas his successor and Roger, who is expressly affirmed by Fordun to have been the son of that Baron who slew the Comyn" [1].

No. 7 Thomas; his heir, for his father's and his own special services to his King and Country, got the lands of Bridburgh in the Sheriffdom of Dumfries by charter from King Robert Bruce I dated Lochmaben 24th May, the fourteenth year of His Majesty's reign, that is 1319/1320[2].

Sir Thomas then apparently a young man was said to have attended his father on the second occasion when he was employed on treaty negociations with England.

This small land holding was part of the forfeited lands of the Comyn, which King Robert I was then distributing amongst those who had served him, and it was classed as a "two penny" land, being granted under the charter "for the service of two archers". This showed the small nominal charge on the crown land, and the personal feudal service demanded[3].

This charter runs:- 24th May the fourteenth year of His Majesty's reign; that is 1319[4].

"Robertus dei gratia Rex Scotorun omnibus probis hominibus totius terre sue salutem. Sciatus nos dedisse concessisse et hac presenti carta nostra confirmasse Thome de Kyrkpatryk militi, dilecto et fideli et fideli nostro pro homagio et servitio suo duos demariatas terre cum pertinentiis in villa de Briddeburgh infra vice comitatum de Dumfres. Tenend: et habend: eidem Thome heredibus suis de nobis et heredibus nostris in feodo et hereditate et in liberam Baroniam per omnes rectas mectas metas et divisas suas, libere, quiete, plenarie et honorifice cum omnibus libertatibus, commoditatibus, asiamentis, et justis pertinentiis suis. Faciendo inde nobis et heredibus nostris dictus Thomas et heredes sui servitium duorum Architenentium in exercitu nostro, et tres sectas ad curiam vicecomitis nostri de Dumfres per annum tantummodo ad tria placita capitalia singulis annis ibidem tendenda.

In cujus rei testimonium presenti carte nostre Sigillum precipimus apponi. Testibus Bernardo Abbate de Aberbrothick Cencellario nestre. Walters Senescallo Scotie, Jacobo Domino de Duglas, Johanne de Meneteth. Roberto de Keith, Marescallo nostro Scotie, et Alexandro de Seton Militibus, Apud Lochmaben Vicesimo quarto die Maii, Anno Regni nostri Quarto Decimo".

This No. 7 Thomas de Kirkpatrick was the first Sir Thomas Kirkpatrick of Closeburn and Bridburgh. He is seen to have been alive in 1355, for his name is found in a Carlyle writ[5], wherein John of Grame, son and heir of Sir John Grame Laird of Maskesseura narrated that he had mortgaged the whole retal of land of Overdryffe in Hotoun in Annandale to Roger of Kyrkpatrick Laird of Torthorwald for £200 stg. Paid to the grantee in his necessity. A witness signing was Thomas Kirkpatrick, Laird of Kylosberne. This transaction is also recounted by Dr. Clapperton as being of date 1355.

I imagine it was perhaps the too readily accepted assumption that the Closeburn charters were totally lost in 1748, that caused the Historical Mss. Commission to seize on the name of this Sir Thomas Kirkpatrick as the only definitely Closeburn personality emerging from the Annandale Kirkpatrick charters, whom they could link with "the memorable encounter" in Greyfriers church, when, as their report reads, "Sir Thomas Kirkpatrick played such a prominent part, that it has ever since been a matter of family and national history" ! If Sir Thomas did do so, why did they not tell us more about it, instead of befogging the more common tradition? Otherwise it looks like guess work! He was a Closeburn Kirkpatrick, and under ten years old in 1306, I reckon for other reasons!

One of the various Roger Kirkpatricks of those early days is mentioned in "Transcriptions from the Vatican at Rome, (1290-1418)", in Register House, Edinburgh, where there is a mandate, (No. 21), to grant dispensation from the marriage of Roger de Kyrkpatryk, Sheriff of Dumfries and Egidia Beth, (or Keith?) dated 30th June 1356.

This Roger, sheriff of Dumfries in 1356, had a worthy descendant in Sir Thomas Kirkpatrick 5th Baronet of Closeburn, who, in 1844, was sheriff of Dumfries, whose portrait now hangs in the County Court buildings there.

Diagram of Relationships

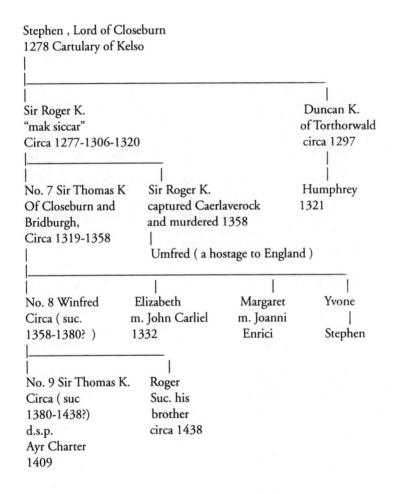

Stephen , Lord of Closeburn
1278 Cartulary of Kelso

Sir Roger K.
"mak siccar"
Circa 1277-1306-1320

Duncan K.
of Torthorwald
circa 1297

No. 7 Sir Thomas K
Of Closeburn and
Bridburgh,
Circa 1319-1358

Sir Roger K.
captured Caerlaverock
and murdered 1358

Umfred (a hostage to England)

Humphrey
1321

No. 8 Winfred
Circa (suc.
1358-1380?)

Elizabeth
m. John Carliel
1332

Margaret
m. Joanni
Enrici

Yvone

Stephen

No. 9 Sir Thomas K.
Circa (suc
1380-1438?)
d.s.p.
Ayr Charter
1409

Roger
Suc. his
brother
circa 1438

The Roger of 1356 must have been either Roger Kirkpatrick of Nyddersdale, the hero who retook the castles of Dalswinton, Durrisdeer and Caerlaverock, driving the English out of Nithsdale in 1355, and who was murdered in Caerlaverock soon after-or-he may have been the Roger, Laird of Torthorwald 1355, you have just read about.

He most certainly was not the shady character also of that name, of whom nothing is known in Closeburn records, but who will be referred to later.

Charles Kirkpatrick Sharpe wrote a ballad about "the murder of Caerlaverock" which appears in Sir Walter Scott's "Minstrelsy of the Scottish border". From this it would seem that Charles Kirkpatrick Sharpe, in recounting this dramatic tale in verse, connected the story of this murder with Bowmaker's description of the incident. See note page 64.

His Mss. history has thrown fresh light on the succession of Closeburn at this period, which has confused certain historians.

A reference to the Diagram of Relationships, on the previous page, and to the 1409 charter, (later quoted) will facilitate understanding of explanations below.

No. 7 Sir Thomas Kirkpatrick of Closeburn[6] and Bridburgh had two sons, Winfred and Ivone; and two daughters, Elizabeth and Margaret.

It is important to note that in the Ayr charter of 1409, Winfred's brother Ivone was specified by No. 9 Sir Thomas, as one of his possible successors, should his first heir Roger fail. (His brother Roger did actually succeed).

For the purpose of this record however, I must deal first of all, with the daughters of the first Sir Thomas. It appears that (No. 7) Sir Thomas "contracted" his daughter Elizabeth to Sir John Carliel, (ancestor of the Lords Carliel of Torthorwald), son of Sir William Carliel of Torthorwald by Lady Margaret Bruce, sister to the King[7].

"The indenture[8] made between the fathers of the young people is dated 8th March 1332; and that he had another; and that he had another daughter Margaret, for, till lately, there existed at the vatican at Rome a dispensation for marriage of Joanni Enrici, domecelle, (domecellus signifies the son of a baron), Glasguem; et Margharita filiae Thoma de Kirkpatrick militis, from Pope Clement VII." (Pope Clements date is given as 1378-1394).

In a footnote to his Mss. Dr. Clapperton refers to John Carliel above as son of Wm. Carliel of Crunington, "Lord of Rons", brother-in-law to King Robert Bruce, thus showing a Carliel-Ross connection, which helps to explain a confusion which was later caused by exchange of lands and marriage. (This will be referred to later).

In Register House, in "Transcriptions from the Vatican", No. 63, Margaret is shown as the widow of Patricius de Moraira Knight, and the date of the dispensation is 14th August 1394.

She may have been a buxom widow of fifty summers when she married, or perhaps the daughter of a second marriage - but in either case, she appears to have been the younger of the two daughters of this Thomas Kirkpatrick of Closeburn and Bridburgh.

Dr. Ramage has commented on the difference of a hundred years between the date given in the report of the Historical Mss. Commission for the indenture of marriage of Sir Thomas Kirkpatricks daughter Elizabeth with John Carliel, and the Closeburn date; which, quoted locally from the writs of Carliel is given as 8th March 1332.

This Historical Commission gives the date as 8th March 1432.

Whoever is responsible for the error in this date, the "Collections for a history of the ancient family of Carlisle" published in 1822, Nicolas Carlisle, (an Englishman not spelling his name Carlyle) refers to this indenture as being in the Drumlanrig muniment room "dated in 1431"[9].

Now the Sir Thomas Kirkpatrick of Closeburn of vintage 1432, was succeeded, according to charter, by his brother Roger. He does not appear to have had any children.

In the indenture, the aforesaid "John Carlell" appears to have been somewhat of 'a backward boy' for it specifies:- "It is also accorded that Schir Thomas with advice of the said William shall get a sufficient scoler to ler (learn) and to tech the foresaid partis ar seen mast spedfull and profitabill to tech him."

The Historical Commission, must have had trouble over this indenture date, for they had refused to accept Bridburgh as a Closeburn charter, while involved this "Sir Thomas" in the Greyfriars brawl!

In the Carlyle genealogy, later published, the 1st Lord John Carlyle (died c. 1500), is shown as marrying the daughter of Sir Thomas Kirkpatrick of Closeburn, Elizabeth Kirkpatrick.

If this were so, a very curious thing must have occurred then, for his father, Sir Wm, Carlyle, appears to have married an Elizabeth Kirkpatrick of another family as seen later.

I am inclined to think that the Closeburn date 8th March 1332 is the correct one.[10]

Goodall, in 1759, (a contemporary of Lord Hailes), uses a further text of Bown, (=Bowmaker - Bowyer), which gives a rather detailed description of Lindsay cutting the throat of the peacefully sleeping Kirkpatrick; and later, has a very detailed account of the death of the Comyn, adding:- 'The said James, (Lindsay), and Roger were first-born, or heirs, of those who took part with Robert Bruce in the killing of John, the Red Comyn, in the Friar's Kirk of Dumfries'. It is to be noted that Bower wrote about the year 1400 A.D.

I have always thought that the motive for the murder at Caerlaverock seemed more attributable to revenge than that of thwarted love, as suggested. No one would sensibly relate this romantically told ballad to reality.

Lindsay had seen Kirkpatrick's son Umfred and his own son handed over to the English as hostages for the payment of King David II's ransom; and knew these youths were likely to languish in prison for many years until full payment was made.

It is quite possible that this James Lindsay knew that his father had not killed the Comyn, and seeing his own son suffering banishment for a crime his grandfather had not committed, visitted his fury on Kirkpatrick by killing him as he lay asleep in Caerlaverock Castle. Surely a much more comprehensible motive for his murder, the details of which may be read in the next chapter.

Notes:
1. C.K.S. see p.28-32.
2. Nisbet's Heraldry; C.K.S. Mss.; Robertson's Index to King Robert I's charters.
3. McDowell's History of Dumfries.
4. C.K.S. Mss. Charta penes Thos. Kirkpatrick de Closeburn Baronet.
5. No. 78 in the Report of the Historical Mss. Commission.
6. C.K. S. Mss.
7. C.K.S. Mss; Dr. Clapperton Mss;
8. "Indenture Thos. Kirkpatrick of Closeburn with Will. Carliel containing ane promais of marriage betwix John, son to the said Will. Carliel and Elizabeth

daughter to said Thom. Kirkpatrick vide writs of Carliel;. Stewart's House of Stewart; Hailes Annals.

9.Dr. Ramage observed this too, but he did not note this indenture at Drumlanrig.

10. Dr. A. Mure MacKenzie in her "Bibliography" records that Fordun left very copious notes covering this time, which were later worked up by Walter Bower, Abbot of Inchcelm, in a supplement called Gesta Annalis. "It is customary and justifiable to refer to their joint work as either "Fordun" or "Scotichronocum" [Robert Bruce King of Scots., Dr. A. Mure MacKenzie C.B.E., M.A., D.Litt.].

Chapter 8

Caerlaverock

I must now return to Roger the younger brother of No. 7 Sir Thomas Kirkpatrick, whom "Fordun" refers to as son of the Baron who killed the Comyn.

Of him, C.K.S. wrote:- "The loyalty and valour of his ancestors did not languish in his person - for, while King David II was in captivity, and King Edward and his troops driven back by a famine into England, he, with what forces he could collect, besieged and took the castles of Durrisdeer and Caerlaverock, then held by the English, bringing all Nithsdale under the command of its rightful sovereign - An. Dom. 1355." " Gulielmus Duglassius Gallovidiam, Rogerius a Cella Patricii, Nithiam, Joannes Stuartus Filius pre regis Annandaim Scotis hoste expulse restituerunt"[1]. ord Hailes[2], wrote concerning this, that, while "Roger de Kirkpatrick obtained possession of Nithsdale. John Stewart, eldest son of the Regent, obliged the inhabitants of Annandale to yield submission to the Scottish government."

This indicated that the inhabitants of Annandale, unlike their near neighbours in Nithsdale, had little inclination at that time to take up arms in support of the Regent and the then existing Scottish government. Amongst possible reasons for this it may be surmised that one was the lack of proper local leadership.

Sir Roger of Caerlaverock's story must be told later, but it was his son Umfred who was a hostage to England for the payment of King David II's ransom two years later. The confusion as to this name's name, which has been created by various writers, must therefore be cleared up[3].

No. 8 Winfred succeeded his father No. 7 Sir Thomas Kirkpatrick of Closeburn and Bridburgh[4]. It has now to be remembered that the 18th and 19th centuries were the heyday of Scottish Antiquarians, and the Zenith of such study was only reached in "Fraser's Cycle of family histories". There must then have appeared to these historians a clear field for real - and speculative - research, in the story of the Kirkpatricks, all of whose records were reputed to have been destroyed in the fire of 1748.

So we find varying accounts, written about what Lord Hailes has termed "the honourable family of Kirkpatrick in Nithsdale", and he refers to the son of Sir Roger Kirkpatrick who was handed over as a hostage to the English in September 1357, as "Humphred", quoting as his authority, "Feedera".

Charles Kirkpatrick Sharpe, on the other hand, quoted from the agreement signed about these hostages at Newcastle on 13th July 1354, giving the name of Sir Roger's son as "Umfred", and Charles Kirkpatrick refers to "Rymer" as an authority.

Some not too careful historians I expect, reading these two records, appear to have considered "Umfred" and Humphrey" as two seperate men, when it is obvious that both references apply to "Rymer's Foedera", (the standard work) so that, "Umfred" and "Humphred" were clearly one and the same hostage.

The matter was further complicated, as there was a Humphrey (or Umfredi), Kirkpatrick, a cousin, of Torthorwald; albeit he lived 35 years earlier in 1321, who could not possibly, in 1357, be called "a youth of first quality", which was the specification each hostage had to fulfil.

It was however left to Richard Godman Kirkpatrick to complete the confusion, in "Kirkpatrick of Closeburn". In 1858, he wrote:-

"Winfred succeeded his father. Playfair thinks Nesbit and Grose are mistaken and that this should be "Umfred" - but Playfair confounds Winfred, with his cousin Umfred, mentioned above, as one of the hostages for the King's ransom"!

I am content to forego any further headache over this relationship, and to accept Charles Kirkpatrick Sharpe's straightforward account, that Winfred succeeded his father as Baron of Closeburn, and that "Umfred", the hostage, was Winfred's Cousin.

The Prior of Lockleven wrote thus of "Roger Kirkpatrick" who reconquered Nithsdale, in A.D. 1355[5].

"Hoge [The g is soft] of Kyrkpatryke, Nithsdale

Held at the Scottis fay all hale.
Fra the castle of Dalswynton
Wes taken, and syne dwyn down
Syne Karlaverok tane had he.

He wes a man of gret bownte
Honorabil, wys, and rycht worthy:
He couth rycht mekil mekil of cumpamy. "
Wynton 13.8 Chap. 43.

"It is evident that Roger Kirkpatrick, (slain later in Caerlaverock), was taken prisoner at the Battle of Durham. In King Edward's order for bringing to the Tower of London the Scots warriors made captive in that fight, Roger de Kirkpatrick is mentioned as the prisoner of Edmund de Hastings, de Kynthorp, John de Kirkeby and the executors of the testament of Radulph de Hastinges[6], who died of His wounds, and bequeathed the body of his prisoner to his joint legatees"[7].

"In the agreement made at Newcastle on Tyne 13th July 1354, concerning the liberation of King David Brus, among the hostages to be given for payment of the ransom, is the son and heir of Roger de Kirkpatrick. And accordingly, Umfred, son and heir to the said Roger, was delivered to Lord Percy, together with John, son and heir to the Lord High Steward of Scotland, in the year 1357[8] There were in all, twenty youths of quality given up at that time. Roger de Kirkpatrick, Miles, was present at the Parliament held at Edinburgh 26th September 1357, as the following article from Rymer proves". (This gives names of those present, which includes Jacobus de Lindesay, Dominus de Crawford, and Rogerus de Kirkpatrick, milites. "To this Kirkpatrick's seal is appended")". "Again, Rogerus de Kirkpatrick Domicellus, appears in "obligatio Praelatorum de exequendocensuras ecclesiasticus centra infracteres conventionum pro redemptione David regis Scotorum", at Berwick upon Tweed. 26th October 1357[9]. (This relates to the interests of the church in the payments)

Lord Hailes states that the treaty was finally concluded on 3rd October 1357, when the hostages were presumably handed over and King David, on release, at once ratified the treaty anew at Scone on 6th November 1357.

When King David II obtained his freedom, he gave Roger Kirkpatrick, as a reward for his devotion and bravery in recovering the place, Caerlaverock Castle and grounds, which had formerly been held of the Crown by the Maxwells, to whom it subsequently reverted[10.]

In his Castle of Caerlaverock, Roger Kirkpatrick was murdered by James Lindsay, in completion, as it was believed in that superstitious age, of a prophecy of vengeance heard in the Greyfriars church at Dumfries after the slaughter of the Red Comyn. - on 10th Feb. 1306[11].

Bowmaker, (an early historian of circa 1400 A.D.), narrated the strange legend that the corpse of the Regent on the night after his death was watched in the church by the Dominicans, with all the usual ceremonies; but towards the approach of morning, the whole of the friars fell asleep, saving one ancient monk, who, with, the greatest astonishment and dismay, heard a voice like that of an infant in distress exclaim: "How Oh Lord, shall vengenance be deferred?" A response was made in a dreadful tone - "Endure with patience, till the anniversary of this day shall return for the fiftysecond time". The story gives, that "exactly fiftytwo years after the Cummins decease, James of Lindsay, son of Him who had entered the Dominican church with Roger, was hospitably entertained at his Castle of Caerlaverock by Roger Kirkpatrick, sprung for his father's friend. At midnight, for some reason unknown, Lindsay arose, and mortally stabbed in his bed, his unguarded host; he then took horse and fled - but, after riding till daybreak, he was seized, by a strange fatality only three miles from the Castle, and by command of King David, suffered death for his crime at Dumfries.

Wynton, who lived from 1350 till about 1420, is reputedly accurate as regards events of his own time, and he relates the story of the murder as it is given above.

He ends by writing:-

"His Wyf[2] passyd til the King Dawy
And prayed him of his realte
Of law that sche mycht serqyd be
The King Dawy then also fast

Til Dumfries with his curt he past
As law wold, quhat was thare mare
This Lyndesay to deth he gert do thare".

Realte or regality was the exclusive right of administering justice within a man's own lands. This, wich gave rise to great abuse was put an end to by Act 43 of Parliament in 1455[13].   The verse above is quoted, as it proves that the date of his murder which is given by Rymer as 24th

June 1357 is wrong. McDowell the accurate Dumfries historian stated:-
"There is good reason to believe that this date is wrong, and that probably 24th June 1358 was therefore the real date."

This is an important issue for the Closeburn family, because Lord Hailes, in his Annals (1797), when relating the story of Caerlaverock, has propounded a strange theory with regard to the murder of Comyn in Greyfriars Dumfries in 1306.

His theory is obviously based on an erroneous date for Caerlaverock.

Lord Hailes wrote:- "Fordun remarks that Lindsay and Kirkpatrick were heirs of the two men who accompanied Robert Bruce at the fatal conference with Comyn".

"If Fordun was right as to this particular, and as to the time of the murder of Kirkpatrick at Caerlaverock, an argument arises in support of a notion I have long entertained, that the person who struck a dagger in Comyn's heart, was not the representative of the honourable family of Kirkpatrick of Closeburn in Nithsdale."

"Roger de Kirkpatrick was alive on 6th August 1357, for on that day "Humphrey", the son and heir of Roger de Kirkpatrick, is proposed as one of the young gentlemen who were hostages for David Bruce. 'Foedera. T. vi. P. 35'.

"Roger de Kirkpatrick was present at the Parliament held at Edinburgh 26th September 1357". 'Foedera T. vi. p. 43', and he is mentioned as alive on 3rd October 1357. 'Foedera T. vi. p. 48'. It follows, of necessary consequence, that Roger de Kirkpatrick murdered in June 1357, must have been different person".

This conclusion can only be accepted if the date of the murder at Caerlaverock was June 1357 and not 1358; and the evidence for the correct date being 1358, is very strong, as seen below.

In any case, how he related the date of Caerlaverock to his "notion" that it was not Sir Roger 'Mak siccar' who killed the Comyn in 1306 is not explained. Perhaps he assumed it was Roger 'Mak siccar' who was murdered in Caerlaverock? If so, he must have been about 82 years old then, for it would seem that Roger 'Mak siccar' may well have been about 30 years of age in 1306.

It must be clear that -

(i) This Caerlaverock murder could not possibly have occurred before 3rd October 1357, when King David II obtained his release from captivity at Newcastle. He signed the treaty there on that date, when the hostages were handed over to Lord Percy for his release.

(ii)   After his release he bestowed Caerlaverock on Roger de Kirkpatrick of Nyddysdale for his services in recapturing that castle [Wynton and Buchanan].

(iii)   According to Wynton, "King Dawy" personally rode to Dumfries, and saw that Lindsay was executed for his crime of Caerlaverock, so that this murder could not possibly have happened before the late autumn of 1357. Thus the argument that because Sir Roger Kirkpatrick was alive in August, September and October, 1357, it could not be him that was murdered in Caerlaverock, falls to the ground.

The murder took place after those dates; possibly, as McDowell indicates in 1358.

(iv)   Lord Hailes, a few pages earlier in his book has pointed out that the commission originally appointed at Perth to deal with the ransom of the King, obtained a passport from King Edward III dated 28th March 1357, and that Rymer had printed the commission, as if it had been granted in January 1355-1356 instead of in January 1356-1357. He wrote; "this error in a single date has occassioned considerable confusion - Abercrombie did not remark the error, and by that means he has exceedingly perplexed the narrative".

It appears that a similar mistake was also made at that time in recording the year of the Caerlaverock murder, with even more perplexing results, as may be seen below.

(v)   It may be added that the legend about the vengeance for Comyn's death being fulfilled 52 years afterwards, would hardly have been handed down to posterity as narrated unless the latter tragedy has occurred in 1358 and not 1357, (February 1306 the date of Comyn's murder).

Should the reader have followed my theme so far, perhaps he will agree with my opinion that the inaccuracy of the comments on the Closeburn Kirkpatrick history as given in the report of the Historical Mss Commission, together with the faultily conceived "notion" of Lord Hailes seen above, appear to be indeed the foundations for the story, already referred to, which has been evolved by a writer within my life time - namely, that the Closeburn Kirkpatricks were not the main line of the family, but had annexed for themselves the motto and traditions of another and senior branch of the Kirkpatricks which has died out in some unspecified way.

To establish his accusations, against the Closeburn family, the author first makes the assertion that it was another Roger Kirkpatrick who gave the death blow to Comyn connecting him with this crime; apparently because ten months after the Greyfriars murder this Roger borrowed £1000 from the then English governor of Annandale, which it would seem was never repaid. There were other "Rogers" then.

It need hardly be pointed out that the connection between the Greyfriars murder and this act of dishonesty is hardly apparent, and cannot be admitted as evidence of complicity in the major crime. It has nothing to do with the case.

Notes:
1.C.K.S. Mss.; Buchanan History fol. 95 prim edi. Hume of Godscroft "History of the House of Douglas" 4th edition; 10 Mkland of Kirkpatrick and lifting stane where stands the chapple of Kilpatrick called Cella Patricii; Mss. Hist of Penpont.
2. Vol II p. 289
3. C.K.S. Mss.
4. C.K.S. Mss.; Nisbet; Grose.
5. C.K.S. Mss.
6. Rymer,
7. C.K.S. Mss. "Among those slain at the battle of Durham, Knyghton mentions Reginald Kirkpatrick".
8. Rymer.
9. C.K.S. Mss. Lord Hailes Annals.
10. "Kirkpatrick of Closeburn".
11. C.K.S. Mss. Lord Hailes Vol II p. 293 Fordun L. xiv. c. 20.
12. Kirkpatrick's wife.
13. C.K.S. Mss.

Chapter 9

The Succession continued

No. 8 Winfred succeeded his father, Sir Thomas Kirkpatrick of Closeburn and Bridburgh[1].

We know little about Winfred, and still less of the fate of his cousin Umfred, the hostage to England for the payment of King David's ransom.

We are told that when King David died in 1371, there was still half of his ransom unpaid[2].

It is not known if the young hostages were then still languishing in English prisons, or if death had brought them release from their troubles. It is unlikely Umfred ever saw Closeburn again.

No. 8 Winfred had two sons, Thomas and Roger[3]. Thomas is shown as dying without legitimate issue (D.S.P.), sometime after 1438[4], but he had a natural son, George, of whom accounted must be given, as he obtained the lands of Pennersax and confusion has thus arisen. He never possessed Closeburn.

It is seen in "a quit claim" that Edward of Crawford "renounced to a worshipfull Lord, Sir Kyrkpatrick Lord of Closeburn and to George Kyrkpatrick, 'his sone naturell', all right he had to lands and toun of Dalgarnock etc. 21st Nov. 1433[5].

"This Sir Thomas made a resignation[6] of the Barony of Closeburn and Bridburgh into the hands of Robert Duke of Albany, Earl of Fife and Monteth, and Governor of Scotland, for a new charter of confirmation and tailzie to him and his heirs male, whilk failzieing, to his brother Roger Kirkpatrick and his heirs male, whilk failzieing, to Ivone Kirkpatrick his uncle, younger brother of Winfred, and the heirs male of his body, whilk failzieing, to Stephen Kirkpatrick, son of his uncle Ivon, whilk failzieing, to David Kirkpatrick, his cousin German and the heirs male of his body - (and the said Duke did grant the said charter). Dated at Air 14th October 1409." (Actually, his brother Roger succeeded)[7]. The witnesses to this charter were "Reverende in Christo patre Gilberto Episcope Aberdonensi

Cancellario Scotie. Johanne Seniori Domino de Buchane filio nestro. Jacobo de Sandilands de Caldero nepete nestro, Roberto de Maxwel de Calderwod" - etc.

In a charter dated at Edinburgh 1410, granted by Sir Robert Maxwell of Calderwood to Sir Alexander Gordon of Stichell, ancestor to the Viscounts of Kenmure, Sir Thomas appears amongst witnesses - Archibalde Comite de Douglas, Domino Thomo de Thomo de Kirkpatrick domino de Closeburn, etc[8].

I find a Record by Dr. Tait Ramage that the Earl of March, who was in possession of the Old Barony of Tybaris, (in Penpont Parish), granted in 1424 to Sir Thomas de Kyrkpatric, the lands of Auchenleck and Newton.

This is the first mention in our records of Closeburn possession of the lands of Auchenleck and Newton. (In the 1232 charter, Auchenleck was expressly excluded).

Here we find a good example of the custom of making a resignation of crown land, prior to its bestowal; for Charles Kirkpatrick Sharpe records[9]:-

"In the year 1424, Sir Thomas Kirkpatrick resigned the lands of Auchenleck and Newton into the hands of George Earl of March and Dunbar, who granted him a new charter, in which he is styled the Earl's dearest cousin[10]". "This George was the last of the mighty race of Corspatrick that bore titles of nobility". (Factsimile in family possession - on it the seal of the Earl of March is seen - a horse's head and shoulders with supporters). "The Earls of March were related to the Kings of England. George, the father of the last Earl writes thus to King Henry IV:- 'and excellent prince, syne that I clayme to be a kyn tyll yhow, and it peraventour nocht known on yhour parte, I schew it to your Lordship be this my lettre, that gif Dame Alice the Bewmont was your graunde dame, Dame Margery Comyne, hyrr full sister, was my graunde dame on tother syde; so that I am bot of the feirde degre of kyn tyll yhow, the quhilk in alde tyme was callit neir. Etc., dated at the castle of Dunbar 18th Feb. 1400".

Sir Thomas[11] was one of the Commissioners that met at Hauden Stank on July 12th 1428 for mutual redress of injuries between the two Kingdoms of Scotland and England at which meeting Sir Thomas was nominated as one of four to whom particular reference should be made in case of any future disputes between the deputies concerning trespass done in the marches. He was also one of the Plenipotentiaries for confirming the peace with the English at Lochmabenstane, anno 1429, and again, in a truce concluded between James II and Henry VI, he was a conservator[12], together with Archibald Duke of Touraine and Earl of Douglas, the Earl of Angus etc. A.D. 1438   It is noteworthy I think, that in 1314, after Bannockburn, one of our ancestors, Sir Roger Kirkpatrick, was one of four Scots Commissioners appointed by King Robert Bruce to discuss peace terms, with Edward II of England personally - and that, something over a century later, another ancestor, Sir Thomas Kirkpatrick should likewise have acted as plenipotentiary for confirming the peace between Scotland and England in 1429.

It has now to be remembered that Sir Thomas Kirkpatrick's forebears, Yvone de Kirkpatrick and Stephen de Kirkpatrick both received grants of land in Pennersax - (Yvone a £20 grant, and Stephen, the land of the "Preste" of Pennersax with mill and portinents.)

There is a charter (102) given in the Report of the Hist Mss. Commission Of this Thomas of kyrkpatrick Kt., Lord of Kyllosbern, wherein he grants his well beloved brother Roger all his lands of Pennirsax with the pertinents - sealed at Kyllosbern - (date heregiven is 21st November 1423). This charter probably refers to the lands above mentioned.

Ramage also stated that in Drumlanrig muniment room, there is a charter by Archibald, Earl of Douglas and Longneville, granting to his kinsman Sir Thomas, Lord of Kylosbern the patronage church of Pennirsax dated 5th May 1428.

Ramage likewise stated that a Drumlanrig charter showed that, thereafter, the same Earl Douglas, then Duke of Tourraine, granted George Kirkpatrick, upon the resignation of his father, the lands of Pennirsax. Charter No. 103 as given the Report of the Historical Mss. Commission shows Archibald, Duke of Tourraine granting "to his cousin George of Kyrkpatrik, son of his cousin Sir Thomas of Kyrkpatrik, Lord of Kyllosbern, the whole lands of Pennirsax, to whom failing to said Sir Thomas Kirkpatrick, who failing to Roger"; and other entail as seen in Sir Thos's own entail given in the Ayr charter.

This Pennirsax charter is dated 13th June 1432.

Fortune it would seem smiled upon "George" the natural son,

for, as previously related, in the following year, he, with his father obtained rights in the lands and town of Dalgarnock.

During his short reign at Pennersax, "George" has been referred to elsewhere as "Lord of Pennirsax", a somewhat grandiose title for so small a place! Could it be that he was only "dominus" there?

Ramage states that some lands of Dalgarnock came to Sir Wm. Douglas 6th Baron of Drumlanrig from Adam de Kirkpatrick of Pennersax and grandson of Sir Thomas Kirkpatrick of Closeburn, in 1423. (This must be Sir Thos. Kirkpatrick of Closeburn No. 7)

Upon the resignation of Adam Kirkpatrick of Dalgarnock in 1499, Simon Carruthers received by charter the £20 lands of Pennersax with the advowson of that church.

In the time of James VI these lands passed to the Douglases; and Buchanan writes that the Earls of Nithsdale seem to have claimed rights of passage to the patronage of the church of Middlebie - "Inquis special" 344.

It was an involved situation as regards Pennersax, which I think may be the cause of certain writers suggesting that, at about, that time, Closeburn also held Torthorwald. Charles Kirkpatrick Sharpe's Mss. history does not suggest this was the case.

Before leaving the period of the Scottish War of Independence, I must repeat the story, told at some length by Jean Froissart in his 'Chroniques', and also by Barbour, regarding the heart of Robert the Bruce.

Froissart was in Scotland in 1365. This is the story as given in "Kirkpatrick of Closeburn", attributed to Froissart.

"King Robert Bruce had made a vow to go to the Holy Land, to expiate the death of Comyn. Upon his death bed he regretted exceedingly having, by the contests in which he was incessantly engaged in supporting his throne, been prevented from fulfilling his vow, and desired that his heart might be taken to Jerusalem. Douglas, with the heart suspended from his neck in a silver casket, accompanied by a son of Sir Roger Kirkpatrick and other knights, undertook the commission.

For want of a vessel sailing direct to Palestine, they passed through Spain, and arrived at Andalusia, at the time the Spaniards were besieging Teba. Thinking it an excellent opportunity to prove their seal against the Infidel, they joined the Spanish standard, and at the critical moment of the assault, Douglas hurled the casket into the midst of the Moors, crying, 'Noble heart, go as thou hast always gone, the first into the fight, Douglas and his knights swear to follow or die'. "The Scots," says the historian, "challenge for the Royal heart, the chief glory of the defeat of the Moor and the capture of Teba."

Dr. A. Mure Mackenzie quotes Lord Berner's version of the story as given in fifteenth century English - a fuller, and more sober account of the action.

In this account the Scots were finally surrounded by the Saracens and killed to a man - William Keith, kept out of the fight by a broken arm, rescued and embalmed the body of Douglas and took it together with the heart of Robert Bruce back to Scotland. The heart was laid to rest in Melrose Abbey. As is well known, the King was buried in Dunfermline Abbey.

In this adventure there were with Douglas, "in his company, a knight banneret and seven other knights of the realm of Scotland, and twentysix young squires and gentlemen to serve him".

There may be some truth then in the tradition that a Kirkpatrick was one of the party.

In this chapter, some involved relationships are given the terms "germane" and "consanguinean" being quoted, and I think this needs to be noted.

Authorities on Scottish law agree that a "brother germane" is "a brother" through both parents" - "a real brother" - "by the same marriage".

Brother germane and cousin consanguinean are further defined in the Hon. John McLaren's book[13] on the law of Rules and Succession.

These are legal terms used when determining the rightful heir and succession by blood relationship.

Definitions of these as given by McLaren are:-

(1) "Full Blood" - (a) Brothers and sisters germane by the same marriage of the defunct. (b) Also brothers and sisters germane of any ancestor of the defunct, in the paternal line and their issue.

(2) "Half Blood" - Consanguinean. (a) Brothers and sisters consanguinean of the defunct, by the same father, but by a different mother. (b) Also brothers and sisters consanguinean of any ancestor of the defunct, in the paternal line, and their issue.

(This makes provision for "step" relationship. N.B. The person need not be "defunct" before a prospective heir is designated. e.g. the case of a bachelor with property in entail to the nearest blood relation, without brothers of his own.)

In the case of a premature death, (more frequent perhaps in early days), provision was thus made for determining the "lawful heir", by tracing back up the direct line of ancestors to find such.

No. 10 Sir Roger Kirkpatrick of Closeburn succeeded his brother Sir Thomas[14]. He was one of the barons of inquest serving William Lord Somerville, heir to his father Thomas Lord Somerville, holden before Sir Henry Preston of Craigmillar, sheriff Principal and Provest of Edinburgh on 10th June 1435[15]. To this retour[16] is appended his seal, bearing his arms - the shield couché, and thereon a saltier and chief charged with three cushions. For supporters two lions guardant, holding up the helmet on the sinister point of the shield[17].

Sir Roger was made Commissioner of the West Borders by King James II in the year 1455[18]. He married the Hon. Lady Margaret Somerville, daughter of Thomas, first Lord Somerville and Janet, daughter of Alexander Stewart Lord Darnley, ancestor of King James VI.

(This ancestress of ours appears to have had a distinguished pedigree, which I have seen represented as streaching back through sixteen generations to King Alfred, who burnt the cakes! I have not been able to check up on that, though the sequence given is quite intriguing!)

By his lady, Sir Roger had two sons, Sir Thomas and Alexander of Kirkmichael. (Also, I believe, a third, Henry as shown later)[19].

Sir Roger Kirkpatrick's widow married secondly, Thomas Ker of Ferneyhurst, ancestor of the Marquis of Lothian, vide Douglas Peerage[20].

Having dealt so far with the Closeburn succession, I wish now to emphasized the fact that during the 15th and 16th centuries, the succession is very well documented.

Records of this period, quoted later, also show that the desendants of the early Annandale Kirkpatricks were, in middle of the 16th century, still able to put 165 men into the field against the English if needed. They had by no means "died out" then!

(It will be remembered that the Closeburn family were accused of annexing the motto and traditions "towards the close of the 15th century").

Inquisition taken at Dumfries
re Thomas Kirkpatrick, dated
March 1585, with 8 seals attached.

*Facsimile Charter showing the Findings of a Commission of Enquiry
to Determine the Succession of the main Line of Closeburn,
from 1502 to 1585*

In the next few pages, I include among other evidence of this period, two important documents, which, between them, cover the period from 1424 to 1585; i.e. a charter of 2nd August and an "Inquisition" dated 1585 the latter proving continuous succession from 1502 to 1585.

No. 11 Sir Thomas Kirkpatrick, eldest son of his father Sir Roger, succeeded.

He resigned[21] his Barony of Closeburn and Bridburgh and his lands of Auchenleck and Sundrum into the hands of King James III, having constituted William Lord Borthwick, Robert Lord Colvyl, master David Guthry, and David Campbell, his procurators, to that effect, by two writs dated at Newerk of Finlayston 15th September 1470; and on 14th October following, the King granted a new confirmation charter[22] of the aforesaid lands and baronies to him and to Maria de Maxwell, his spouse "et eorum alteri diutius viventi" - Testibus. Bishop of Glasgow, Aberdeen etc.

Amongst Charles Kirkpatrick Sharpe's papers, I have found a drawing of the seal attached to this "procuratorial resignation to Lord Borthwick".

The seal, obviously, that of this Sir Thomas (1470), shows the family arms. The seal, only partially complete, shows the name Kyrkpatrik.

By the Parliament which sat in Edinburgh 2nd April 1481, No. 11 Thomas was made Keeper of Lochmaben Castle, having a hundred men under his command[23].

Sir Thomas sat in the Parliament of James III, which commenced 29th January 1487 and continued till 5th May - and in that one, beginning 1st October the same year[24].

From the above, the conclusion may certainly be drawn, that he was the chief of the Kirkpatrick family in Dumfriesshire then.

When James, the ninth and last Earl of Douglas, weary with a tedious exile, and anxious to revisit his native land had vowed that on St. Magdalene's day he would present his offering on the high altar at Lochmaben - and accompanied by the Earl of Albany had entered Scotland in a warlike guise, the borderers flocked together to oppose him, and he was defeated at Burnswark in Dumfriesshire. Whoever should kill or bring captive the person of the Earl was to receive a thousand marks and an estate of an hundred marks yearly rent; and for killing or taking any of his party, if a gentleman, the reward was to be twenty pound, if a yeoman ten. Alexander Kirkpatrick, brother to Thomas of Closeburn, made the Douglas a prisoner with his own hand[25].

The Earl desired to be carried to the King, saying to Kirkpatrick, "thou art well entitled to profit by my misfortune, for thou wast true to me while I was true to myself", in allusion doubtless to some bend of man rent, then so common, which he had obtained from Alexander[26] - but the young man burst into a passion of tears, and offered to fly with his captive into England. The Earl refused his proffer, and only desired that he might not be given up to the King till his conqueror had made sure of his reward. Kirkpatrick generously went further. He stipulated for the safety of the antient Lord and received the estate of Kirkmichael for his own services, while Douglas was permitted to retire to the abbey of Lindores - "sit illis terra levis" [27].

The grant to Alexander of the lands of Kirkmichael forfeited by Lord Crichton and his brother Gavin is dated 2nd October 1484, and may be seen at length in Lord Haddingtons collections in the J.S. library of Edinburgh. The King also gives to him "terras de Lochelbrageane extend; ad viginti liberas et octodecem liberatas terrarum de Duns cum pertinentiis - infra vice comitat: nest: de Berwic -" which belonged to the Duke of Albany [28].

(Note - In *History of Dumfries* it is noted that Kirkpatrick apparently received his full stipulated £100 land. At any rate £90 land is included in the charter of 2nd October 1484 in R.M.S. (ii) 1603. C.K.S. does not accept Mr. Pinkerton's story that the Earl was taken captive by a mean hand). "Alas - poor Alexander - "hei mihi quantum mutatus ab illa"[29]. In the acts of the Lords of the Council 19th January 1484 Vol I page 95 Alexander Kirkpatrick of Kirkmichael, Henry Kirkpatrick and Sir Thos. Kirkpatrick of Closeburn are called brothers, the occasion being that Robert Charteris of Annisfield was sueing for one third share in Alexander's profits when he obtained Kirkmichael. (Elsewhere C.K.S. notes that Alexander got the lands of Kirkmichael from the King in 1483. Perhaps the mistake is in the year, as often found).

In some family pedigrees, a Henry's name is seen in the succession of Closeburn. There is nothing to show that he ever succeeded, and he is not thus shown by Charles Kirkpatrick Sharpe who was somewhat puzzled as to his connection.

He married "Elizabeth Grier", who was the daughter of Roger Grierson of Lag. Her father was killed at Sauchieburn in 1488, and one of her brothers was killed at Flodden.

Henry and "his spouse" had a baddish record though.

King James V granted to Henry Kirkpatrick and his spouse Elizabeth "Grier" a full remission, for conspiring with the Earl of Angus to seize upon the King's person and that of his brother at Stirling Castle[30].

Also for treasonable correspondence with David Hume of Wedderburn, his brothers and accomplices. Dated at Edinburgh 1527.

Henry and his spouse had once before (in 1517), received a full remission from James V for a crime of violence they were accused of being mixed up in, in the previous year[31].

Sir Thomas Kirkpatrick of Closeburn No. 11, who died 1502, left issue by his lady, Maria de Maxwell, who, I am greatly inclined to believe, was the daughter of Herbert, second Lord Maxwell, by Isobel, daughter of William Lord Seton, and the same lady that is termed Mariotta in the Tailzie Carnsalloch 1475 (vide Douglas Peerage)[32].

There have been doubts as to whether there were two or three successive Thomases who now succeeded.

In an inquisition which was later held at Dumfries to determine the succession, four generations are shown within the period 1502-1585, and the finding was, that No. 14 Thomas Kirkpatrick of Closeburn was the great grandson of No. 11 Sir Thomas Kirkpatrick of Closeburn 1502, (four generations).

The summary below will make the text, I think, easier to follow.

No. 11 Sir Thomas Kirkpatrick of Closeburn married Maria de Maxwell 1470, died in 1502. He left issue by her:-

No. 12 Thomas. He got a brief from the King's chancery in 1515 to be served heir to his father. (there was another brother Henry)[33, 34].

Thomas was taken prisoner at the battle of Solway Moss 1542. He married Dame Margaret Sinclair, daughter of the second Earl of Caithness. According to sasine record he was succeeded by his son Roger.

No. 13 Roger succeeded 1552, married Elizabeth, daughter of Hamilton of Stenhouse. Died between 1581- 1584 - succeeded by his eldest son Thomas No. 14[35]. In his old age, this Roger apparently tried to marry again. There is a contract of marriage[36] dated 1st April 1580 as between him and Alexander Gordoun of Trochquhane in which settlement is made for his marrying Margaret, the daughter of Alex. Gordoun. Then, after settlement of certain debts, Roger bound himself "in June year" to infeft Margaret Gordoun, his future spouse, by charter "in life rent or conjunct fee and to the heirs lawfully got, in all and hail, ane annual rent of ane hundreth merks money, uplift at two times in the year of the ten pound land of Bridburgh with the pertinents" etc. Witnesses Richard Kirkpatrick servant of the said Roger, Johne Gordoun of Trochquhane younger, James Gordoun of Crage, William Gordoun brother.

It would appear that Roger must have died very shortly afterwards; and perhaps this marriage was reason for the inquisition, as given below, being taken.

INQUISITION TAKEN AT DUMFRIES RE THOMAS KIRKPATRICK OF

CLOSEBURN,

dated 30th March 1585, with 8 seals attached.

"The inquest[37] was made in the Tolbooth of the Burgh of Dumfries before an honourable man William Creichtoun of Liberie, Sheriff depute of the Sheriffdom of Dumfries, specially constitute, on the penultimate day of the month of March in the year of our Lord 1585, by these honourable men and others subscribing, namely Charle Murray of Cokpule, Roger Grierson of Lag, Alexander Kirkpatrick of Kirkmichael, John Gordon of Troquhane, John Kirkpatrick of Allisland, James Creichtoun of Carco, Mr. Horner Maxwell of Speddek, Thomas Paidzeane of Newtoun, Mathew Wilson of Troghrig, John Grierson of Halidayhill, Roger Kirkpatrick of Aldgirth, James Gordoun of Crogo, John Sitlingtoun of Stanehous, John Chartouris in Riddingwod and William Cunynghame in Lincleuden, who, sworn, say that the deceased Thomas Kirkpatrick, now of Cloisburne knight, great grandfather of Thomas Kirkpatrick, now of Cloisburne, bearer of these presents, died at peace and faith of the deceased James IV of that name, King of Scots, of blessed memory, in the month of November in the year of the Lord 1502: And that the said Thomas Kirkpatrick now of Cloisburne, is lawful and nearest heir of said deceased Thomas Kirkpatrick of Cloisburne knight, his great grandfather, and, that he is of lawful age.

In witness whereof the seals of those who were present at the making of the said inquest are appended to those present, closed with the seal of said sheriff of the sheriffdom of Dumfries, the royal brieve being enclosed on the year, month, day and place as above".

(The signatures of the jury follow with their seals.)

The one matter which is clear from the inquisition and other evidence, is that the line of succession never went out of the main line of Kirkpatricks of Closeburn.

The members of this court of enquiry were all men of high standing in the counrty and connected closely with Closeburn, as can be seen from their signatures; and their verdict must obviously be accepted as a determining factor. Nevertheless, Charles Kirkpatrick Sharpe was puzzled to account for two papers he found among the Closeburn records.

(a)   How Lord Sanquhar was brother in law to Sir Thomas Kirkpatrick No. 12.

(b)   What relation to his predecessor Roger was, who succeeded in 1552.

As regards (a) - It was later explained that a sister of Lord Sanquhar married John Sinclair. If her name was Margaret, it would appear that she, as widow of John Sinclair, married Sir Thomas, whose wife is named as Dame Margaret Sinclair, and who is referred to by Charles Kirkpatrick Sharpe as "of the Roslin family".

The matter of (b) is much more complicated; and some fresh light is thrown on this now by certain Closeburn records deposited in Register House Edinburgh in the spring of 1952, by the solicitors of the monteth family.

These records must have been in their hands since 1783, when Rev. James Monteth bought Closeburn from Sir James Kirkpatrick; consequently they could not have been seen by Charles Kirkpatrick Sharpe.

There is record[38] of a sasine entry, showing that Roger Kirkpatrick of Closeburn, No. 13, who succeeded c 1551, was son of his predecessor Sir Thomas, and therefore was not his nephew, as inferred from a paper[39] Charles Kirkpatrick Sharpe had found , in which "Dame Margaret Sinclair Lady Closeburn, relict of umquhil Sir Thomas Kirkpatrick of Clozeburn

Knight, grants a discharge of her jointure" to her dearest and best beloved 'nephew' Roger Kirkpatrick of Closeburn 156 - A.D." C.K.S. suggests, "word nephew sometimes signifies grandson, but if Roger was such to her his son Thomas, of course must have been her great grandson, but his retour proved that his great grandather died in 1502". Dame Margaret Sinclair was not that Sir Thomas's widow, and it would therefore appear that there might have been a third successive thomas somewhere, which might be borne out by the wording of the charter grant of Robertmure, (copy in my possession). Charles Kirkpatrick Sharpe also considered whether Henry Kirkpatrick might not possibly have had a so called Roger, who as a nephew might have succeeded to Closeburn; but this supposition is now barred by the evidence of the sasine entry above referred to.

In amplification[40] of the story after No.11 Sir Thomas died in 1502, it appears that, No.12 his son, Thomas, (a minor), was served heir to his father, by a Brief from the king's Chancery dated 22nd June 1515, (John Kirkpatrick of Alisland being his tutor or guardian). He was taken prisoner at the Battle of Solway Moss 1542. He married Dame Margaret Sinclair

In the list[41] of prisoners taken at the Battle of Solway Moss, as published by Lodge, are:- "pledges lately bestowed in Yorkshire, by the consaile there" 'Larde of Closeburne, of an hundres pound (land) sterling and more; his pledge Thomas Kirkpatrick his cosyn, for 403 (men), a proof of the opulence and power of the family at that time.

In the above mentioned list of prisoners, is the note:- "Oliver Sincler. Alexander Synclair, James Synclair, being of small lands and good substance; their pledges, the Larde of Closeburn's sonne and heyre, whose father is of c. pounds sterling. Lands and more".

The Oliver mentioned was the fatal favourite of the King[42].
"The 'sonne and heyre' I take to have been Roger Kirkpatrick, who succeeded to Thomas, and gives a confirmation Charter[43] of the lands of Allisland to an honourable man Thomas Kirkpatrick of Allisland of Allisland and Janet Gordon, his spouse, the Reddendo, unum donarium in festo pentecostis nomine Albe firma dated 1553. This charter was granted with consent of John Grierson of Lag, Kirkpatrick's curator and guardian. Testibus Johanne Griersone, Cuthberto Grierson, Cuthberto Kirkpatrick etc." The three prisoners, Synclers, were obviously near relatives of Dame Margaret Sinclair, wife of the Laird of Closeburn, who was himself

prisoner of the English, so it was natural to find Roger quoted as pledge.

There is a "letter of gift"[44] dated 29th November 1509 "by Robert Lord Crechtoun of Sanquhare, superior of the lands of Robertmure in the Barony of Sanquhar and sheriffdom of Dumfries to an honourable man and his brother in law, Sir Thomas Kirkpatrick of Closeburn, his heir and assignees, for good and thankful services done, and to be done, of the ward of the 10 merklands worth of the said lands, viz. Clanry, Spangok, Garley, Friermynnyn, now in the hands of the grantee through the death of Thomas Kirkpatrick of Closeburn, last tenant and possessor thereof, with all the mills and profits during the said ward, till the entry of the laeful heir at Edinburgh - Witness John Crechtone of Harlwood - James Wauch of Schawis, George Dalzell and Paul Watsone. Signed Robert Crechton of Sanquhar

(The lawful heir was presumably Thomas (No. 12) granted Brief from the King's Chancery in 1515 as heir to his father.)

Sir Thomas was one of the convention of Prelates, Earls and great Barons appointed to meet in Edinburgh on 24th June 1545 by an act of council dated 7th June 1545; and he was, at that time adherent of Mary, the Queen Regents' party[45].

From a charter, as given below, it is obvious that certain Closeburn lands had been previously wrongly alienated, and that irregularity had to be corrected by decree. This charter refers to the lands of Auchinleck and Newton, for which, on resignation, as far back as 1424, Sir Thomas Kirkpatrick of Closeburn No. 9 received a new charter of confirmation, from George, Earl of March and Dunbar.

Charter dated 2nd August 1545[46].

"Charter by Thomas Kirkpatrick of Closeburn and superior (dominus) of Auchinlek and Newtoun narrating that whereas the lands of Auchinlek and Newtoun in the barony of Tibberis, sheriffdom of Dumfries, pertained to deceased Thomas Kirkpatrick of Closeburn, Kt. His father, and were recognised to the crown in the time of James IV, on account of alienation of the major part thereof without licence, consent or confirmation of the King or his predecessors, in terms of a decreet of the Lords of Session, and were decerned to be at the disposition of the crown, and whereas said deceases Thomas paid a composition to the Treasury before the death of James V, and that said deceased Thomas died before uplifting said infeftment, therefore sid James V being unwilling that said Thomas should suffer hurt or prejudice in his heritage of said lands, but rather should help him, infeft him *de novo* in all and whole the said lands of Auchinlek and Newtoun as is contained in charter under the Great Seal of date at Perth 12th May 1539, and whereas deceased Simon Padzane of Newtoun, father of Thomas Padzane now of Newtoun, paid his part of said composition to said deceased Thomas for new infeftment in said lands of Newtoun and also died before uplifting the infeftment, wherefore said Thomas Kirkpatrick, unwilling that said Thomas Padzane should suffer hurt or prejudice in his heritage of said lands of Newtoun grants and confirms him de nov in all and sundry, the said lands of Newtoun, in the barony of Tibberis and sheriffdom of Dumfries adjoining the lands of Auchinlek, to be held of said Thomas Kirkpatrick in fee and heritage forever, paying therefore yearly one penny Scots on Whit Sunday in name of blench farm if asked.

Dated and sealed at Closeburn 2nd August 1545 (seal appended)".

This charter is one of these in the box of Closeburn writs mentioned as deposited in Register House in 1952.

It was pointed out to me that there was a small difference in this seal in the Closeburn Arms, as there was a small object (an animal) at the base of the shield indicating it was the seal of a cadet branch.

Differences in seals in charters are dealt with in Macdonald's work, "Scottish Armorial Seals".

He writes:- "seals are not always used by the person for whom they were made, but are not infrequently used by several generations of a family where the christian name remained the same".

If you read the context of this charter, you will see that a most involved situation was being dealt with, because the lands of Closeburn had been wrongly alienated by someone in the early part of that century.

This most probably happened during the minority of No. 12 Thomas, his trustees or guardian making a mistake.

In 1542, Thomas was taken prisoner at Solway Moss. He may have lost his own seal then.

It could be the seal of the Trustee or Guardian (John Kirkpatrick of Alisland), attached to this charter correcting the original unfortunate omission. (There was also apparently a Thomas Kirkpatrick of Alisland about that time).

Macdonald, an expert on seals, and a common sense man it would appear, continues:-

"It also happened that though a person had a seal of his own, it got mislaid, and if an ancestor's seal was at hand, it was made use of. In such instances the granter of the charter is mentioned" (as is done here). Macdonald, accepting human fraility, even says:- "It is not an unknown thing for a wrong date to be found on a charter, and thus it is not always conclusive evidence that a man was alive at a particular date because a charter by him exists with that date".

Which all shows that one should not jump to conclusions when dealing with heraldic difficulties or ancient history.

It would appear from this that the diference in this seal does not necessarily mean any break in the succession of Closeburn then; and the inquisition held in 1585 to establish the succession of Closeburn during that century is seen to give no indication whatsoever that any such thing as a break occurred at that period.

In 1547 a savage incursion[47] took place into the West Borders led by Lord Wharton. They burned and ravaged the country side of Annan and Dumfries and "lifted" the flocks. "An immense tract of Dumfriesshire and Selkirkshire was turned into a howling desert"[48], and Lord Wharton compelled the Barons and Clans on the West Border to give pledges that they would serve his master the King of England.

A record has been preserved of the chiefs of Dumfriesshire and their followers who then swore fealty to England. Nithsdale The Master of Maxwell 1000 and more men. Kirkpatrick of Closeburn 403, Grierson of Lag 202, Laird of Kirkmichael 222, and in Annandale The Laird of Ross 165, The Lord Carlyle (Torthorwald) 101, the Irvines of Pennersacs 40, and many others[49].

Despite this, fighting again continued the next spring. Kirkmichael was found guilty of high treason by the Lords of Session in Edinburgh 12th June 1548 and outlawed.

The above record of the number of men each laird could mobilize, shows very clearly the comparative standing of the family at that time; Closeburn by far the most powerful; with Kirkmichael and Ross a supporting second and third the Carlyle's of Torthorwald then made a poor showing; and where is "the Lord of Pennersax?".

By then the Kirkpatricks of Annandale were not yet defunct, nor had they had their motto filched from them!

Such a 'parade state' is useful as maintaining a sense of proportion in all things.

In the "inventory of the Barony of Closeburn and Dalgonar, from Roger Kirkpatrick in 1552 to Thomas Kirkpatrick of Closeburn 1672," we find the first entry is a record of "sasine of the £48 land of old extent of the Barony of Closeburn, under the great seal, for infefting the said Roger Kirkpatrick as heir served of the deceased Thomas Kirkpatrick of Closeburn, his father therein, and which sasine is dated 4th June 1552. Witnesses Lady Grierson of Lag, etc.

No. 13 Roger[50] son of Thomas above, married Elizabeth daughter of Hamilton of Stenhouse by a daughter of Lord Semple - and by sasine agreement of 7th April 1562, he and his wife, Elizabeth Hamilton, with the consent of the Convent of Halpudhouse, in consideration of a payment of 200 marks, obtained the Kirkland's of the vicarage of Dalgarnock and attachments.

Issue of this marriage was Thomas, Samuel of Auchenleck, and Alexander.

It appears[51] that this Baron came speedily into the measures of the Reformation and his name is recorded among others in "ane contract of the Lords and Barons to defend the liberty of the Evangell" dated at Edinburgh 27th April 1560. The reformers were then skirmishing daily with the French troops, the Queen Regent being in the Castle of Edinburgh

Though Closeburn himself was ready to adopt the novelties of Knox, his cousin[52] of Kirkmichael seems longer to have retained the ancient creed. At the first general Assembly of the reformed Kirk of Scotland, holden at Edinburgh 20th December 1560, it was thought expedient to ask Parliament for exchowing of the wrath and judgement of the eternal God and removing of the plagues threatened in his law, that sharp punishment be made upon the persons underwritten:-

"the Laird of Kirkmichael - who causes messe to be said and images to be holden up and idolatrie to be maintained within his bounds"[53]

Roger Kirkpatrick of Closeburn, whom Douglas by mistake, styles Sir

Robert (peerage p. 370) entered into a contract[54] with the predecessors of the Duke of Queensberry, and Earl of Dumfries with Sir William Grierson of Lag, Sir John Gorden of Lochinvar, etc. etc., whereby they were bound to stand by one another against all mortals to keep together in all assemblies, armies and wars, and to submit all differences amongst themselves to the majority etc". This was in the year 1561.

When the rebellious Lords Argyll, Murray, etc. made an attempt, under the mask of religion to overthrow the Queen's authority, and by Marie's courage and wisdom, had been compelled to fly into Enland for a shelter under Elizabeth, the gentlemen of Nithsdale and Annandale subscribed[55] a bond to defend the King, Queen and their lieutenants to resist the rebels - to resist, and invade England, etc - which bears date at Edinburgh 21st September 1565, and contains the following names: - Johnstoun (ancester of the Marquis of Annandale) Closeburn - John Jardine of Applegirth - James Johnstoun of Corre, William Kirkpatrick of Kirkmichael, "with my hand at the pen, led by Alex. Hay, nottar, at my command" etc.[56]

Though to the bond of association for support of the Regent Murray entered into July 25th 1567, the signature of Closeburn appears, Thomas Kirkpatrick of Alisland and William Kirkpatrick of Kirkmichael are also bonders of that time; the latter still "with his hand at the pen"! yet it is evident that he was one of many, who, in compliance with the ruling party, subscribed that paper, and afterwards espoused the Queen's cause.

On the 8th May 1568, nine Earls nine Bishops eighteen lords and others obliged themselves by bond to defend the Queen's majesty etc. etc. This is dated at Hamilton, and subscribed by the Baron of Closeburn, whose loyalty cost him dear - for during Marie's confinement in England, the Earl of Sussex, with four thousand men invaded the Border, purposely to oppress her adherents. "and destroyed with poulder Cloisburne and divers utheris houss, and carried away great spulzie."

Roger Kirkpatrick died between 1581 and 1584, his son Thomas succeeded, vide inquisition held in Dumfries 30th March 1585, earlier quoted.

No. 14 Thomas[57], proved heir to his great grandfather Sir Thomas Kirkpatrick of Closeburn d. 1502 by inquisition 30th March 1585. He married first Lady Jean Cunningham, widow of George Haldane of Gleneagles and daughter of William Earl of Glencairne. Secondly Dame

Barbara Stewart widow of John Kirkpatrick of Alisland and daughter of Alexander Stewart of Garlies, by which marriage he obtained the lands of Alisland

In the "Inventory of the Barony of Closeburn" deposited in Register House in 1952, there are some interesting entries regarding this period.

In addition to two sasine entries already mentioned, there are the following entries:-

No. 4. A sasines in favour of Roger Kirkpatrick and Elizabeth Hamilton his wife, dated 26th April 1576.

No. 5 a confirmation under the great seal 14th April 1581 (of above sasine grant).

No. 6 charter by the said Roger Kirkpatrick for resigning the £10 land of Auchenleck in favour of Thomas Kirkpatrick his son and apparent heir, and Jean Cunningham, the future spouse; and also the Barony of Closeburn, in favour of Thomas and his heirs, under the reservation of Roger's Life rent right of the Barony of Closeburn 13th June 1577.

No. 7 contract of marriage between Thomas, son of Roger Kirkpatrick of Closeburn, and the Hon. Lady Jane Cunningham daughter of William Earl of Glencairne, and widow of George Haldane of Gleneagles. She was grand-aunt[58] to James first Duke of Hamilton, and to William Earl of Glencairne, Lord High Chancellor Scotland. This gives a Stewart connection. No. 8 sasine thereof 4th September 1577.

No. 9 Procept under the great seal for infefting said Thomas Kirkpatrick as heir served of the said deceased Roger to £48 land and Barony of Closeburn "which has been in the Kings Hands about two years", dated 27th March 1585.

No. 10 Sasine thereon 29th May 1585.

No. 11 Charter, under the great seal, to Thomas Kirkpatrick of Closeburn of lands and Baronies of Closeburn and Bridburgh, Auchinleck, sundum laire, and Morton - 40/- land of Alisland and 40/- land of Kirklands of Dalgarnock etc., as given by Alexander II. Date in index omitted (- ?1585).

No. 14 Thomas Kirkpatrick of Closeburn succeeded[59] his father Roger, as shown. By his first wife, Lady Jean, he had three sons, Thomas, John and George, and a daughter, Margaret. The contract of his second marriage to Dame Barbara Stewart is dated Haliewood 17th December

1614. His bride as already stated was a daughter of Sir Alexander Stewart of Garlies, (killed at Stirling in 1571 ancester of the Earls of Galloway) by Catherine daughter to Andrew, Lord Herries of Terregles.

Sir Thomas had another son and daughter; Alexander of Barnmuir and Susanna; but whether by the first or second wife is not clear.

King James the sixth understanding that there had been continual depredations committed upon the baronies of Closeburn, Bridburgh, Auchenleck, Alisland etc., pertaining to Sir Thomas Kirkpatrick, was pleased to constitute[60] him Justiciar in that part, with full power to take, try and punish delinquants according to law - and in the case of resistance from those pursued, to convoke the lieges in warlike manner, to raise fire, etc., with a full remission should wounding, mutilation or slaughter arise from such proceedings. The commission, which was to last two years, is dated Edinburgh 26th May 1589.

On the 24th of the same month, Closeburn[61], together with the Lords Hamilton, Angus Merton, Atholl, Mar, Marshall, Seton, Somerville, Dingwall, Cathcart and Barons Pittarow and Lag and the Constable of Dundee, sat as one of the Assize on the trial of Lords of Errel, Huntly, Crawford and Bothwell.

Again in the year 1593, the King issued forth another dreadful writ[62] of fire and sword against certain persons at variance with the Baron of Closeburn Grierson of Lag, Thomas Kirkpatrick of Closeburn, Sir John of Lochinver and Hew Campbell, Sheriff of Alyth, were ordered by James III to take drastic action against all rebels

In the year 1590, among the persons named[63] by the Privy Council to put into Exection the Act of Parliament made against Josuits, sominary priests, etc., are Robert Lord Sanquahr, James Douglas of Drumlanrig, and Robert[64] Kirkpatrick of Closeburn within the Sanquahr, or even of Nithsdale.

On 23rd October 1593 Sir Thomas Douglas entered into a bond with Robert Maxwell of Castlemilk and Thomas Kirkpatrick of Closeburn binding themselves to stand firmly by each other in the execution of the Royal Commission against[65] Sir James Johnstone of Dunskellie. (Calderwoods History Vol v p.256).

"In 1593 Sir Thomas (then not knighted), joined Lord Maxwell to oppose the Laird of Johnstone, and was present at the battle[66] of Dryffe

Sands, from which he escaped with the lairds of Drumlanrig and Laig, by the fleetness of their horses! About the year 1589, Thomas Kirkpatrick was made gentleman of the Privy Chamber, by King James the sixth. The regulations for this office, written on Parchment and superscribed by his Majesty, are still preserved among the family archives" [67]

There is a comprehensive list of the Closeburn Estates at this time, given in the Index to Closeburn papers now in Register House, where an entry shows the resignation and issue of a charter to Thomas Kirkpatrick of Closeburn, under the great seal, dated 16th September 1594 which specifies :- "The baronies of Closeburn and Brideburgh, - and freed tenandries of Auchenleck, Sundum and Newton - the 40/- land of Haliesland (Alisland) and 40/- of land called the Kirkland of Dalgarnock with the mills, fishings, and pertinents." There is an entry:- "Resignation of the original lands of Closeburn granted by, Alexander II to Thomas Kirkpatrick's predecessers, as also containing a dissolution of the parish churches of Closeburn and Dalgarnock with the teinds, Profits and tithes - parsonage and vicarage of same, from the monasteries of Kelso and Halpudhouse to which they belonged, and granting the advocation and right patronage of the said two churches, parsonage and vicarage to said Thomas Kirkpatrick, uniting the same to the barony of Closeburn; for the fourth of the services of a soldier in .... of Closeburn etc. etc." The faulty alienation of lands done by some one without authority, as shown in the charter of 1545, seems now to have been rectified.

In 1596, King James "grantis and gevis licence to one trusty and familiar servator Thomas Kirkpatrick of Closeburn and his eldest son to depairt and pas furth of our realme to the parties of France, Flanderis and utheris beyond sea, and thair in, for the space of five years; meanwhile their lands, stedings, possessions, offices, tenants, sevants, to remain in our special protection, to be unharmit, untroublit unmolested or unquieted in any sorte be any person or personis for quhat somever cause" etc. etc.

Perhaps Sir Thomas took a wise precaution in taking a long holiday with the safety of his property thus guaranteed!

King James granted Sir Thomas a patent of the Denizon within the kingdom of England dated at Winton 24th November, the first year of the King's reign in England, 1603.

He was knighted[68] before the year 1612, but his affairs got into great disorder, partly from domestic misfortune, partly from foreign foes.

Whereupon, King James wrote that, "by reason of certyne deadlie feyods before our coming into this kingdom, and by attending our service here, he should be given the space of a year to pay his creditors."

Sir Thomas was one of the Commissioners named by the King for repressing border rapines. 1618[69]. He died circa 1628.

No. 15 His son, Thomas, succeeded[70] - he married Dame Agnes Charteris, daughter of Sir John Charteris of Annisfield, by Lady Margaret Fleming, daughter of the first Earl of Wigtown. Eleven children - The eldest son Thomas died young. Remaining issue:- John, Robert, Samuel, Roger, Charles, Margaret, Jean (married to John Corsane of Muckleknox vide Nesbit), Janet, Barbara and Sarah.

"Thomas Kirkpatrick of Closeburn, together with the Earl of Queensberry, Lord Dalzell and other county gentlemen borrowed considerable sums of money, the bonds for repayment of which are dated 1640" [71]. "These peers and gentlemen composed what was termed 'the committee of War' of Dumfries, and were compelled by the assembly to borrow money to defray the expenses of the deluded clowns trained up to rebellion under the banners of the covenant[72]". The family finances appear to have been considerably depleted thereby.

This Baron died before the year 1648, and was succeeded by his son John about 1645[73].

No. 16 John, this second son, who succeeded, died in the month of October 1646, as appears in the inventory of his effects and goods "pertinit" to Mr. John Kirkpatrick, younger of Closeburn.

This inventory[74], which exhibits a long list of cattle and grain, hath the following passage:- "and as touching the rest of the inventrie, guidis, silver worke and other vessel within the place of Closeburn, the samen were by Robert Dougles of Tilliquhillo, Lieutenant Colonel to Sir Johne Browne, (this Johne Browne was a Whig), of Fardel, and Lieut. Vauss, with utheris, their accomplices, at the direction and warrant of the said Robert Douglas plunderrit and taken away quhat was any way transportable". (This was the second "sacking" of Closeburn. (1646).

This Sir J. Brown was one of the Major Generals of that "True Blue Army of the West"[75], which collected itself after the Duke of Hamilton's defeat 1648.

Charles Kirkpatrick, Captain of Horse, was taken prisoner at the battle of Dunbar 10th September 1650[76]. Here I find it essential to quote

Sir Thomas Kirkpatrick,
3rd Baronet of Closeburn,
1720-1771

more fully from this John's wills and bequests as given in full by Charles Kirkpatrick Sharpe. The will is certainly a curiosity as given:-

"Item - I mak nominat and constitute Robert Kirkpatrick, my brother, my only executor.

Item. I leave in legacie to Roger Kirkpatrick my brother, fourtie sheip pastured upon the landis of Auchenleck, and that giff at the pleasure of God he returns to this Kingdom of Scotland.

Item. I leave to Charles Kirkpatrick, my brother, my grey hors.

Item. To Johne Kirkpatrick my uncle, my auld broune hors. etc.

Sic subscribiture Mr. John Kirkpatrick with my hand at the pen, led by the notaris undersubscrivand at my command, because I cannot wryte myself in respect of my present weakness and infirmitive of my handis" etc. Charles Kirkpatrick Sharpe comments:-

"This poor gentleman appears from his testament to have suffered much through the turbulance of the times. He died while his father was yet alive, who, leaving these children before mentioned, was succeeded by his son, Robert Kirkpatrick of Closeburn".

Here it is obvious Charles Kirkpatrick Sharpe made a slip. It was a mistake in the use of the possessive pronoun! Robert was obviously the brother of Johne, as quoted in the will. I have taken it as being such in the pedigree.

There is now a curious and significant reference made by Charles Kirkpatrick Sharpe to the eldest son Thomas, of this family of Thomas Kirkpatrick and his wife Dame Agnes Charteris. He writes:- "The eldest son Thomas is only mentioned in a contract between Robert Charteris of Kelwood brother german to Sir John Charteris of Amisfield Knight and his father Thomas Kirkpatrick; being styled "oy" to Sir Thomas Kirkpatrick of Closeburn KNIGHT 23rd March 1624". "He died early and his brother John seems to have been in possession of Closeburn Castle and part of the estate during the life of his father".

Note. "oy" was the word used for grandson in those days - so that his grandfather was the one I show as No. 14 Sir Thomas, who died "circa 1628".

It is to be noted that it was to Sir John Charteris of Amisfield the father of Agnes Charteris (Kirkpatrick) of the eleven children, that William Kirkpatrick of Kirkmichael sold part of his estates in 1622.

(This would mean nothing to Charles Kirkpatrick Sharpe in

98

1811, but often the recording of such facts helps future generations to elucidate the history of a later period).

We know that "Thomas" and John's father was alive in 1640, and John himself died in 1646.

I am told it was a common thing for landowners then to make over portions of their estates to members of their family before their own deaths, in order that they should be able to vote for members of Parliament.

Here we have in any case, three brothers, of the same marriage, Thomas, John and Robert, who were "brothers germane".

So, it was, No. 17 Robert, brother of John, and third son of No. 15 Thomas, who succeeded.

He married Dame Grizzel Baillie (her mother was Grizzel, daughter of Sir Claude Hamilton of Elieston, son to Claud Lord Paisley and brother to James, Lord Abercorn. Nisbet Heraldry Vol.2) daughter of Sir William Baillie of Lamington, a direct descendant of the illustrious Sir William Wallace, by whom he had the following off spring:- Sir Thomas (the 1st Baronet), John of Apine, who died young, Grizzel who married Grierson of Barjarg, Jean, Marion and Agnes.

This Robert is named as one of the commissioners for setting the militia of Dumfries, together with Lords Nithsdale, Carnwath, Annandale, Drumlanrig etc., 1668, having been before, made justice of Peace by an Act of Council dated 8th October 1663.

He greatly revived the family affairs, which had long been much deranged, and yielding to fate sometime betwixt the year 1673 and 1679, was succeeded by his eldest son Thomas.

(This brings the record down to the first BARONET created 29th March 1685).

Notes:
1. C.K.S. Mss Nisbet.
2. Dr. A.M. Mackenzie "The Kingdom of Scotland".
3. C.K.S. Mss.
4. See Ayr charter showing that the succession passed to his brother.
5. Report of Hist.Comm. Volume XV charter 104.
6. C.K.S. Catalogue of family writs penes me
7. Charter penes Thom. Kirkpatrick de Closeburn Baronet A.D. 1409.

8. Charter penes R. Laurie de Maxwelltown Baronet.

9. C.K.S. Mss. Charter penes Thomas Kirkpatrick de Closeburn (5th) Baronet.

10. "Consanguineas" as in charter Latin generally signifies "cusin german" C.K.S. Mss.

11. C.K.S. Mss.

12. Rymer Ramage.

13. Judge of the High Court published in 1894.

14. C.K.S. Mss.

15. C.K.S. quotes in full what appears to be Somerville's extract from the Provost's records himself shows the year as 1445; possibly after verification.

16. charter penes Dominus Somerville.

17. It has already been mentioned that Nisbet testified to having seen this retour carrying this seal. "System of Heraldry" Vol. I.

18. C.K.S. Mss.

19. C.K.S. Mss.

20. History of the Somerville Family in the possession of Lord Somerville.

21. C.K.S. Mss

22. Charter penes Sir Thomas Kirkpatrick de Closeburn Baronet 23. C.K.S. Grose and Ridpath.

24. C.K.S. Mss. Carmichael's tracts concerning the Peerage of Scotland. "Members of Parliament for Scotland" Foster.

25. C.K.S. Hume of Godscroft Duff's History of Scotland.

26. "By the Parliament held at Stirling 1467, David Kirkpatrick (shown in tailzie of succession to Closeburn Barony in Ayr charter 1409) and the Laird of Drumlanrig were named to take inquisition of the avale ilk mannis rent within the shire of Dumfries". Records Parl. p.151) 27. C.K.S. Mss..

28. Exchequer Rolls 1487 and in 1495 Alex. Gets sasime of the lands William K. likewise in 1550.

29. C.K.S. Mss..

30. C.K.S. Mss.

31. R.S.S.I. (i.b.i. 3894) 27th Dec. 1517 R.S.S.I. App. 2646 16th Oct. 1516.

32. C.K.S. Mss..

33. C.K.S. Mss. charter penes Sir Thomas Kirkpatrick de Closeburn Bt..

34. His wife's grandfather was Verdost Grierson, son of Gilbert Grierson, who married Elizabeth daughter of Sir Duncan Kirkpatrick, Laird of Torthorwald.Lag records.)

35. Closeburn records, Register House; C.K.S. Mss..

36 Marriage contract in family possession

37. C.K.S. Mss. Copy in Family possession.

38 Inventory of Barony of Closeburn, H.M. Register House

100

39. C.K.S.Mss Paper in Possession of Sir Thomas Kirkpatrick.

40. C.K.S. Mss. Charter penes Sir Thom.K. of Closeburn 5th Bart..

41. Illustrations of British History Vol. I p. 38 Lodge.

42. C.K.S. Mss.

43. Charter penes Thos de K. de Closeburn Bart.44. Charter chest of Closeburn. In margin of charter ("ane gift of ye non entries of lands of Robertmure") Copy in family posssession..

45. C.K.S. Mss. Keiths History of Scotland.

46. For reference dates are James V died 1542. James IV (1488-1513) James III (1460-1488) James II (1437-1460) James I (1406-1437).

47. McDowell's History of Dumfries.

48. Hollingshed's Scottish Chronicle p. 243.

49. Also Bell's Mss. preserved in Carlisle Cathedral.

50. C.K.S. Mss.

51. C.K.S. Mss.

52. C.K.S.Mss.

53. Keiths History of Scotland p. 499.

54. C.K.S. Mss..

55. C.K.S. Mss..

56. It appears that very many gentlemen of that time could not write their own names. The Lord Carliel of Torthorwald was in the same predicament - vide Duff's History and Crawford's Peerage.

57. C.K.S. he appears to have been in possession of Closeburn in 1583.

58. C.K.S. Mss..

59. C.K.S. Mss

60. C.K.S. Mss..

61. Spottiswode p. 376.

62. Given in full in C.K.S.Mss..

63. C.K.S.Miss Calderwood page 251

64. Robert here must be a mistake for Thomas, C.K.S.

65. The laird of Closeburn was a Deadly enemy of the Laird of Johnstone. Vide Myses' Mem. p.220.].

66.The Affray took place on 6th Dec. and it is said that Lord Maxwell after having his hand cut off, was slain by the wife of Johnstone of Kenton, who found him lying on the ground half dead. She knocked him on the head with the key of her tower, having sent out all her servants to know the issue of the fray, and finally sallied forth herself to the scene of conflict..

67.This was written in 1811 by Charles Kirkpatrick Sharpe. He gives the text in full in his Mss.

68. Charter penes Thos. K. of C.; Rymer Vol. 16 p. 559.

69 Rymer.

39. C.K.S.Mss Paper in Possession of Sir Thomas Kirkpatrick.

40. C.K.S. Mss. Charter penes Sir Thom.K. of Closeburn 5th Bart..

41. Illustrations of British History Vol. I p. 38 Lodge.

42. C.K.S. Mss.

43. Charter penes Thos de K. de Closeburn Bart.44. Charter chest of Closeburn. In margin of charter ("ane gift of ye non entries of lands of Robertmure") Copy in family posssession..

45. C.K.S. Mss. Keiths History of Scotland.

46. For reference dates are James V died 1542. James IV (1488-1513) James III (1460-1488) James II (1437-1460) James I (1406-1437).

47. McDowell's History of Dumfries.

48. Hollingshed's Scottish Chronicle p. 243.

49. Also Bell's Mss. preserved in Carlisle Cathedral.

50. C.K.S. Mss.

51. C.K.S. Mss.

52. C.K.S.Mss.

53. Keiths History of Scotland p. 499.

54. C.K.S. Mss..

55. C.K.S. Mss..

56. It appears that very many gentlemen of that time could not write their own names. The Lord Carliel of Torthorwald was in the same predicament - vide Duff's History and Crawford's Peerage.

57. C.K.S. he appears to have been in possession of Closeburn in 1583.

58. C.K.S. Mss..

59. C.K.S. Mss

60. C.K.S. Mss..

61. Spottiswode p. 376.

62. Given in full in C.K.S.Mss..

63. C.K.S.Miss Calderwood page 251

64. Robert here must be a mistake for Thomas, C.K.S.

65. The laird of Closeburn was a Deadly enemy of the Laird of Johnstone. Vide Myses' Mem. p.220.].

66.The Affray took place on 6th Dec. and it is said that Lord Maxwell after having his hand cut off, was slain by the wife of Johnstone of Kenton, who found him lying on the ground half dead. She knocked him on the head with the key of her tower, having sent out all her servants to know the issue of the fray, and finally sallied forth herself to the scene of conflict..

67.This was written in 1811 by Charles Kirkpatrick Sharpe. He gives the text in full in his Mss.

68. Charter penes Thos. K. of C.; Rymer Vol. 16 p. 559.

69 Rymer.

70. C.K.S. Mss
71. C.K.S. Mss.
72. For a full account of the Puritan devices in this particular - vide Spalding Vol.2 page 245"
73. C.K.S. Mss.
74. C.K.S..
75. Barnet's Memoirs. Of Duke of Hamilton p.370
76. Cromwell's letter from Dunbar.

Wrought Iron Gate
inside Closeburn Castle

Chapter 10

Closeburn Castle

"Closeburn Castle is of great antiquity though we have no date by which we can determine its precise age" [1]. The present Tower, "the keep", is the only part of the original Closeburn Castle remaining, for, in 1690, the first Baronet, Sir Thomas Kirkpatrick, pulled down all but the stronghold tower, and built himself a "new Mansion", using the stones and material from the old castle for this purpose.

At the same time, he made considerable repairs to the present tower, as seen in a claim by Alison and Cook as recorded.

"These masons bound themselves (1689), to take down the old hall of Closeburn, timber work and sclate thereof and to build one square battlement round the old tower of Closeburn conforme to the height, breadth and workmanship of the tower of Glencairne, pertaining to Sir Robert Laurie of Maxwelltown; as also to flag and cover the said tower and the *volt grof (?)* [2] - and also to raise one chimney vent upon the south side of the said tower from the middle *volt grof (?)* - to raise and clean the chimney......(?) to sufficient height for venting, etc. etc."

It is evident that, at that time, the old tower was without a proper roof, while the castle was in decay.

Also, a reference to a contract for work on the new mansion, (given below), is dated 17th December 1696.

Since then, many alterations have transformed and modernized the old tower, into the highly attractive residence it is now.

(Here I think I should explain that in relating the story of Closeburn Castle from the scant information we have about it in the old days, a certain amount of repetition information already given in these notes, seems to me to be unavoidable).

The charter of the lands of Closeburn granted to Ivone Kirkpatrick by King Alexander II dated 15th August 1232 very clearly indicated the boundaries of these lands; so well indeed, that my great grandfather, Sir James Kirkpatrick the 4th Baronet of Closeburn, won a land case against Charles, Duke of Queensberry for the retention of his lands of Thriepmuir at Dumfries on 24th July 1773, by producing the original charter of 1232 before Mr. James Ewart, the arbiter, in Dumfries, as stated by him in his judgement.

In the wording of this charter, King Alexander II referred to these lands, "as we held them and Affrica before us". Affrica, the natural daughter of King William the Lion, who married Roger de Mandeville a Norman Knight, received as her dowry, the Barony of Tynwald and the temple lands of Dalgarno and Closeburn[3].

There must have been a stronghold of some sort on these crownlands of Closeburn, possibly of Norman type as connected with Roger de Manderville.

We are told, on a descriptive survey[4] of old Scottish buildings, that the early baronial Scottish castles of these times generally consisted of a strong enclosure wall, 20 to 40 feet high and several feet thick, conforming to the site, which usually consisted of a rocky table or island or a piece of dry ground surrounded by swamps, just as Closeburn must have had. .

Towers were often placed at the corners. These had several floors reached by stairs, usually in the thickness of the wall, which led to battlements which crowned the walls. There were no windows. Within the enclosure, families and cattle were housed. The entrance was by a fairly wide arch defended by a portcullis, with a moat and drawbridge.

Closeburn Castle was very strong, built on a site very similar to the above description.

The castle was on a small rising plot of land, about four or five acres in extent, and in those days, immediately west of the castle, a loch existed. This lock "was measured on ice eight acres, in the midst of a spacious bog"[5]. The water could apparently be taken round to the east of the castle by a moat, and the main entrance was no doubt that side, where the drawbridge must have been, the existence of which we hear of in a traditional story, which is as follows

"In former times, many precautions were taken towards security during meals" [6]

In 'orders for household servants' first devised by John Haryton in 1566 is the following ordinance:- 'that the courte gate be shutt eache meale, and not opened during dinner or supper, without just cause, on pain the porter forfet for everie time one penny' [7].

106

"An estate was lost by one of the lords of Closeburn, who, while at dinner, would not allow his drawbridge to be lowered to admit the visit of his cousin the Laird of Ross.

It appears that the irate laird desired the porter to tell his master, that, by his refusal, 'a better dinner had slipped away from his mouth than ever went into it', and rode on to Drumlanrig, where he altered his will, and instead of settling the estate of Ross on Kirkpatrick, according to his first intention, bequeathed it to his kinsman, Douglas, ancestor of the Duke of Queensberry, whose title Viscount of Ross is taken from this estate".

The lands of Ross are shown by Ramage as passing to the Douglases in 1573.

The tradition is that the Closeburn family always referred to the Ross people as their "cousins", dating back no doubt to the time when Roger Kirkpatrick of Torthorwald exchanged his lands for those of the Carliels of Ross and this Roger is seen to have been descended from Duncan Kirkpatrick of 1297 of Closeburn and Torthorwald, who married Isobel daughter of Sir David Torthorwald.

In 1568 many Scottish nobles and gentlemen bound themselves to defend the cause of Queen Mary. Amongst these was Sir Roger Kirkpatrick of Closeburn of that time.

"His loyalty cost him dear" [8], for in 1570, the Earl of Sussex with four thousand men invaded the borders, sacked and "destroyed with poulder Cloisburne and divers utheris houses". (This probably meant that the main entrance gateway was blown in, with some of the outer defence wall, and inner buildings) In 1646 Closeburn was plundered by the Douglas, "who took away anything transportable".

By 1690, as narrated, the old castle was in such a state of decay, that reconstruction of the tower became necessary and a "new mansion" was also built.

"The house of Closeburn was begun to be built on the 1st day of December 1693. The pavilions thereof were built by Will Lukup, who commenced his work Monday 27th May 1706." [9].

This "new mansion" had a short life, for on the night of 29th August 1748 it was burnt to the ground, through the carelessness of the servant of a guest[10].

It has frequently been stated that in that fire all the family property and papers were destroyed. That was not the case. Some valuable charters were saved, which were later lithographed and thus record has been preserved for posterity. In 1951, two boxes of Closeburn recordes of date 16th century and later, were deposited in Register House Edinburgh, which give records of later years. After the fire, Sir Thomas,3rd Baronet took up residence in the tower, where he died in 1771.

His son, Sir James, forced to sell most of his estates, rebuilt the old house on his property of Capenoch, which had come to his father by his marriage with Susannah Grierson. Closeburn tower was then inhabited by the factor.

Thus, it was after all these changes that Francis Grose F.S.A., wrote[11] the first full description of the tower of Closeburn, as it was at that time.

"It is", wrote Grose, "perhaps the oldest inhabited tower in the south of Scotland. The building is a lofty quadrilateral tower, all vaulted. The lower apartment was a souterrain: the walls of which are about twelve feet thick; the door is under a circular arch, with a zig zag or dancette moulding, rudely cut out of the hard granite. The only communication with the hall was by a trap door. The second floor originally consisted of a hall: the approach to the door was by a ladder that was taken up at any time, the present outer stair being a very modern erection, though the old iron door is still remaining.

This hall was probably the dining room, the ground chamber and the dormitery of the garrison, when invested by an enemy.

A small turnpike stair, built in the wall led to the principal apartment, for the Governer of the castle.

The fire was made in the middle of the floor, as there is only one stack of chimnies, which are in the centre of the building. Above the hall there are two series of chambers with oaken floors and over them an arched roof crowns the building, which was covered with slate by the late Sir Thos. Kirkpatrick who repaired and inhabitated this tower after his house was burned down."

The slate was afterwards replaced by flag stones from Gateley Brig quarry).

"A way, fenced with a parapet, goes round the top. The height to the battlements is fortysix feet. The base is fiftyfive by thirty three feet.

There is no escutcheon or armorial bearings on it - an additional proof of its antiquity - as it is not probable that the lord of the castle would have omitted placing his arms on some conspicuous part".

I think that the explanation for this omission, (which Grose would not have known about), was that the arms would have been over the main entry through the old enclosure wall, which was probably blown in with powder in 1570.

Dr. Ramage gives some more detail:- "The walls are of extraordinary thickness, even in the upper stories being six feet thick. They are filled, not with rubble work in the centre, but with large stones throughcut, imbedded in mortar, so well prepared that the whole is not less strong than if it were a rock".

"Originally, there had been mere slits in the wall, for air rather than light, some of which still remain in the higher floors, but in later times the wall has been excavated to make windows to give what light could be get through such deep perforation".

This is said to have been done when after the fire of 1748, the family took up residence in the tower.

"The ground floor had a well in it, sunk so as to supply the inhabitants with water if they were besieged."

I have given this description in full, as it can be seen how well it accords with the description of the earliest types of Scottish castles, as classified by Sir John Stirling Maxwell. He does not instance Closeburn in his book; for he is unlikely to have known the history of this castle through the centuries, as told above.

Grose wrote:- "From the plan on which it was built and the style of the mouldings of the door, which are the only ancient ornaments now remaining about the building, it seems that the date of its construction cannot be later than the beginning of the twelfth century". Seven years after Grose wrote this, Sir James died in Capenoch.

Dr. Hill Burton in his "History of Scotland", at a later date, remarked "In Dr. Grose's 'Antiquities' there is a drawing of a doorway of Closeburn Castle thoroughly Norman. On a pilgrimage to the spot, no such doorway and no vestage of Norman work could be found. The castle is just a featureless Scottish peel tower of the fifteenth or sixteenth century". Dr. Hill Burton's cursory "pilgrimage" and attempt to discredit Grose, was answered by Dr. Ramage:- "It is to be recollected, as I have already said, that the doorway has been long disfigured by plaster, so that its original appearance cannot now be discovered. I confess that I think that the form of the archway is Norman".

Later antiquarians appear to believe that the tower, (the only bit of the old castle now standing, and much renovated)was built, about the fourteenth century.

Let the antiquarians argue it out; but this only shows that James Balfour Paul was right when he advisd:- "Before sitting down to write a family history, it is of course necessary to know something about the family whose history you are going to write"; and that applies also to the history of their old castles, and how the centuries have dealt with them.

"Those who are familiar with the place know that the loch was drained in 1859, and that now:-

"................in its place
A meadow streaches firm and dry
Where waving crops and reeds replace
That grew luxuriant, rank and high".

It was a tradition[12], that previous to the decease of any of the Kirkpatricks, a swan was seen upon the loch. One of the Barons, after having had a son by his first marriage, married a second time.

"On his father's wedding day, the young man walked forth from the castle, and chancing to turn his eyes towards the lake, descried the fatal bird; returning, overwhelmed with melancholy to the bridal chamber, his father rallied him on his despondent appearance, alleging these second nuptials as the occasion of his sadness. The young man only answered - "Perhaps before long you also may be sorrowful" - and expired suddenly that very night"!

"In "Scottish Armorial Seals"[13] Sir Thomas Kirkpatrick of 1526 is shown as having a seal with a swan on it. This bird has a long tradition with Closeburn. In Edward I's time swans were considered sacred, and we read that when this king heard of Comy's death, he publicly, at a banquet, had two swans covered with golden network placed upon the board; and standing, he "vowed to God and to the sacred birds that he would forthwith avenge the murder of Comyn and visit all rebel Scots with condign punishment". Perhaps he put the curse of a swan on Closeburn, and this Sir Thomas had a seal, with it seen as a talisman? At times, it would not appear to have been very effectual though, so this had better be classed as a traditional fable!

Macdonald's remarks on "differences" in seals, quoted on page 90 of this book, appear relevant to this fable, as warning that undue attention should not be paid to occasional "differences".

When the loch was drained in 1859, a number of relics were found. Amongst these, was an oak canoe 12 feet long in a good state of preservation. This was sent to the Antiquarian Museum in Edinburgh. The tradition is it was used to carry the dead of the Kirkpatricks across the loch to the family tomb in Closeburn kirkyard.

The 3rd Baronet had the family coat of arms carved over the gateway of the tomb, with the Grierson fetlock impaled, (his wife's coat of arms; the addition confirming to heraldic custom).

The words on the stone, read:- "vanitas omnia vanitas", and inside, on the walls over the gateway, is inscribed:-

"Nos, nostraque Norte debemus
Majoribus posterisque
De Closeburn Baronetus
Extratruendum curavit. 1742".
"Sic transit gloria mundi".

Signifying, Sir Thos. Kirkpatrick Baronet of Closeburn caused this to be erected A.D. 1742.

"We and our relatives
have all to die".
Thus earthly glory passes".

Hardly an original thought, but a true prophecy, for his house went up in flames six years later, and he lost all his possessions.

The last Baronet of Closeburn to be buried in the family tomb was his grandson, Sir Thomas Kirkpatrick 5th Baronet, the sheriff of Dumfries, who is reputed to have added the last four words to the tomb, before his death in 1844; for by then Closeburn had passed into the possession of others.

Only a certain amount[14] is known regarding "the new mansion", which was destroyed by fire in 1748. A reference to a contract reads:- "Be it kent, etc, me, John Lachore of Birkenshaw, mason - forsamuckle as by ane former agreement betwix Sir Thomas Kirkpatrick of Closeburn and me, I was bound to work and set up the roof upon the house at Closeburn toun built by me to him; and to lath the said roof, lay jests for platforme of lead and sark and cover the same sufficient for the load, make the two outter entree doors in the .... house etered to the platforme - and sich lyke, to caise ye haill windows of the said house they all being to be with bound boards, the under half of the windows, excepting the windows of the second and third stories of the fore front of the house, which are to be with chess boards, and a chak in the inner side for darkening boards - and in case it shall please God that I, the said John Lachore, be removed by death, etc. etc. Dated at Closeburn 17th December 1696".

The house was therefore three stories and we have two inventeries showing the disposition of the furniture within ten rooms and the "pavilion".

The house of Closeburn was begun to be built[15] on the first day of December 1693. The pavilions thereof were built by Will Lukup who commenced work on Monday 27th May 1706.

The first inventory, taken from the records of the local historian Dr. Clapperton, is given as follows:-

"Ane account of what is under Mary Sydserf her charge and delyvered to her at the terme of Mart 1717".

There is the "linnens"of Baronet; amongst which were:-
24 linen night shirts.
18 Holline and linnene slips for night caps.
3 pair of holline lugs for slips.
2 Woolen night caps and 3 quilted ones,
and a vast number of shirts and "gravats".

A note to the inventory was added later:- "Upon the 23rd May 1720, when all the blankets within the house were counted, there was exactly four score and sixteen pair, besides 4 pair which Thomas Gay gott at Whitsunday 1719 and was to bring back again. There is also 13 half blankets, and there is a pair of old blankets which if they be not given to James Miller herd, are to be broken for any necessar use about the house.

The rooms were fully furnished, headed:-

In the high dining roume. 3 tables, 16 chayres bottomed with redleather; A teatable, silver and china, clock, curtains etc. The general "ware" seems to have been "pother" (pewter). Furniture in the best bedroom was japanned.

In the lemon roume.............................
In the Whyte roume..............................
In the orange roume.............................
In the dark roume...................................
In the Bairnes roume............................
In the Red roume...................................
In the Blue roume..................................
In the low dyning roume........................
In the 2nd storie of the south pavilion.....
In the upper storie, where the servants lye...
In the low roume opposite to the kitchen.....
In the woman house...................................

The second inventory was "transcribed" at a much later date as seen below; "from the records in the sherriff clerks office Dumfries, dated September 1721; (after the death of Sir Thomas Kirkpatrick 2nd Baronet). It is very similar to the one above, with the addition of "the Chaplain's room". This inventory is not quite complete; Charles Kirkpatrick Sharpe writing at the bottom of it:- "The rest of the inventory has not been transcribed by my niece, 1824". The niece was probably daughter of his sister Mrs. Bedford). So much for the house as it was ; and for the accuracy of Dr. Clapperton as a local historian, with contacts then with Closeburn, as seen later.

(Accomodation for the chaplain was needed as, by Act of Parliament in 1672, Sir Thomas Kirkpatrick had been granted the patronage of the United Kirks of Closeburn and Dalgarnock).

There is mention of the new mansion in the marriage contract of Sir Thomas 2nd. Bt. In that, he was bound to infeft his bride to be in a just and equal half of the new mansion in her widowhood. If she was to marry after her husband's decease, she was "to renounce possession of it immediately after her marriage, to another husband; being infeft in half of the old mansionhouse in lieu thereof."

In John Lachore's statement mention is made of the house that he built "at Closeburn toun".

In his Reminiscences of Closeburn Parish, R.M.F. Watson wrote in 1901 of "Closeburn town":- "there is now only a cottage or two standing, and these are of modern execution".

There is some reason to think that the site of the "new mansion" that was burned down in 1748, was in the close vicinity of the Menteth's derelict "Closeburn Hall", for at the suggestion of Mr. John Galadstone, the present owner of Capenoch, who is much interested in our family history, we together interviewed a cottager by the old stables.

She at once said that her father, Walker by name, had been coachman to Brown, the factor, just across the road, and north of the dismantled "Closeburn Hall", as being the site of the mansion house that was burnt down.

This was a very likely site, near the stables and old walled garden, and her father, she said had frequently spoken about it. She also indicated the small stone bridge over the burn where she had been told the gibbet formerly stood. (This was possibly in use as such, when, with the countryside much disturbed, Sir Thomas was constituted Justicier by James VI, and given full powers to deal with anarchy and disorder in that part of the border.)

Air photographs later taken failed to disclose signs of foundations, but a very large and distinct "T" shows up in the photographs, just where the house would appear to have been, for which no explanation so far has been suggested.

Most likely the stones of a house built on that site would have been utilized to build "Closeburn Hall", which is so close at hand, thus accounting for the sign of the previous existence of the older mansion.

I remember the ancient oak tree, of great girth, seventeen feet round the base, which stood at the corner of the avenue, close by the Castle.

It was reputed to be 800 years old; and it was the custon of many generations of Kirkpatrick children to link hands and dance around it.

Alas, it is now no more, for when I last visited Closeburn, I was told that it fell some time during the second World War.

In 1783, Sir James Kirkpatrick was forced to sell his Closeburn estates, (with the exception of Capenoch and Thriepmuir) to the Rev. Stuart Menteth.

Grose mentioned in 1797 that "this gentleman has built himself a handsome seat near the Castle, in the midst of a beatiful plantation".

This house was "Closeburn Hall".From him, Mr. Douglas Baird

of Gartsherrie bought Closeburn in 1852. Mr. Baird did not live long, and his two married daughters succeeded. What was then known as the "Villiers estates" finally sold the properties to a syndicate about 1921, which levelled much of the beautiful woodlands.

"Closeburn Hall" was left derelict, after being dismantled by the builders. Now it is a mere blot upon the landscape.

Mr. Stevenson from Glasgow bought the estate itself in 1924, and spent a lot of money restoring and adapting it to modern requirements as a residence.

When he died in 1944, Mrs. McWharrie, (now Lady Pigott), bought the Castle.

She in turn has made structural improvements and fully modernized the interior of the old tower.

With most artistic decoration and skilful treatment, the blending of modern and ancient construction has produced a charming result.

Outbuildings, alongside the Castle, have been utilized to accommodate an up to date and pleasing "home farm".

The scene would cause the ancestors great satisfaction, could they see the transformation effected in their ancient stronghold, for their fortunes varied so greatly through the centuries, from occasional and moderate affluence to, more often, financial distress.

In those days of border raids and forays, their goods and chattels were few and were seldom left with them for long, being at the mercy of invading armies from across the border, or local raiders.

Would that these walls could tell the story of those bold Knights and fair ladies who lived there in that romantic past.

Notes:
1. Ramage Drumlanrig and the Douglases.
2. Possibly this means that they boarded over the vaulted stone roof of the top story room to give a floor, and built a roof to the top of the tower, above the height of the battlement; as it now exists. In ancient days, the battlements would have no roof, which would hinder active defence.
3. McDowell's History of Dumfries..
4. Shrines and Homes of Scotland. Sir John Stirling Maxwell 1937
5. R.M.F. Watson "Closeburn"

6. "Kirkpatrick of Closeburn".
7. History Cumberland p.232.
8. C.K.S. Mss. Hist of King James the Sixth..
9. C.K.S. Mss..
10. C.K.S. Mss.
11.The Antiquities of Scotland First Volume, published 15th April 1797, latest edition..
12. C.K.S. Mss.
13.Scottish Armorial Seals - Macdonald; McDowell History of Dumfries.
14. C.K.S. Mss.
15. C.K.S. Mss.

Chapter 11

The last of the Torthorwald and Ross Kirkpatricks

This presents an intriguing and difficult genealogical issue. In writing his history of Closeburn, Charles Kirkpatrick Sharpe had not much to say about the Torthorwald and Ross Kirkpatrick branches of the family.

The fact is there is little known about them for reasons seen later; and the Carlyle records are singularly uninformative.

I shall try and trace something of their history from the fragmentary records below:-

Roger Kirkpatrick, Laird of Torthorwald, got a charter from John of Graham granting him and his heirs an annual rental of 40/- out of the lands of Over Dryffe dated 355. The report of the Historical Commission Shows this charter was signed, as witness, by Sir Thomas Kirkpatrick of Kylosberne. This was clearly Sir Thomas Kirkpatrick of Closeburn and Bridburgh whose daughter Elizabeth we think was contracted to marry John Carliel in 1332[1].

It is also noted that amongst the names of the conservators of the peace with England, "as from the 1st May" [2], (with reference to the agreement signed on 3rd October 1357 regarding King Davids ransom), is the name of Sir Thomas Kirkpatrick.

The above Roger Kirkpatrick of Torthorwald had a donation[3] from John of Corrie of the lands of Wamphray and Dundreth with the advocation of the Kirk of Wamphray, ratified by Robert Stewart of Scotland Vice regent for the King (David II) dated 16th June 1357. (It is quite obvious from the following paragraph why John Corrie made this "donation")

The name Roger "excambs" [4], (exchanges), the lands of Torthorwald for the barony of Ross, with the Carliels; by which means they became possessed of Torthorwald, and his, (Roger's) posterity took the title of Ross"

Of the Carliels, Charles Kirkpatrick Sharpe wrote[5] that they were "antiently Knights of Combquinton in Cumberland. William Carliel, (Temp Edward I), sold most of his English lands and of him the Barons of Carliel of Scotland were lineally descended". Elswhere he wrote that "the English Carlisles seem to have had nothing to do with their Scottish namesakes". This would appear to be the case, and Charles Kirkpatrick Sharpe spells the name "Carliel" for the Scottish, and "Carlisle", for the English, families Burke's Peerage, giving the lineage of the present Earl of Carlisle Viscount Howard, makes no reference to any early Scottish connection of this family.

John de Corry and his wife Susannah are seen to have been given part of the lands of Torthorwald later, by David II in 1363.

Charles Kirkpatrick Sharpe is seen to have had small regard for Nicolas Carlisle's book, published in 1822 in London, in as far as the Scottish Carliel's history was concerned. He found inacuracies and "verily believed he was related to none on them".

I only refer to this because of the difficulty in fitting Duncan, the last Kirkpatrick of Torthorwald, into the jigsaw of Torthorwald and Ross, In any case, the Scottish Carliels[6], (who were 'historically' lost for quite a number of years) lost all their lands in Dumfriesshire, through, it is said extravagance and litigation over their succession.

Charles Kirkpatrick Sharpe, was I think quite naturally puzzled in trying to connect an exchange of lands which appeared to have taken place before 1372 with the fact that a "Sir Duncan Kirkpatrick" received a grant of the Barony of Torthorwald in 1398 from King Robert III, on resignation.

Thus he wrote:- "In the reign of Robert II or III, (i.e. between 1371 and 1399), the Barony of Torthorwald went, (by exchange it is said), into the possession of the Carliel family".

He considered that Roger Kirkpatrick of Torthorwald's son "seems to be William of Kirkpatrick, who grants a charter to John of Garroch of the twa merk land of Glengip and Garvillgill within the tenement of Wamphray, dated 27th April 1372".

Dr. Clapperton's Mss., records this as "vide writs of Carliel".

The Historical Commission records[7] this charter as "in an inventory of writs of Torthorwald and Carlyle 1686", but shows elswhere a charter in which "Duncan of Kirkpatrick" granted John of Carruthers 2 1/2 merks of land of Glengepp and Gorardgille on the very same date. (27th April 1372).

A statement by McDowell[8] that William Kirkpatrick of Ross was the grantor of this charter of 27th April 1372 seems to support Charles Kirkpatrick Sharpe's view. So "William of Kirkpatrick" and "William of Ross" appear to be one and the same person   The line of the former Torthorwald Kirkpatricks therefore followed by Charles Kirkpatrick Sharpe became that of "the Ross Kirkpatricks":-

(i) "Some time after the year 1400, a Roger Kirkpatrick of Ross grants liberty to Johnstone of Esbyshools to carry off the water of Ea for serving his miln". (perhaps a son of William?)[9.]

(ii) John Kirkpatrick grants a seasine of the lands of Rochillhead, Carthwatt and Cogries, to William Lord Carliel, "ay and guill the said William has pay off ane sum of money for the relief hereof" dated Annan 11th May 1503 (writs of Carliel).

(iii) Roger Kirkpatrick gets a precept of seasine of the lands of Knock, from Patrick Earl of Bothwall, Magnus Admirallus Scotiae, and John Prier of St. Andrews, his tutor testamentary 1522.

Fifty years later, these lands are seen to have passed to the Douglases of Drumlanrig; But there were Kirkpatricks resident later in Knock and Glenkiln in the parish of Garrell, which about the middle of the 17th century, was amalgamated into the parish of Kirkmichael, becoming part of that borony.

A "Thomas Kirkpatrick in or of Knock", whose name appears in a grant of arms, of the date 16th May 1791, is believed to have lived there about the year 1649.

It can be seen that there is no connected chain of descent for Ross; but, as earlier shown, there was a Kirkpatrick, Laird of Ross, as late as 1547, who could raise 165 men for battle.

It must have been only a few years later, that the Laird of Ross, wishing to arrange for the disposal of his lands, is reputed to have ridden over to see "his cousin", the laird of Closeburn, whom he found so inhospitably inclined, (as is later described), that he rode on to Drumlanrig, where he arranged to dispose of his land to the Douglase (It was shortly after the above date that the last of the Ross lands were transferred).

But apparently there were still plenty of the Ross connection in 1547.

Sufficient to have protested if the Closeburn family had dropped in and tried to filch their motto and traditions from them. They never questioned the position of Closeburn as the main line of the family.

To revert to Torthorwald. There is still less shown in our records about its history after 1357, quite naturally; and the history of the last Kirkpatrick to be laird of Torthorwald, "Sir Duncan Kirkpatrick", is largely a matter for speculation. Charles Kirkpatrick Sharpe does not mention him; but, if I do not try to bridge the gap which then occurs in Torthorwald history, someone else may start speculating as regards this, with possibly even less family information than I have acquired, to guide him.

I shall indicate what I think may be deducted from records.

First of all it would appear that William and Duncan Kirkpatrick above referred to, who each signed a charter on 27th April 1372, were brothers; sons and heirs of the Roger Kirkpatrick of Torthorwald of 1355, who got the rental of Over Dryffe for himself and his heirs.

In the charter which Duncan granted, he made a significant reservation; that:- "if those lands should be justly alienated from the said Duncan.......... the grantee and his heirs should enjoy an annual rent of 40/- from the lands of Over Dryffe due to said Duncan and his heirs by the Laird of Over Dryffe".

Now this rental was the heritage of William and Duncan from their father Roger of Torthorwald!

Duncan was apparently not quite certain that he might not default in respect of the 2 1/2 merks of land he proposed to hand over, for 20 merks sterling. They may have been part of the exchanged lands!

It was a curious transaction, leaving one in doubt as to which of the two brothers was the elder.

William appears to have succeeded his father in the Barony of Ross, but I am certainly doutful if Duncan had any cause to be styled "Lord of that ilk" then, as given in the English rendering of the charter quoted, in the report of the Historical Commission.

He was certainly not in possession of Torthorwald and he was not holding the Barony of Ross. Both he and his brother William are referred to as "of Kirkpatrick", which may be "de Kirkpatrick", or "of Kirkpatrick", (Juxta).

I think Duncan 'was a wily fellow'! He certainly "played his cards well" thereafter.

He married Isabel Stewart of Castlemilk "an heiress" by whom he

120

had three daughters only, who were all married.

The eldest married Sir William Carlyle of Kynmount, Janet married Graham of Auchencas, and Isabella married Gilbert Grierson younger of Lag.

At that time, the chaotic situation on the border has to be considered, as it must have been an ever ruling factor in the lives of those living there then.

In 1332, war with England had started afresh, and when King David II, a bad King, died in 1371, he left the prestige of the Crown much damaged[10].

His successor Robert II had little influence as regards the intrigues and quarrels of his nobles, where there were divided loyalties. There was tension and war throughout his reign, bringing raids and counter raids on the border, until the battle of Otterburn 1388.

Land tenure in Annandale must have been most uncertain with constant changes of ownership.

In his old age, Robert II went blind and virtually abdicated, before his death in 1390[11].

Robert III, who succeeded, is described as "a kindly and gentle cripple". As such, he was still less able to deal with the confused internal situation and was desposed in 1399.

In these circumstances, we find a charter[12] issued by him in 1398 as follows:-

"To his beloved and faithful Duncan of Kirkpatrick, Knight and Isabel, his spouse, and the longer liver of them, the Barony of Torthorwald in the sheriffdom of Dumfries, which belonged to Duncan, hereditably and was resigned by him into the Kings hands in presence of most of the chief men, barons and nobles of the Kingdom. To be held by the said Duncan and Isabel the survivor of them.

The King's seal is commanded to be affixed. At Dumbretane 10th August, ninth year of the King's reign, (1398)." Witnesses a number of high nobility. The remark is made in the Historical Commission Report. "The charter is not in the register of the great seal".

From the wording of this charter it appears as if Duncan was making a bid to regain the lands of Torthorwald, which had belonged to him "hereditably".

He was certainly his father's son, but had the lands ever belonged to him?

From the phrasing, it would appear that he had nothing to show that he had received a grant of those lands between 1372 (when he was not in possession) and 1398, when, claiming an hereditary right to them, he, in the presence of many witnesses before the King, tendered his resignation of these lands.

It may be that the King thought it fit to mention in this charter that there were many witnesses, "most part of the chief men, barons and nobles of the kingdom", if there was any doubt as to whether Duncan's claim could be sustained.

But where were the Carliels and the descendants of those who had exchanged Torthorwald lands with Duncan's father Roger, or the descendants of Elizabeth, daughter of Sir Thomas Kirkpatrick and John Carliel, who in Closeburn records are shown as under contract to marry, 8th March 1332, "vide writs of Carliel"?

That can only be considered later.

Meanwhile, I must make a "guess" 'off the record', in American parlance, that there was a break in the ownership of Torthorwald about this period, and that the Carliels were otherwise engaged then. Duncan had apparently many Scottish friends to support his claim, in those troubleus times. Moreover, it was unlikely that the lands of Torthorwald would lack an owner for long; so I make a second 'off the record' "guess" that Duncan had already, before 1398, seized his opportunity, and been in unofficial possession of these lands, when he offered his resignation of them to King Robert III in 1398.

By then Duncan was an elderly man, in high favour, apparently, with the King - with no heir, but his eldest daughter, Elizabeth, was married to Sir Wm. Carlyle of Kinmount.

The King may have thought it politic to grant this charter, being advised of the circumstances, and that when Duncan died, the lands would go to the Carlyle family, as indeed they did; for on Duncan's death Sir Wm. Carlyle assumed the title of Laird of Torthorwald, in virtue of his wife's heritage, and, in the Torthorwald section of the Carlyle pedigree, it appears as if their son John became the first Lord Carlyle of Torthorwald, when that peerage was created circa 1475.

Moreover, in that pedigree, he is shown as marrying Elizabeth Kirkpatrick, daughter of Sir Thomas Kirkpatrick of Closeburn. It would

122

appear that a father and a son each married an Elizabeth Kirkpatrick; but of different families!

Possible, but I find it a little difficult to accept! It may be a mistake due to a difference of a hundred years in the date of the second marriage, previously remarked upon.

It is still difficult to account for the absence of any information as to what happened to Torthorwald towards the end of the 14th century.

Here reference must be made to the records of Nicolas Carlisle and Bain.

Nicolas Carlisle wrote[13] that amongst the gallant body, of nobles who fought and died around King David II at the Battle of Nevill's Cross in 1346 was Thomas de Carlile.

"He and his brother James were witnesses to the Earl of Carrick's grant of land to augment the park at Kynmount. He is also a witness to a charter concerning the fishing of the water of Annan, when he is styled Dominus Thomas de Torthorwald".

Both these charters are seen, without date, in the report of the Historical Comm; and if they were granted after the exchange of lands, this Thomas de Torthorwald would be entitled to call himself such.

Again, Nicolas Carlisle refferring to Sir William de Carlelle, (father of John, who is shown as marrying Elizabeth, daughter of Sir Thomas Kirkpatrick of Closeburn), wrote:- "This Sir William de Carlelle appears to have been the first who possessed Torthorwald; at least we hear of him as its possessor for the first time in 1436".

There does indeed appear to be a complete lack of any record of the Carlyles' holding Torthorwald before the 15th century.

Now Dr. A.M. Mackenzie suggests that the crumbs of information which fall from the historical tables of Joseph Bain "should be handled with care", as the bald statements in his compendious "Collection of documents", have to be related to their historical surroundings; and I feel that the quotations below, while adding to the confusion about Torthorwald, may nevertheless yield some explanation of Sir Duncan Kirkpatrick's possession of Torthorwald under the charter of 1398.

Here are some extracts from Bain. It does look as if, besides changing their coats, some people changed their names as well, when they crossed the border!

Sir James de Torthorwald[14] - His widow acknowledges gift of grain for sustenance from King Edward, 8th Dec. 1314 (close 4 Edward m. 7).

Sir Andrew de Harcla[15] knight, as warden with three other knights, held the city of Carlisle against his countrymen. Restoration of 22 horses to Sir Thomas de Torthorwald and others killed in St. Andrews raid on the Scots near Redecros on Steymore on 4th August. Four died in Carlisle - £1746 - and those of Sir Thomas and 10 others killed on raid on Pennersax in November £83:6:8. (Col).Exchequer Q.R. miscellaneous Army No. 35/20.

Warrant[16] of Exchequer to pay Sir Thomas Torthorwald £10 on account of £20, which King Edward owes him (Newcastle on Tyne). Tower 16. Ed III file 6.

The King[17] to the magnificent Prince, Sir Robert by the grace of God, King of Scots begs him his favourable consideration of his well beloved John de Torthorwald, who claims certain lands and tenements in Scotland, and is about to proceed thither in quest of his heritage. (Privy Seal Tower.)

King Edward grants[18] his liege, John de Torthorwald whose father James de Torthorwald a willing adherent to the late King, and lost his lands in Scotland and was killed thereby in his service, a 100/- a year from the farming of Ixning in Suffolk for his support, as attested by persons whom the King trusts. (Privy Seal, Tower, 4 ES III File 2).

It is known[19] that after Bannockburn King Robert I had deprived certain Scots who had lands in England of their Scottish lands, on the plea that, as English subjects, they were likely to prove disloyal to authority; and such were driven across the border.

The Comyns and Baliols in Northumberland and David de Torthorwald, Gilbert de Carlile, and Walter de Corry in Cumberland, were in a like case[20] in England, when Edward I, in 1296, dealt with the Scots his side of the border who would not swear fealty to him, and who held lands there.

When the treaty of Northampton was signed in 1328, there were hopes entertained that the ejected Scots would regain their lost lands. As this did not ocur, war broke out afresh in 1332 and "John de Torthorwald" must have waited in vain for his lands.

In any case, Lord Hailes writes[21] that in 1355, while Roger Kirkpatrick "of Nyddysdale" obtained possession of Nithsdale, John

Stewart, eldest son of the Regent "obliged" the inhabitants of Annandale to yield submission to the Scottish government.

Roger Kirkpatrick of Nyddysdale regained[22] that valley by force of arms, but Annandale was long under English domination; and Jedburgh was not free from English occupation until the local people rose and took it in 1407. It had been in English hands since 1346. Such was the state of the border then; and the English would be unlikely to reinstate previously ejected Scots in such circumstances .

I am only prepared to speculate about my own, and not about other peoples' family histories; so I shall confine myself to stating that I think that Sir Duncan Kirkpatrick probably seized his opportunity in the absence of the Carliels, to lay claim to the lands of Torthorwald, formerly held by his father, which could be considered ownerless due to the hazards of war.

He does not come into the picture of the main line of Closeburn; but it had to be shown why this was probably the case.

Dr. Clapperton gave this description of the arms of Torthorwald in 1784 which were then to be seen "cut on a formal shield, hung by the dexter corner, by a belt issuing from a rose, upon a stone brought from the old castle of Torthorwald, new built in the east gable of the miller's house there; as also on another formal shield, supported by a sword, with the Scots thistle in form of a cross flovy, paralel with the sword, with a broken inscription in latin in antient characters, on a stone dug from the foundation of the old church of Torthorwald, and now to be seen on the south volt of the new one, which was built last year".

Charles Kirkpatrick Sharpe also quotes from the Mss. of Grose, a description of the arms:- "in the end of a cottage near the ruin; a stone with a shield and the following bearings cut upon it. Beneath a chief charged with three pellets, a saltier - the crest like a rose; and in the wall of the church is a tombstone on which are neatly carved; a cross, a sword and shield with the above bearings".

No - I do not think the Closeburn Kirkpatricks borrowed anything from Torthorwald; and the full story of that place remains untold. The Carliels appear not to have recorded their doings there for many years, but left this to Bain until the beginning of the 15th century.

Very negligent of them if they wanted a place in the history of that time. The Ross Kirkpatricks, save one Duncan before mentioned,

125

seem to have struck to their Ross Barony acquired by exchange, until their lands passed finally to the Douglases in the middle of the 15th century. There is not a hint that any other family supplanted them and took their motto!

The infamous Sir Roger Kirkpatrick Kt. Of Auchencas had no apparent connection with Torthorwald at any time either in 1306 - 1313 or 1332, (when we hear about him) - and his arms when he borrowed money from the English Governer of Annandale one day in 1306 and affixed his seal to the bond. This had a Trefoil three shields meeting at a point; which does not relate him to anyone in Torthorwald; or in the Church of Greyfriars Dumfries!

There certainly appears to be doubt as to the correctness of certain dates as given in records regarding Scottish Carliels: and Charles Kirkpatrick Sharpe confined himself in 1811 to a very brief summary of the Torthorwald history, as can be seen at the bottom of page 18 of this book.

He connects the passing of the Barony of Torthorwald with the death of the third Baron of Drumlanrig in 1464; correctly it would seem from the following, which I have from an official source:-

"The date of the death of William Douglas, third Baron of Drumlanrig, is given in the Historical Mss. Commission Report XV on the Buccleuch Muniments appendix VIII page 4, as in the year 1464.

The pearage article, however, in the Scotts peerage VII on Douglas Duke of Queensberry, p. 116, casts some doubt on this, and suggests the third Baron was alive in 1466, but the reasoning in the pearage articol is somewhat suspect".

Thus the Torthorwald history remains uncertain.

Notes:
1. C.K.S Mss..
2. Dr. Clapperton Mss..
3. C.K.S. Mss.; Report of Hist Commission.
4. Dr. Clapperton Mss..
5. C.K.S. Mss.; Denton's Hist of Cumberland.
6. Nicolas Carlisle.
7. Report of the Historical Commission.
8. History of Dumfries.

9. C.K.S. Mss..

10. Dr. A.M. Mackenzie C.B,E., D. Litt..

11. Dr. A.M. Mckenzie.

12. Report of Historical Mss. Commission.

13. "Collections for a history of the ancient family of Carlisle". Pub. 1822.

14. Bain (406) 8 Dec. 1314.

15. Bain (403) 8th July, 30th Nov. 1314

16. Bain (725) 16th Sept. 1322.

17.Bain (958) 1328.

18. Bain (1020) 1330-31

19. Dr A.M. Mackenzie The Kingdom of Scotland.

20. McDowell History of Dumfries.

21.Lord Hailes Annals of Scotland; Wynton.

22. Dr. A.M. Mackenzie. "The Kingdom of Scotland".

Chapter 12

The Baronetcy of Closeburn

No. 18 Sir Thomas, 1st Baronet, created 1685, is shown as succeeding before the death of his father No. 17 Robert, probably for the same reason as his grandfather No. 16 John, was previously given early possession of Closeburn and some of the estates.

Sir Thomas was infeft and seased in the Barony of Closeburn 17th May 1667.

In 1671, Sir Thomas resettled his estates by charter, ratified by Parliament in 1672, to include the united kirks of Closeburn and Dalgarnock. He re-registered[1] his arms at the office of the Lyon King of Arms in Edinburgh in 1673, according to the arms shown in Sir David Lindsay of the Mount, Lyon King's Register of 1542, as requested then to be done by Act of Parliament of 1672 1.

"He supported the importance of his family with much splendour and hospitality, continuing true to the Crown and mitre through the chameleon reigns of Charles and James"[2].

Simpson in his "Traditions of the Covenanters" tells a pleasing story of Sir Thomas.

One day a party of troopers were sent to the mansion of Sir Thomas Kirkpatrick, for the purpose of demanding aid in searching for Whigs in his woods. The woods, linns, and cottages of Closeburn furnished shelter for many a wanderer.

Sir Thomas was obliged to comply with the demands and accompanied the soldiers to the woods. He pursued the nearer routes to the supposed hiding places of the Covenanters, using narrow footpaths, while the horsemen were obliged to take more circuitous routes.

In winding his way through the thicket, Sir Thomas came upon a man fast asleep by the side of the path, obviously one of those for whom the soldiers were searching. Nearby was a heap of newly cut bracken. This, Sir Thomas turned over with his staff, to cover the sleeping man.

His action was seen by one of the troopers, who cried out that the guide was doing something suspicious, but before any of the party

Sir James Kirkpatrick,
4th Baronet of Closeburn,
1771-1804

had time to dismount and investigate, Sir Thomas turned round, and, in an indignant tone, asked if he could not be permitted to turn the loose bracken and withered leaves of his own forest without their permission, and so the matter ended and the man remained undiscovered.

"Sir Thomas had a confidential domestic servant, whom he employed to give warning to the Covenanters seeking shelter on his property; and for the protection thus afforded by the family, they were endered to the whole countryside. It is easy therefore to understand how, notwithstanding their attachment is the Stuart dynasty and their little sympathy with the excesses of fanatics, they would shrink from abetting any attack on the reformed religion"[3].

In 1684 Sir Thomas was one of the Commissioners of the border empowered to try several persons accused of horsestealing and other crimes; and together with Lord William Douglas and others he took the "Test" at Dumfries "in conforme the Act of Parliament in all points"[4].

His position must at times have been a very difficult one; for later, according to Charles Kirkpatrick Sharpe, he was "classed among the persecuters of the Godly in the cloud of (false) witnesses;" having exacted 700 pounds in fines from the Covenanters of Nithsdale , to insure their peaceable behaviour and conformity with the established mode of worship; and thereby, their immunity from the fatal musket, or more destructive noose!"

"His efforts in the service of his country were so exceptable to the throne, that King James VIII was graciously pleased to create him a Knight baronet of Nova Scotia by a patent dated at Whitehall 26th March 1685. It is said that at the Revolution, he had the offer of a Peerage with the style and dignity of Earl of Closeburn, but he refused it, doubtless for some good reason, which is not apparent to his posterity"[5].

In "Kirkpatrick of Closeburn", this explanation is offered:-

"It may at first sight appear inconsistent that Sir Thomas Kirkpatrick, a staunch supporter of the Stuarts, and rewarded by them with a baronetcy, should have had an offer of a coronet from William III; but, it should be borne in mind that the family had been for more than a century warm advocates of the Reformation, strengthened by the connection by marriage with the family of the Earl of Glencairne a most strenuous supporter of the cause.

It may be easily understood that Sir Thomas felt a delicacy

Sir Thomas Kirkpatrick,
5th Baronet of Closeburn,
1804-1844

in accepting the personnal reward of an Earldom, which might be misconstrued into his having for selfish objects assisted William against the Stuarts, who had so recently bestowed on him a baronetcy; and it is also a tradition in the family that he preferred remaining what his forefathers had been, a leader among the ancient gentry, rather than be lost as a new made 'Peer' ".

Sir Thomas Kirkpatrick, the first Baronet, was made Lt. Colonel of the Dumfriesshire Militia in 1691 and was M.P. for the country 1695 and 1698.

He married first the Hon. Isabel Sandilands, daughter of John Lord Torthicon descended descended from Sir James Sandilands, wo married Joan, the daughter of King Robert II. The marriage contract is dated 25th April 1666.

He married secondly Sarah, daughter of Robert Ferguson of Craigdarrock. 7th December 1672.

He married for the third time, in 1686, Grizzel the daughter of Gavin Hamilton of Raploch, and widow of Inglis of Murdiston. By her he had no issue.

His son and heir Thomas, was by his first wife.

Roger of Alisland was by his second wife. It was he, who is said to have been the last to see the fatal swan; and he died a bachelor. There was another son, James, who at the age of 18 took umbrage at his father's third marriage, and after witnessing the ceremony, left his father's house in anger for ever. He went to England married Ann Hoar at Romsey in 1703. They moved to the Isle of Wight, and there settled, founding the branch known as the Isle of Wight Kirkpatricks. As James was 18 at the time of his father's 3rd marriage it appears he must have been born in 1668, as the second son of the first marriage. My uncle, Roger Kirkpatrick of Lagganlees, married Isabella Kirkpatrick of this Isle of Wight family, of which more later.

Sir Thomas was apparently pretty autocratic in his ways.

It will be told in the story of Closeburn Castle how he built for himself a new mansion as he then found the old castle falling into decay; and later he drew up a marriage contract for his son, which runs into six closely written pages about his property. Amongst other matters laid down for the bride was a clause that:- "the heirs female and the descendants of their body who shall happen to succeed to the foresaids lands and estate, shall keep, assume, bear, wear and use the surname, arms and designation of Kirkpatrick of Closeburn, without any alteration as their own proper surname, arms and designation, in all time coming; and if any of the said heirs female or the descendants of their body who shall happen to succeed to the lands etc., shall doe in the contrair hereof, then, and in that case, the person so contraveening, shall ipso facto without any declaration to follow, hereupon amitt, lose and tyne their right, title and succession above specified to the lands and Barony; and the same shall fall and accrese to the next heirs, as if the contraveeners and descendants of their bodys were naturally dead -"

Charles Kirkpatrick Sharpe quotes from some old memorandum books of this and the 2nd baronet's to show what small salaries and wages were paid at that time. The "cook" John Stewart entered 24th November 1690, "to get £24 yearly and a pair of shoes and hosen". Another entry reads "Mr. James Wallis entered my service in the station of Chaplain at Whit's 1703, his fee for a year 40lb. Scots"!

The 1st Baronet died sometime after 1702.

No. 19 Sir Thomas, his eldest son, succeeded him as 2nd Baronet. He took an active part[6] in repressing the Rebellion in 1715, when "the Fencibles" in upper Nithsdale were called out. In September the Duke of Argyll, Commissioner in chief of Scotland sent for volunteers for the Royal Army at Stirling. Under Sir Thos. Kirkpatrick, James Grierson of Capenoch and others, 400 effective men and 100 horsemen rendezvoused at Keir Moss, Penpont. Sir Thos. Kirkpatrick promised to defray all expenses of his tenants, and paid them 8d. a day.

When, shortly after this, the rebels in Dumfriesshire and Kirkcudbright rose and Threatened Dumfries, so firm a front was shown, that the rebels were forced to retire into the north of England and joined with Lord Derwentwater.

Upon this occasion, the men of Closeburn carried a banner, five feet long and four deep, the colour of the family livery, (blue with yellow facings), with the baronets arms fully blazened, surmounted by an inscription:-

"For King George, liberty and religion according to the Scots Reformation".

This flag was bequeathed to my grandfather by Charles Kirkpatrick Sharpe, in whose possession it then was.

I remember it in possession of my father, but he, feeling that such a heirloom should be in possession of the Baronet, as head of the family, sent it to, I believe, Sir James, the 6th Baronet, who was employed at the Admiralty. Before my father sent it, my sister Margaret made a water colour drawing of the flag; but where the flag now is, I have been unable to ascertain.

This flag shows the Talbot hounds as supporters, as in Nisbet in place of the lions formally used as such.

In 1702, Sir Thomas 2nd Bt. Married Isabel, eldest daughter of Sir William Lockhart of Carstairs Bt. and Lady Isabel Douglas, sister to the first Duke of Queensberry, by whom he had the following issue:- Thomas (3rd Bt.), born 1704, James who died at Calcutta a bachelor; William, and Robert, born 1711 and died an infant; and one daughter, who also died young. William, 3rd son, born 1705, had the estate of Alisland left him by his father. He represented the Burghs of the Dumfries district in Parliament. He married Jean, third daughter of Charles Erskine of Alva, Lord Justice Clerk of Scotland, descended from the family of Mar. William Kirkpatrick died in 1777, issue 3 daughters, Grizzel, Jane and Isabella and two sons; Thomas who died young and Charles, who changed his name to Sharpe according to the writ of Matthew Sharpe, his mother's grand uncle, who bequeathed him his whole estate of Hoddom.

Charles Sharpe married Eleanora Renton. According to the Preface to the two volumes of published correspondence of C.K.S., Charles Sharpe had by his wife, five sons; Mathew, colonel in the army, William John, Charles Kirkpatrick Sharpe, Alexander, and John William - and seven daughters - Susan, Jane, Ellenora, Isabella (I), Isabella (II), Elizabeth Cecilia, and Grace who married Rev. W.K.R. Bedford (I do not vouch for the accuracy of these but all their birthdays are given).

Sir Thomas 2nd Bt. died in 1720.

No. 20 Sir Thomas, his eldest son, succeeded[7] him as 3rd Baronet, at the age of sixteen. He made a tour of France and Italy and returned to bear a great sway in the politics of Dumfriesshire, and, together with Charles Erskine, brought his brother William into parliament, though opposed by the Duke of Queensberry, his second cousin.

It was on 29th August 1748 that Closeburn mansion was burnt down. Only a "pavilion"was said to have been left standing, saved, it is said, by a servant piling 'divits' against a door. It was in the second story of this pavilion that the servants lived, according to the inventory.

After the destruction of Closeburn House, Sir Thomas took up his abode in the tower. There he died in October 1771. He married in October 1727 Susanna Grierson, only daughter and sole heiress of James Grierson of Capenoch by his third wife Catherine Sharpe. By her he had the following children:- Thomas, who died before his father. James, George, William, Isabella married to Robert Herries of Haldykes, Joan and Christian.

Much ruinous expenditure had been incurred[8] at this time in political contests. Various members of the family and and their connections had sat in Parliament for the county or Borough, and they now found their claim disputed by their powerful neighbour the Duke of Queensberry

In all these contests Sir Thomas plunged, with a disregard to expense, which ultimately involved the family in serious difficulties.

The portrait of this Sir Thomas the 3rd Bt., was said to be a copy of the original which was destroyed in the fire of 1748. The copy was formerly with Miss Lumsden a descendant of his and came to our family on her death.

The portrait, together with other heirlooms of this family are the property of my nephew Ivone Kirkpatrick at present in South Africa, now head of that branch of the Closeburn family directly descended from Sir James Kirkpatrick 4th Baronet of Closeburn.

No. 21. Sir James Kirkpatrick 4th Baronet succeeded his father in 1771.

It is not clear when he and his family went to live in "Capenoch". There was a question whether they would not go to "Shaws", the other Grierson property, which came from their mother. Sir James found Capenoch needed considerable reconstruction, and the present owner, Mr. John Gladstone, points out that the thick walls and vaulted roof built without wood, part of the present house, may indicate that this type of building was done to avoid risk of fire.

Certainly the "Capenoch bell", a very large hand bell which I have, is designed "to wake the dead", if rung. It looks as if it was a case of "once bitten, twice shy".

Sir James devoted himself strenuously to restoring prosperity to his estates, which he found crippled by previous extravagance.

He tried[9] to introduce many agricultural improvements. He discovered limestone in Closeburn and established a lime factory; but

136

he met with much opposition to using lime, from the ignorance and prejudice of the tenants; and Sir James found it necessary to compel them in their leases to lime a certain quantity of their land; he furnished them with the lime and even paying the cartage.

Later, other county gentlemen followed his example, his lime factory proven a success. He wrote a pamphlet on estate management and he greatly increased the value of his own estates; but he found himself unable to meet the debts previously incurred.

It is seen that ten years before he had to sell the barony, Sir James upon his own resignation, obtained a new charter under the Great Seal, of the lands and barony of Closeburn, dated 11th March 1774, excepting a number of lands, the superiority of which were previously, or later, disposed within the family, certain of them in life rent.

The above charter is important as showing who had had the superiority of the Closeburn lands then.

I surmise this disposition was done to exercise closer supervision and efficiency of management in the fourteen different properties named, and possibly in the development of the new lime factory.

Meanwhile , the depreciating effects of the war with America had caused a great drop in the value of land. We are told[10]:- "Money was scarce and valuable. Creditors were pressing, and Sir James, a man of nice honour and refined sensitiveness, decided to meet their wants by the bitter sacrifice of estates held by his ancestors"

To satisfy his creditors, my great grandfather made over to a trustee to sell, Closeburn and about 14,000 acres, retaining only Capenoch, the patrimony of his mother, and a few properties including the small piece of moorland known as Thriepmuir, adjoining the Duke of Queensberry's lands.

The trustee effected a hasty sale of the Closeburn barony to the Rev. Stuart Menteth for £50,000 in 1783.

There are papers in my great grandfather's writing which make sad reading, for his debts then amounted to but £38,000 and the potential value of the land was much more.

Extensive improvements were made during the Menteth's tenure of Closeburn and there was a continued rise in the value of land.

In 1852, Sir James Menteeth sold the Closeburn lands to Mr. Douglas Baird of Gartsherrie for £225,000, with £30,000 for "Shaws". My father had a note that the estates were valued in 1875-76 for the Bairds' successors at £500,000.

The estates were disposed of by the Bairds' trustees, and were finally broken up by a syndicate which had bought them, in about 1921.

The Dumfries Courier and Herald of 8th January 1924, in commenting on the sale of the Closeburn barony considered "it would be under the mark in estimating the present, (then), value of the land at sevenfold the original purchase value".

So it was thus that Closeburn passed out of possession of the family, only the small bit of moorland called Thriepmuir still remains in our branch of the family; which was bought in after the sheriff died, by my father, so that a small portion of the ancient property should remain in the family. This is now in the possession of my nephew Ivone Kirkpatrick, the head of our branch at present in South Africa.

Sir James married Miss Mary Jardine, and in his family bible are entered the names of their children:-

Thomas, born 28th October 1768, died young.
Susanna, born 14th January 1771
Isabella born 8th August 1772.
Jeanie born 29th December 1773.
Mary born 18th October 1775.
Thomas born 25th April 1777 (5th Bt.)
Roger born 28th August 1779 (my grandfather).

Sir James died in Capenoch in 1804.

The Dumfries Weekly Journal of 12th June 1804 described him as "the representative of an ancient and respectable family, which had inherited that estate in succession, for upwards of seven hundred years. Descended from this ancient race, he was inferior to none of his predecessors in that generous spirit and fortitude by which they were distinguished. Mild, gentle and courteous in his manners, he possessed at the same time that firmness and stability of mind which made him tenacious of his purposes, constant in his friendships, and steady in his principles. His principles were no other than the two great sources of human excellence - piety to God, and benevolence to man". etc.

In another obituary reference to him, it was said:- "His publick character was strongly marked by disinterestedness by generosity and by a firm determined spirit. Possessing in a high degree all the publick and social affections, he was always amongst the first to promote any measure which he considered as of general utility and never suffered his own private interest to stand in the way of what appeared to him to be a publick good. Warm and steady in his friendships, he never deserted those whom he once attached himself, nor declined any exertions, however inconvenient for himself, that could be beneficial to them.

"Generous and liberal to the full extent of his fortunes, sometimes perhaps beyond it, he denied himself many gratifications to which he was well entitled, that he might have it in his power to do more good to others.

"Armed with uncommon resolution, he bore unmoved the severest strokes of adverse fortune, and, in situations the most trying, retained full command of himself", etc.

Those who read his personal account of his troubles and struggle to save Closeburn, will understand how such tributes came to be paid to him.

His is a record of which his descendants may feel justly proud, and an example which they should do well to remember.

The portrait of him in this book is from an enlargement of a miniature done by Miss Grace d'Arcy a descendant of the 5th Baronet.

No. 22 Sir Thomas 5th Baronet succeeded his father in 1804. He married his cousin Jane Sharpe, sister of Charles Kirkpatrick Sharpe who, it is seen, was dependant on this baronet to a very large extent for documentary proof of the early charters, upon which he wrote his history of the family.

Sir Thomas in his position as Sheriff of Dumfries and having access to various public records, must have given great assistance; as is seen by the very important record of the land case Sir James Kirkpatrick had over Thriepmuir, where the dispositions of the lands of Closeburn in 1773 were so clearly defined.

Also, in this Sir Thomas Kirkpatrick's hands must have been the eldest family pedigree we now have, which was previously referred to as having been drawn up at least 109 years before Charles Kirkpatrick Sharpe wrote his history in 1811. With his great grandfather's signature on this pedigree charter, (who died as 2nd Bt. in 1720), Charles Kirkpatrick Sharpe obviously used his early pedigree as a frame work for his history, from which I take our story. There is only quite slight differences between the early pedigree referred to and that in Charles Kirkpatrick Sharpe's Mss. book.

This Sir Thomas's children were:- Eleanore married to Sir William Hope-Johnstone, Mary Ann married to Henry Lumsden of Auchendoir, James a promising young midshipman, who died at Calcutta only 18 years old to his father's great sorrow, Charles Sharpe (6th Bt.), Margaret married John Ord Mackenzie of Dolphinton, and Charlotte married to Henry Burn, Esq., W.S. Edinburgh.

Sir Thomas had a distinguished career as sheriff of Dumfries and the account of his work as such is best read below.

He died in Capenoch in 1844. His second son Charles succeeding, sold Capenoch in 1846 to James Grierson of Dalgonar. Four years later, Mr. Thomas Stewart Gladstone of Liverpool bought Capenoch, and it has remained in the Gladstone family possession ever since.

This family carried out very considerable extensions to the old building. These additions have provided a very beautiful country seat, set amidst the old oak park, which has been preserved, and thus has escaped the fate which befell so much of the pleasant woodlands of Closeburn at the hands of "the syndicate".

The ancestors may well rest thankful that Capenoch has, as is the case with Closeburn, come into possession of an owner who will regard and develop the dignity and beauty of their domains.

The Dumfries Courier of 4th November 1844, devoted a whole column to an obituary notice describing the confidence and esteem in which Sir Thomas was held as sheriff of Dumfries. "For thirty three years Sir Thomas discharged the duties of sheriff. His character for unflinching integrity and strict impartiality afforded full assurance to his litigants that justice was in all cases, scrupulously administered".

"Indeed his judicial decisions may be said to have given universal satisfaction, not only to the procurators, but also to the litigants, who confided with entire reliance in his sterling uprightness and discriminating judgement, by which he was so peculiarly distinguished".

An extract from another notice reads:- "He was in very truth a man in whom there was no guile. Straight forward honest, unbending integrity and the purest philanthropy characterized every action of his life.

140

Profound sorrow pervades this town and district for the losss of this honoured judge and much beloved gentleman".

I have, for the benefit of my descendants, given the above extracts regarding two of our ancestors for two reasons - the first, an obvious one, is that the knowledge of our ancestors' attributes and their example should be known to our postority, so that they live worthy of them; and secondly - that they may use their own judgement as to whether such men would support our traditional history through the centuries if they did not believe it in their hearts to be true.

At the request of the Procurators of Dumfriesshire, Sir Thomas sat to Sir William Allan for his portrait in his robes. This picture now forms a principal ornament in the County Court House in Dumfries. Sir Thomas also sat to the same artist at the request of a number of his more immediate neighbours for another portrait, which they gave to his daughter. This is now the property of my nephew Ivone and is the one of which a photograph is given in this book.

The continuance of the Baronetcy from the 6th to the present 10th Baronet, Sir James Alexander Kirkpatrick, who is now resident in Kenya, is seen in Burk's Peerage and in the family genealogical table in this book.

Notes:
1. *Vide* Letter of Sir Francis Grant, K.C.V.o. ex-Lyon King of Arms of 16th July 1952.
2. C.K.S. Mss..
3. "Kirkpatrick of Closeburn".
4. C.K.S. Mss..
5. C.K.S. Mss..
6. "Kirkpatrick of Closeburn" in reference to Rae's History of the Rebellion".
7. C.K.S. Mss.
8. "Kirkpatrick of Closeburn".
9. "Kirkpatrick of Closeburn".
10."Kirkpatrick of Closeburn".

Appendix I

The Genealogical Table of the Family of Kirkpatrick of Closeburn

This has been made out in accordance with that given in the text of Charles Kirkpatrick Sharpe's M.S. history of the family, written by him prior to 1811, and brought up to date in places from various family and other records.

The numbers given opposite each name refer to the corresponding number and name in the text of this book, thus establishing connection with the fuller detail of the individual concerned.

1. IVONE KIRKPATRICK. 1141. Witness to a charter of Robert Bruce, the elder to the fishings of Torduff to the monks of Holmeultram.

2. WILLIAM. Son (or brother) suc. Assisted Gilbert in war in Galloway. Killed c. 1187.

3. IVONE. Son suc. Charter of Closeburn 1232 from Alex. II m. Euphamia dau. of Robert Bruce Lord of Annandale.
HUMPHREY KIRKPATRICK. Got lands of Colquhoun in time of Alex. II. -- INGRAM took surname of COLQUHOUN. -- ROBERT --
ROBERT -- HUMPHREY COLQUHOUN. M. heiress of Luss 1394.

4. ADAM. Son suc. In Kelso chartulary shows as having lawsuit with Abbot over the advowson of Closeburn Church. 1264.

5. STEPHEN. Son suc. In Kelso chartulary styled dominous de Kelosbern, filius et haeresdomini Ada de Kirkpatrick. Made an agreement with monks over Kelosbern Church 1278. Two sons Roger and Duncan.

6. ROGER. Son suc. "vetus amicus" of Robert the Bruce. Slew

the Red Comyn in Greyfriars Church Dumfries. 10 Feb. 1306. After Bannockburn, was commisioner for peace with England 1314, and again negociated in 1320. Two sons. Thomas and Roger. This Sir Roger took the Castles of Durrisdeer, Dalswinton and Caerlaverock from the English in 1355, and was murdered in that Castle 1358. His son Humphray was one of the hostages to England for payment of King Davids ransom in 1357.

DUNCAN. C. 1297. M. Isobel dau. and heiress of Sir DavidTorthorwald. -- HUMPHREY. Son suc. Charter of lands 1321. -- SIR ROBERT KIRKPATRICK prisoner at battle of Dupplin 1333. -- ROGER KIRKPATRICK Lord of Torthorwald 1355. Exchanged lands for Barony of Ross. (Apparently two sons, William of Ross and Duncan).

7. THOMAS. Son suc. Received charter of lands of Bridburgh from King Robert Bruce for services- 24th May 1319. He had two sons Winfredus and Ivone, who had a son Stephen. Also two daughters, Elizabeth and Margaret.

8. WINFREDUS. son suc. He had two sons Thomas (9) and Roger (10).

IVONE. -- STEPHEN.

9. THOMAS. Son suc. In charter dated Ayr 14th Oct. 1409, he dep. Received new charter of Barony of Closeburn and Bridburgh and tailxie for his heirs male, whom failing to his brother Roger, whom failing to his uncle Ivone, whom failing to Stephen son of Ivone. Whom failing to David Kirkpatrick his cousin Germane and his heirs male. He was one of the Commissioners for peace at Hauden Stank in 1428 and Plenipotentiary for peace with England 1429. Again Conservator for peace with Earl Douglas and Angus in Truce of 1438. Died d.s.p.

10. Sir ROGER. Brother suc. Commissioner of the West Borders 1455. One of the Barons of inquest to his brotherr in law Lord Somerville. To the retour his seal was appended with arms of Closeburn. (Nisbet). M. Hon. Lady Margaret Somerville, dau. of Thomas 1st Lord Somerville. Two sons - Thomas and Alexander of Kirkmichael, who took 9th Earl Douglas prisoner at battle of Burnwark 1484 and received the lands of Kirkmichael. From him are descended the Irish Kirkpatricks.

11. SIR THOMAS. Son suc. Keeper of Lochmaben Castle 1481. Sat in Parliament of James II in 1487. Confirmation charter for himself and wife Maria de Maxwell dau. of 2nd Lord Maxwell 14 Oct 1470. Died 1502.

12. THOMAS. Son suc. Got a brief to be served heir to his father 1515 from the King's Chancery. Taken prisoner at battle of Solway Moss 1542. M. Dame Margaret Sinclair of the Roslin family, (Lord Creighton's younger sister). She had just married a Sinclair - one of Convention of Prelates, Earls and Great Barons. Edin. 24 June 1545.

13. ROGER. Son suc. One of the association of Earls, Barons and others who, on 8th May 1568, bound themselves to defend Queen Mary. In revenge, the Earl of Susses's Army sacked Closeburn and other border castles, carrying away "great spulzie". He married Elizabeth Hamilton of Stonehouse- died 1584. Succeeded by his son Thomas (who was proved heir to his grandfather Sir Thom. Who died 1502, by inquisition, held at Dumfries 30 Mar. 1585).

14. THOMAS. Son suc. Commissioned by King James VI as Justicial on border 1589. Again in 1592, issued with writ of Power to suppress outrages by fire and sword. Took part in Battle of Dryffe Sands. Gentleman of the Privy Chamber to James VI. Comme. To repress Border rapine 1618. M. Lady Jean Cunninghame, dau. of Wm. Earl of Glencairn and widow of Haldane of Gleneagles - 2nd mar. Dame Barbara Stewart, relict of John Kirkpatrick of Alisland. Died circa 1628. Lady Jean was grand-aunt to James 1st Duke of Hamilton. Thomas was knighted before 1612. He died circa 1628. By 1st mar. sons Thomas, John and George and 1 dau. Also son Alexander of Barnmuir and 1 dau. Susanna.

15. THOMAS. Son suc. In order to support measures of the Reformation he together with the Earl of Queensberry and others, borrowed money on bonds in 1640 to his great harm. Mar. Dame Agnes Charteris dau. of Sir Wm. Charteris of Amisfield. Issue eleven children (including John (16) and Robert (17)). Died before 1648.

16. JOHN. Son suc. Possessed Closeburn in life time of his father-In 1646 Castle plundered by the Douglas. John died same year d.s.p.

17. ROBERT. Brother suc. J.P. Dumfries 1663. Comms. For militia 1668, together with Lords Nithsdale, Carnwarth, Annandale, Drumlanrig etc. Greatly retrieved the family affairs. Issue by his wife Dame Grizzel Baillie, dau. of Sir William Baillie of Lamington, descendant of Sir William Wallace- Thomas (1st Bt.), John of Apine, died young, Grizzel, who married John Grierson of Barjarg, Jean, Marion and Agnes. Died betwixt 1678-79.

18. THOMAS. Son suc. 1st Bt. created 26th Mar. 1685. Was infeft in Barony of Closeburn 17th May 1667. A Commr. for the Border empowered to deal with offences 1684. Lt. Colonel in Dumfriesshire militia 1691. M.P. for County 1696 and 1698. M. 1st Hon. Isabel Sandilands dau. of Lord Torphichan, descendant of Sir John Sandilands and Joan, daughter of Robert II. M. 2nd 1672 Sarah dau. of Robt. Ferguson of Craigdarroch. M. 3rd 1686 Grizzel dau. of Gavin Hamilton of Replock and widow of Inglis of Mudiston - son 1st Mar. Thomas. 2nd Mar. Roger of Alisland and another son James. Died circa 1763-4

19. Sir THOMAS. Son suc. 2nd Bt. Deputy Lieut. of the county. Took an active part in public affairs. When, in 1715 Rebellion, disturbances occurred he raised a contingent of Closeburn men, who then carried a family banner inscribed "For King George, liberty and religion according to Scots Reformation. Mar. 1st Helenor dau. of Sir William Stewart of Ravenshaw, Wigton. No issue. Mar. 2nd Isabel Lockhart dau. of Sir William Lockhart of Carstairs Bt. by Lady Isabel Douglas, sister to the 1st Duke of Queensberry. Issue - Thomas b. 1704, James died unmar., William of Alisland, Robert b. 1711 and died an infant and one daughter. also died young. Sir Thomas died 1720.

20. Sir THOMAS. Son suc. 3rd Bt. at 16 years of age. Took much part in county politics and brought his brother William into Parliament 1737 though opposed by Duke of Queensberry, his second cousin. On 29th Augt. 1748, the house of Closeburn was burnt to the ground. Thereafter, Sir Thomas lived in the Castle, where he died in 1771. He

146

married Susanna Grierson only dau. and heiress of James Grierson of Capenoch, m. 172/. Issue - Thomas, Sir James, George, William (m. Isabel Irving), Isabella m. Robt. Herries of Holdykes, Grizzel m. to Hon. Capt. Sandilands, bro. To Lord Torphichess, Jean, Christian. Eldest son Thomas died before his father.

21. SIR JAMES. Son suc. 4th Bt. He rebuilt Capenoch and lived there after debts had forced him to sell the Baroney of Closeburn (with the exception of Capenoch and Thriepmuire) in 1783 - He married Mary Jardine. Issue 3 sons 4 dau. Thomas 1768 died an infant, Thomas 1777, Roger 1779 m. Lilias d/o Robert Anderson of Stroquhan (Nov. 1817) - Sir James died 1804.

22. SIR THOMAS. Son suc. 5th Bt. Sheriff of Dumfries - Lived in Capenoch which was sold on his death in 1844, m. Jean Sharpe dau. of Charles Sharpe of Hoddam. Issue 2 sons 4 dau. James midshipman, d.s.p. young, in Calcutta, Charles 6th Bt.) b. 1810 died 1867- Eleanor m. Wm. Hope Johnstone Admiral R.N., Mary Ann m. Harry Lumsden of Auchendoir, Margaret Hope m. John Ord Mackenzie, Barbara Charlotte m. Henry Burn W.S.

23. SIR CHARLES. Son suc. 6th Bt. m. Helen Kirk d/o Thos. Kirk of Keir Mill Dumfries - 8 sons- Thomas 7th Bt (24)., James 8th Bt., (25) Roger, Charles Wm Sharpe, Robert Herries, Stewart, Arthur, Yvone. 2 dau.- Jane, Charlotte Barbara. Died 1877.

24. SIR THOMAS. Son suc. 7th Bt. m. Sophia Blanton d/o Wm. Blanton of Frampton on Severn. Died d.s.p. 1874.

25. SIR JAMES. Brother suc. 8th Bt. m. Mary dau. C. J. Fearnley of Peckham- 4 sons- Charles Sharpe, H. Fearnley Lt. Col. D.S.O. The Buffs, Yvone, Athol. 2 dau. Josephina, Margaret Hope m. Wilfred Stilgoe solicitor Lond. Died 1899.

26. SIR CHARLES SHARPE. Son suc. 9th bt. m. Alice Mayne d/o John Parnell Mayne of Ramsgate, Kent. She obtained a divorce 1910 - d.s.p. 1937.

Lt. Col. . FEARNLEY D.S.O. m. 15/12/1914 died 1918. Clara Agnes Clutterback only daughter J.W. Alexander I.C.S.

27. SIR JAMES ALEXANDER. B. 26/10/18. Nephew suc. 10th Bt. in 1937. Resident in Kenya. M. Ellen Gertrude dau. of Capt. R.P. Elliott late R.N.R. sons Ivone Elliott, Robin Alexander.

Appendix II

Our own Family Story

My father, James Kirkpatrick, was the eldest son of Roger the second son of Sir James Kirkpatrick, the 4th Baronet of Closeburn. He sailed for India about 1840, and joined the medical service of the Hon. East India Company in the Madras Presidency, retiring after 32 years service as Deputy Surgeon General.

In all that time, he only twice got furlough, once to South Africa, and once he took two years furlough at home.

Such a voyage in a sailing ship with a young family was then a considerabe undertaking, for furniture and a cow had to be installed on board for a voyage of some months, round the Cape of Good Hope.

In 1854, he married my mother, Margaret Jane Proctor, daughter of Lieutenant William Proctor late 21st Light Dragoons of Kilkenny and Drooge Vlei, S. Africa.

The family were in India during the Indian Mutiny. Luckily the Madras Presidency was unaffected thereby.

The family came home in two batches. The first of five, the second of three children, (one child died as an infant), and I, a very late comer, was born in Edinburgh several years after my father retired, so I know little of his life in India, and he died when I was ten years old.

Three brothers and myself thereafter served out there. Our services are given below.

My father's only married younger brother, Roger Kirkpatrick of Lagganlees, had a family of five, but none of these, our first cousins, married, and they are all now dead.

These cousins were blood relations of both the Isle of Wight and the Conheath branches of the family, and the relationships are seen in the table of family conections, which gives details down to my generation. The next generation will, I trust, continue the narrative hereafter.

Services of the Sons of
Deputy Surgeon General
James Kirkpatrick, M.D., H.E.I.C.S.

1. Colonel Roger Kirkpatrick, C.B., C.M.G., M.D.,
R.A.M.C., died 1933.
  War Services:-
Burma medal with 2 clasps 1885-7 and 1887-9.
N.W.F. India medal with 2 clasps.   Punjab Frontier 1897-8.
                                     Tirah 1897-8
South African War medal 2 clasps 1901-2
    "   "   Queens medal 4 clasps. Transvaal.
                                    Relief of Ladysmith
                                    Tugela Heights
                                    Cape Colony
War 1914-1919.   1914-15 star.
        G.S. medal
        Victory medal
C.B. C.M.G. Twice mentioned in despatches.

2. Major William Kirkpatrick, D.S.O. 1st Punjab Infantry.
Punjab Frontier Force, died 1941.
  War Services:-
Burma medal with clasp 1885-7.
  Mentioned in despatches.
N.W.F. India 1st Miranzai Expedition 1891.
      Gumatti Expedition   1899.
N.W.F. India medal with 2 clasps 1897-98.
      Waziristan   1901-02.
D.S.O. and twice mentioned in despatches.

3. James Ivone Kirkpatrick, C.A., Edinburgh.
Volunteered his services in the war 1914-18, and was employed
in Pay Department of the Army, where his health broke down,
and he died in 1918.

4. Lt. Colonel Edward Kirkpatrick. 59th Scinde Rifles and
Punjab Frontier Force, Khyber Rifles, died 1941.
War Service:-
Tibet medal 1903-4.
N.W.F. of India medal with clasp Waziristan 1894-5.
" "   "   "   "   1908.
War 1914-18.   G.S. medal and Victory medal

5. Major General Charles Kirkpatrick. C.B., C.B.E.
Thirty six years service in the Indian Army.
Q.V.O Corps of Guides and 53rd Sikhs, Punjab Frontier Force.
Assistant Commandant Chitral Scouts 1907.
Commandant 2nd Bn. Khyber Rifles 1908.
Commandant 3/12th Frontier Force Regt. 1923-26.
Brigade Commander 1926-30. Rawal Pindi, and Kobat Brigades.
   District Commander officiating Kobat District in 1927-28.
Promoted Major General 1929.
Commander Sind Independent Brigade Area 1931.
Officiated G.O.C. in Chief, Western Command, India 1934.
Was A.D.C. to King George V 1927-29.
Retired 1935.
War Services:- War 1914-15.
(1) Operations Tochi and Derajat 1914-15. D.A.A. and
Q.M.G., Derajat Brigade.
(2) Operations against the Mohmauds 1915.
Mesopotamian Expeditionary Force 1916-19.
Brigade Major 34th Ind. Inf. Bde.
G.S.O. II Euphrates Front.
G.S.O. II 13th Division.
G.S.O. I 14th Division.
Operations in Waziristan 1920-1923.
G.S.O. I Waziristan Expeditionary Force.
N.W. Frontier of India 1930. Brigade Cmdr. Kohat Bde.
Brevet of Lt. Colonel and four times mentioned in despatches.
War 1914-18.
Four times mentioned in despatches, Waziristan operations
   1920-23.

War 1914-1918.   1914-15 Star
                  G.S. medal
                  Victory medal.
N.W.F. India medal with clasp.   Waziristan 1919-1921.
N.W.F. India Clasp with clasp.   Waziristan 1921-1924.
N.W.F. India Clasp with clasp.   N.W. Frontier 1930-1931.
C.B. C.B.E.

In continuation of the Table of Family Connections of Closeburn, Isle of Wight and Conheath, the next generation of our family is given below.

1. Children of Lilias Kirkpatrick and Sir Philip James Hamilton Grierson, B.A. Oxon, Advocate, H.M. Solicitor of Inland Revenue, Scotland, Kt. Batchelor 1901, L.L.D.

(i) Margaret Proctor b. 19.2.1882, m. Admiral A.J.B. Stirling CB Has Issue.

(ii) Philip Francis b. 15.4.1883, m. Margaret d/o J.G. Bartholomew, L.L.D. Geographer Royal, Scotland, B.A. Oxon., Advocate, Captain 5th R.S.F. and Staff Captain 1914-1918 War. Judge of High Court Khartoum. Advocate General Sudan Govt. Sheriff Substitute Moray, Nairn and Inverness since 1936. M.B.E. Has issue.

(iii) Lilias Constance b. 19.2.1885, d. 22.1.1950.

(iv) James Gilbert b. 1.5.1887, killed in action Gallipoli 12.7.1915. B.A. Oxon. W.S. 2/Lieut R.S. Fus.

2. Children of James Ivone Kirkpatrick, C.A. b. 1866 and Elizabeth Margaret Thomson d/o David Thomson, Edinburgh.

(i) Ivone, W.S. 1933. W/Cmdr. A.A.F. War 1939-45, b. 1907, m. 1936 Ruth d/o W.R. Peterson of East London, S. Africa. Has issue.

(ii) Margaret Jean b. 1912.

3. Children of Major General C. Kirkpatrick, C.B. C.B.E. and Elsie Isobel d/o H.J.H. Fasson, I.C.S.

(i) Herbert James, Group Captain R.A.F., C.B.E., D.B.E., D.F.C. War 1939-45 (despatches twice) b. 1910, m. Pamela d/o Lt. Col. H.D. Watson, I.A. Has issue.

(ii) Hilda May b. 1920, m. Major J.M. Jourdier, East Surrey R. Has issue.

Appendix IIa

Lieutenant (Acting Captain) Andrew Wetherby Beauchamp-Proctor,
V.C., D.S.O., M.C., D.F.C.,
No. 84 Squadron, R.A.F.

I must not fail to set down for our posterity the wonderful record of my mother's Grandnephew, in the war of 1914-1918.

The official citation which won him the Victoria Cross is as follows:-

"Lieut. (A/Capt.) Andrew Weatherby Beauchamp-Proctor, D.S.O., M.C., D.F.C., No. 84 Squadron, R.A.F."

"Between August 8th 1918 and October 8th 1918, this officer proved himself victor in twenty six decisive combats, destroying twelve enemy kite balloons, ten enemy aircraft, and driving down four other enemy aircraft completely out of control.

Between October 1st 1918 and October 5th 1918, he destroyed two enemy scouts, burnt three enemy kite balloons, and drove one enemy scout completely out of control.

On October 1st 1918, in a general engagement with about twenty eight machines, he crashed one Fokker biplane near Fontaine and a second near Ramicourt. On October 2nd he burnt a hostile balloon near Selvigny; on October 3rd he drove down an enemy scout near Mont d'Origny and burnt a hostile balloon; on October 5th the third hostile balloon near Bohain.

On October 8th 1918, while flying home at a low altitude after destroying an enemy two seater near Marets, he was painfully wounded in the arm by machine gun fire, but, continuing, he landed safely at the aerodrome and after making his report, was admitted to hospital.

In all, he has proved himself conqueror over fifty four foes, destroying twenty two enemy machines, sixteen enemy kite balloons, and driving down sixteen enemy aircraft completely out of control.

Captain Beauchamp-Proctor's work in attacking enemy troops

on the ground and in reconnaissance during the withdrawal following on the Battle of St. Quentin from March 21st 1918 and during the victorious advance of our armies commencing on August 8th, has been almost unsurpassed in its brilliancy, and as such has made an impression on those serving in his Squadron and those around him that will not be easily forgotten.

Captain Beauchamp-Proctor's was awarded the Military Cross on 22nd June 1918, D.F. Cross on 2nd July 1918, Bar on the D.F.C. on 16th September 1918 and the D.S.O. on 2nd November 1918."

This very gallant young fellow lost his life very shortly after the Armistice in a flying accident.

So modest was he, that when he came over from France to receive his decorations and stayed with my mother for some days, he left without any of my family knowing he had particularly distinguished himself.

I MAKE SURE

Sir Thomas Kirkpatrick   of Closeburn.

Kirkpatrick of Closeburn,
in the Parish of Closeburn
and County of Dumfries
(Nisbet's Heraldic Plates

Appendix III

Heraldry.

The use and assumption of armorial bearings were in early days vested in the Lyon King of Arms jointly with his heralds, but, since 1672, in Scotland, his duty has, by act of Parliament, been exercised by the Lord Lyon or by his Deputy. The Lord Lyon under the Sovereign is the supreme judicial authority in all things pertaining to heraldry in Scotland.

The earliest official register of arms in Scotland, Sir David Lindsay of the Mount, Lord Lyon's Register of 1542, in which our arms were registered, was approved by the Privy Council in 1630.

Seton's "Scottish Heraldry" describes this book as "exhibiting in their proper colours, the armourial bearings of 114 noblemen and about 320 of the principal families in the Kingdom, unaccompanied however by any exterior ornaments in the shape of crest, motto or supporters".

The shield, or escutcheon, is the main part of a coat of arms, upon which the wearer's armorial signs appear; for, the origin of arms is associated with the wearing of mail armour, when the leader's faces being hidden, their distinguishing arms were worn on their surcoats or "blazoned" on the shield.

Nisbet states that the Kirkpatricks of Closeburn bore the chief and saltire of the Bruces, the same as do the Jardines and Johnstons, with different tictures and additional figures.

It appears, that after 1542, there was no Lyon Register kept for over a century; and Seton writes that no regular system of armorial visitation appears to have been adopted at that time by the heralds of Scotland to collect records, as was enjoined by an Act of 1592.

Consequently, many irregularities occurred, and spurious arms adopted. To remedy matters, another Act of Parliament was passed in 1672, requiring all persons to register their arms and to show authenticated warrants for their use.

It would seem indeed regrettable, that just at the time this registration was ordered to take place, old records of the Lyon King's Office should have been temporarily lost for a period of years, and not been recovered till the end of that Century; as related in the preface.

In such circumstances registration could hardly have been satisfactory. By the time these records had been found, we can read in "Seten" that "Nisbet had contrived to collect the armorial bearings of most if not all of those surnames and families that ever made any considerable figure in Scotland. There is no doubt that Scottish Heraldry is materially indebted to Alexander Nisbet".

With regard to the Lyon King's list of registrations then, Nisbet wrote much later "It was not so complete as is to be wished. Many of our most ancient and considerable families have neglected to register their arms notwithstanding the Act of Parliament, so that, were it not for ancient records, blazons etc, to which I have had recourse with great labour, the armorial bearings of sundry considerable families in Scotland had been entirely lost".

Seton observes that probably one of the most delicate and touchy points in Scottish Heraldry is involved in the question relative to the right to bear "supporters".

This point, raised in 1672, was still a matter of inquiry in 1821, as described at length in Seton.

Supporters are classified by Nisbet as "exterior ornaments of the shield". He traces their origin to certain ceremonies performed at tournaments. These animals, birds or figures it was written were afterwards adopted as "armorial supporters".

According to Sir George Mackenzie, and other authorities of that period. Supporters were not hereditary, but may be altered at pleasure. By heraldic custom, a peer bore these as a distinction and addition to his arms. Though thus restricted, many of the old Barons of Scotland who were not peers, and particularly the chiefs of clans or names, had been in the habit of using them, as they had been borne by their ancestors for centuries. Under the Act of 1672 it became illegal for anyone under a peer to bear supporters, unless especially designated by the Lyon King of Arms.

Nisbet records the following as bearing supporters in the capacity of Chief of Clans or representatives of ancient barons, their use of these appendages being instructed by seals, old books of blazon etc. The Homes of Wedderburn, the Kirkpatrick of Closeburn, the Murrays of Touchadam, the Haigs of Bermerside etc., twenty two in all, and Sir George Mackenzie names four others.

Nisbet wrote later "I think it very hard that a person cannot by right carry the arms which his progenitors used, legally perhaps, the authority or warrant being lost through time, more especially when accounts of them are so indifferently taken and kept by one provincial heralds, and, in later times, as indifferently preserved".

It would appear that Sir Thomas Kirkpatrick of Closeburn re-registered his arms in 1673, but that then his lions, as supporters, were objected to.

Most probably at that time he had no adequate proofs to support his claim. Then, Nisbet's later evidence as to his having personally seen Sir Roger Kirkpatrick's seal of 1435 in the possession of Somerville of Drumm, quoted by me previously, was not in existence, and the Lyon King's register of 1542 did not include representations of supporters. In any case it was then apparently lost to knowledge in Denmylne castle.

"Kirkpatrick of Closeburn", published in 1858, referring to the registration of 1672 mentioned that many of the Scottish Barons protested against being compelled to discontinue supporters which had been borne by their ancestors for centuries, and this is seen to have been the case.

It went on to say that "the matter was not pressed, and their families have since continued them without opposition".

In the exercise of his office, the Lord Lyon appears subsequently to have made concessions as regards those who could show "ancient usage" or special circumstances.

Seton shows in a table, that, of 133 Scottish baronets existing between 1625-1707, ninety-seven are given as using supporters and just thirty-six had none.

In 1685 when Sir Thomas was created a baronet, he had to register his arms afresh. By that time the ruling had been given that baronets, as such, were not entitled to supporters. He appears to have tried again to get his lions recognised, for there is a second entry:- "But it was not as a baronet that Sir Thomas Kirkpatrick and his descendants claim the right. They claim, as old Scottish barons who having from the earliest period, used supporters, protested against being compelled to discontinue, and were tacitly permitted to retain them".

It was about the close of the century that Nisbet visited Closeburn. Referring to the old arms, Nisbet wrote that the family now used hounds as supporters, and he drew his plate accordingly, as shown in Heraldic plates.

I surmise that the Sir Thomas got tired of finding his claim refused while his position vis a vis the other baronets of that time was certainly equivocal. The family flag, which I earlier mentioned as being carried in 1715 by the men of Closeburn under the 2nd Baronet, had the arms with hounds as supporters on it. Perhaps like another Baron who much later contested his claim on grounds of immemorial usage, he refused to pay fees demanded for registration. There is a rumour current in the family somewhat to that effect!

I have mentioned the entry which the 1st Baronet made in his eldest son's marriage contract - i.e. that should there be any failure by the bride or her descendants "to keep, assume, bear, wear and use", the surname and arms of Kirkpatrick of Closeburn, disinheritance of the Barony would follow at once- so maybe his approach to the Lyon King was not as tactful as it might have been! He had suffered much provocation.

If there were any family records of this, they were probably burnt in the fire of 1748; with the subsequent sale and break up of the Barony, no further action would appear to have taken place, and the arms as registered now show the arms, crest and motto but no supporters.

Note:- Since writing this chapter on Heraldry, I find that Nisbet, when writing elsewhere of seals, again mentions Sir Roger Kirkpatrick of Closeburn's seal, and adds that his son Thomas in the year 1470 carried the same arms.

I wrote earlier in this book that I had found a rough drawing of a seal shown as attached to "the procuratorial resignation" of Sir Thomas Kirkpatrick of Closeburn 1470, with the family arms on it, amongst the papers of Charles Kirkpatrick Sharpe.

I did not realise till now what a good of corroborative evidence this is, for Charles Kirkpatrick Sharpe does not make mention of this seal in his history. His drawing of the seal was on a single sheet of paper, along with other rough notes he had evidently jotted down for his history.

The drawing of the seal is the size of a half crown. In the centre is the shield; thereon a saltier with three cushions. The name Kyrkpatrik is inscribed half round the circumference.

Appendix IV

Coat of Arms of Kirkpatrick of Closeburn

The illustration is taken from Alexander Nisbet's "Heraldic Plates".

Alexander Nisbet was born on 25th April 1657, and died on 5th December 1725.

These plates were prepared by him in 1696, for issue originally with his work "System of Heraldry", first published in 1722; but, at that time, expence prohibited this being done.

They were reprobuced in 1892, with indroduction and notes, genealogical and historical, by Andrew Ross, Marchmont Herald and Francis J. Grant, Carrick Poursuivant later, Lyon King of Arms.

The following is the heraldic description:- "Thomas Kirkpatrick of Closeburne bears, argent, a St. Andrews Cross azure, on a cheife of the second three cushons or, with helmet and mantleing as is usuall; crest, a hand holding a dager destilling drops of blood; the motto "I make sure".

Matriculated 5th December 1673. Note: The plate shows supporters, two dogs collared, (Talbot Hounds)."

Major William Kirkpatrick, D.S.O., son of Deputy Surgeon general James Kirkpatrick M.D. who was grandson of the 4th Baronet of Closeburn, matriculated at the court of the Lord Lyon on 7th April 1937.

His ensigns armorial are this described:- "Argent- A saltire argent, on a cheife of the second three cushions or, a crescent also of the second for difference. Above the shield is placed a helmet befitting his degree, with a mantleing azure doubled argent, and on a wreath over his liveries is set for crest a hand, holding up a dagger distilling drops of blood proper, and in an escrole over the same, the motto. "I make sure".

Appendix V

The Collateral Branches of Closeburn in Dumfries-shire

Space does not admit of my giving in this book, accounts of the various offshoots of the main branch of Closeburn.

Besides the Torthorwald branch of the family, which has been dealt with at some length in this book, Dr. Ramage in "Drumlanrig and the Douglases" adds, as appendices, accounts of the following families:-

(1) The Kirkpatricks of Ross.

(2) The Kirkpatricks of Alisland and Friar's Carse.

(3) The Kirkpatricks of Auldgirth.

(4) The Kirkpatricks of Kirkmichael.

(5) in Annandale, (2) and (3) in Nithsdale, (4) South of Queensberry hill.

There are also:-

(5) The Irish Kirkpatricks.

(6) The Conheath Kirkpatricks. (see App VI)

(1) The Ross Kirkpatrick family has been dealt with earlier in this book. Their story is unfortunately disjointed; but Ramage also repeats the story, as told in our history, that Roger Kirkpatrick of Torthorwald exchanged his lands with the Carliels for the Barony of Ross; which was in the parish of Garrel. The first of this family was William Kirkpatrick of Ross 1372, who we think was a son of the Roger Kirkpatrick above.

Besides the record of this family earlier given, there is mention of a Henry de Kyrepatricke of Knock who was witness to a charter of Sir Edward de Crichton of Sanquhar, granting to his son Edward the lands of Kirkpatrick in Glencairn, 28th August 1472.

The next record[1] was that a Roger Kirkpatrick got a precept of sasine of the lands of Knock from Patrick, Earl of Bothwell, Magnus Admirallus Scotie and John Prior of St. Andrews, his tutor testamentary,

1522. "Sasine penes Ducem de Queensbury."

These lands passed to the Douglases in 1558.

(2) The Kirkpatricks of Alisland had a commission by Cardinal Antonius, dated at Rome, 13th September 1465, confirming a charter from the monastery of Melrose to John Kirkpatrick of Alisland, of certain lands in Dunscore, which belonged to the monastery.

The family held these very considerable lands for upwards of two hundred years.

We find[2] a John Kirkpatrick of Alisland as tutor guardian to Thomas Kirkpatrick of Closeburn, who, as a minor, got served heir to his father by a brief from the King's Chancery dated 22nd June, 1515.

It appears that this John Kirkpatrick was involved in some irregular practises in connection with the Closeburn lands of his ward.

He is mentioned as being the half brother of Henry Kirkpatrick, whose record of undetected crime was a very bad one.

During John's guardianship early in this century, Henry seems to have gained illegal possession of Closeburn lands, and he and john Kirkpatrick of Alisland must be held responsible for the wrongful alienation of the Closeburn lands of Auchenleck and Newton to a certain Senior Padzean and his son Thomas, as seen in a charter of 1545, where "a seal with a difference" is noted as being upon this charter (an easily explainable matter now).

The Crown first proceeded against Henry in 1518 regarding his service in the Closeburn lands. Despite protest by the Chancellor, James, Archibishop of Glasgow, Henry and James of Alisland escaped Conviction then.

But in 1536, the Crown issued a Commision to Thomas Kirkpatrick of Closeburn to capture, try, and punish John Kirkpatrick and other "tenants" of Closeburn.

The charter of 2nd August 1545, found only now, amongst the charters deposited in Register House in 1952, makes their fraudulent positions clear.

But it was only in 1585 that the trouble was finally straightened out. An "inquisition" was held at Dumfries on 30th March 1585 under the deputy Sheriff, William Crichton of Liberie, with fifteen county gentlemen connected with the family empanalled, to determine the succession to Closeburn, with due consideration of the circumstances of the past eighty three years. The verdict was that the then Thomas Kirkpatrick of Closeburn 1585 was the lawful and nearest heir of his great grandfather, Sir Thomas Kirkpatrick of Closeburn, who died in 1502 - so the succession was truly established at last.

Nearly all Closeburn eldest sons were called Thomas then. Henry and John obviously conspired to usurp a minor's rights.

Henry was in trouble in 1516 on a charge of murder and looting, and in 1527 also, for attempting to seize upon the King's person with the Earl of Angus.

He got "remission" on both occasions!

The Thomas Kirkpatrick of Closeburn thus proved heir to his great grandfather (d. 1502) married[3], as his second wife, Dame Barbara Stewart, widow of another John Kirkpatrick of Alisland and daughter of Stewart of Garlies, by which marriage he became possessed of Alisland.

The property later came into possession of William Kirkpatrick third son of the second Baronet of Closeburn, who was Charles Kirkpatrick Sharpe's grandfather, so the latter was likely to know the facts, (except that he could never have seen the 1545 charter now found). I therefore held to the succession of Closeburn as pronounced by the Inquisition of 1585 and 1545 which covers the 16th century and really goes back to the Auchinleck and Newton grants of 1424 (details on pages 87ff) n 7th December, 1585, James, Commendator of Melrose, infefts John, (son and heir of Thomas Kirkpatrick of Alisland previously mentioned) in the Dunscore lands; a witness being Roger Kirkpatrick of auldgirth. A few years later we hear[4] of John Kirkpatrick, younger, of Friars Carse, These lands apparently passed to John Maxwell of Shaws in 1628.

The families of Alisland, Friars Carse and Auldgirth were thus intermarried, and connections of Closeburn in Nithsdale.

At the time the Closeburn Kirkpatricks from Nithsdale could muster 403 men after "Solway Moss", and Kirkmichael 222. They all intermarried. No wonder their marriage connections are difficult to trace in 1953!!! The Inquisition of 1585 is a better guide.

(4) The Kirkpatricks of Kirkmichael.

Alexander Kirkpatrick, who was the originator of this family, has been previously mentioned[5] in this book (page 84) in connection with the capture of the last and ninth Earl of Douglas at the battle of Burnwark, 1484. He was the brother of Sir Thomas Kirkpatrick of Closeburn, who died in 1502. It would appear that there were three brothers, Sir Thomas, Alexander and Henry, sons of Sir Roger Kirkpatrick of Closeburn, whose seal Nisbet testified to having seen on the retour of Lord Somerville, then in the possession of Somerville of Drum. Charles Kirkpatrick Sharpe also mentions a son Henry, but in the account of Alisland given above, this Henry appears in another light! We have no certainty about him except that he caused much confusion, and had a long run of undetected crime.

The Somerville family records compiled by Lord Somerville in 1679 related[6] that: "this nobleman (the first Lord Somerville), being blessed with several children, his eldest daughter Marie, this year, 1427, he married upon Sir William Hay of Yester- the youngest daughter named Margaret, he marryes upon the Laird of Closeburn in Niddisdale of the sirname of Killpatrick-"

X   X   X   X

"Thus wee see this nobleman happy and fortunate in his owne match, and in the matching of his daughters, being married to gentlemen of eminent qualitie; two of them Chief of their names and families; (i.e. Closseburne and Restalrig)."

(5) The Irish Kirkpatricks trace their descent from the Kirkmichael Kirkpatricks- and from George Kirkpatrick of Knock, who first landed c. 1690 at Londonderry- where he founded the Irish connection; his father being shown as the last Laird of Kirkmichael.

There is a very full story of their descent from their Scottish connections told in the "Chronicles of the Kirkpatrick family" written by Alexander de le Pere Kirkpatrick, published in 1897. As is natural, certain detail regarding the early Closeburn family given there differs somewahat from that given in this book; but their connection with the Conheath branch of the family was traced by Mr. Campbell Gracie of Dumfries, himself a Kirkmichael man, whose mother was a Kirkpatrick, who was a Wilson of Kelton.

William of Conheath, the great grandfather of the Empress Eugenie, married Mary Wilson of Kelton. They had nineteen children, whose births, deaths and places of burial were recorded by the last surviving child of that family, Miss Jane Forbes Kirkpatrick of Nithbank, Dumfries, where she lived until she died at the age of eighty seven, on 22nd December 1854.

Notes;

1. Dr. Clapperton's Mss..
2. C.K.S. Mss.
3. C.K.S. Mss..
4. Dr. Ramage. "Drumlanrig and the Douglases"..
5. C.K.S. Mss; Hume of Godscroft; Duff's History of Scotland; Acts of the Lords of Council 19th Jan. 1484 Vol. I p. 95.
6.C.K.S. Mss. quotation

Appendix VI

Closeburn and the Empress Eugenie of France

(i)

Many books have been written about the romantic marriage of this descendant of the Kirkpatricks of Closeburn.

My own first cousins were blood relations of the Empress, by virtue of the fact that their maternal grandmother was the first cousin of the mother of the Empree, (The Comtesse de Montijo), by a later marriage.

This later connection can be seen in the chart which shows the considerable intermarriage which took place in comparatively recent years, between the Closeburn, Isle of Wight and Conheath branches of the family.

I mention this later connection, because our first cousins, during their lifetime, frequently visited their Conheath relations in Brussels, who are the direct descendants of William Kirkpatrick of Conheath, greatgrandfather of the Empress Eugenie.

Robert Closeburn Kirkpatrick, now the head of that family, served in both world wars in the British army, and lives in Brussels. His married sister has long been resident in Scotland.

The connection of the Conheath branch with Closeburn, from which the Empress was descended was well established on very good evidence, long before the Empress was born.

This is important, as, on her marriage to Louis Napoleon, Emperor of France, in 1853, many different stories as to her lineage were started, and contradictory stories told.

During the century which has elapsed since her marriage, further information has been forthcoming; not the least of which is now available from certain charters relating to her great-grandfather William Kirkpatrick of Conheath, as seen in a box of Closeburn papers recently deposited in Register House. These papers had been retained for nearly 170 years, without our knowledge or access to them, in lawyer's hands, who were unconnected with the family. Much unnecessary confusion has been caused thereby, so I must summarize the evidence upon which the Closeburn connection is founded.

(1) Firstly there is the patent of arms (Appendix VIa, below) granted to William Kirkpatrick of Conheath's eldest son, John Kirkpatrick of Conheath (Culloch), issued by the Lyon King of Arms on 16th May 1791, in order to show his and his family's connection with Closeburn. This undoubtedly had the approval of Sir James Kirkpatrick 4th Baronet.

(2) This grant of arms was given on the indesputable contemporary evidence of Dr. Clapperton, the local antiquarian, who, in 1784, for reasons later explained, produced for William of Conheath a complete pedigree, showing his family connections. At that time, and for its purpose, this pedigree was not required to go further back than approximately 1650; but it was drawn up thirtythree years before the mother of the Empress married the Comte de Teba. (Appendix VIb, below)

(3) Much later research proves the correctness of the relationships shown in the above. (i.e. over a dozen sasine entries in the Dumfriesshire and Kirkudbright official records as later explained).

(4) In 1826, John Kirkpatrick of Conheath on the request of his sister in Dumfries, sent to Sir Thomas Kirkpatrick the 5th Baronet of Closeburn, a full account of his own family connections. With his letter, he encloses the original evidence of Dr. Clapperton referred to above. (Extract from this letter, dated Honfleur, 12 Sept. 1826, is Appendix VIc, below.)

(5) In 1853, when her grandniece the Empress married Napoleon III, Miss Jane Kirkpatrick of Nithbank, Dumfries was then the last surviving member of William Kirkpatrick of Conheath's large family. She died in the following year at the age of eighty-seven. She kept the record of births, deaths and places of burial of her family. (Appendix VId, below.)

In the public display of interest in the marriage, the importance of the patent of arms of 1791, where William of Conheath's genealogy and connection with Closeburn was certified, appears to have been somewhat over-looked, (as shown later).

(6) A notarial document written after William of Conheath's death in 1787, describes the disposition of the Barony of Closeburn under the charter of 11th March 1774, and the infeftment then of Sir James, the 4th Baronet, his two brothers, George and William, and his kinsman William

Kirkpatrick of Conheath in certain lands of the Closeburn barony.

(7) A note in my grand-father's writing elucidates the text further.

(8) The charters of their infeftment in these lands are only now seen in the deposited Closeburn records in Register House.

The above authentic and mutually corroborative evidence from widely different sources cannot be disproved, and it requires Closeburn family knowledge to link this evidence.

This is the first part of the story, and it only needs to be expanded in detail, because I find there are still contradictory stories being published about the Empress Eugenie's Scottish descent.

(ii)

William Kirkpatrick of Conheath, above mentioned who married Mary Wilson of Kelton, Dumfriesshire on 22nd December, 1755, had nineteen children. Some of these died in infancy; several emigrated to Belgium, Spain and America. The eldest son, John, settled as a merchant in Ostend. The third son, William Kirkpatrick, became a prosperous fruit and wine merchant in Malaga, Spain, where he was American Consul for eighteen years.

According to Royal Spanish Academy records, he was recommended to President George Washington in a letter by George Cabot "as a person, who, by his situation and talents was fully able to fulfil in a satisfactory manner the position of Consul of the United States". It is mentioned that as a Catholic he moved in the best Andalusian society.

He married Francoise de Grevignée, daughter of Baron de Grevignée of Liege.

The eldest of their three daughters, Marie Mannela, marrie Don Guzman de Palafox-y-Portocarrero, Count de Teba, and later de Montijo, a Grandee of Spain, of ancient descent with many titles after his name.

The youngest of their two daughters, born on 5th May, 1826, was Marie Eugenie Ignacic Augustina, the future Empress of the French.

When Don Cipriano made proposals of marriage to Maria Mannela Kirkpatrick in 1817, it became necessary for her father to prove to the King of Spain that his ancestry was as such as to justify a Grandee of Spain forming such a connection.

William Kirkpatrick then wrote to his kinsman Charles

Kirkpatrick Sharpe, the well known Scottish antiquarian, no doubt mentioning that his eldest brother John had, many year before, matriculated and obtained a patent of arms from the Lyon King of Arms as a cadet of the family of Closeburn.

Charles Kirkpatrick Sharpe obtained from the Lyon King's office a copy of the patent dated 16th May, 1791, certifying his descent paternally from the ancient Barons of Closeburn. It appears he sent this to Malaga with a pedigree showing the descent of the Spanish Kirkpatricks from the main stem. This he was well able to do, as he had completed writing the history of the Closeburn family from early times in 1811.

(The above is referred to in Antiquarian Notes for 1898-99; and it is to be noted that this patent of 1791 was issued when Charles Kirkpatrick Sharpe was just ten years old, so he had nothing to do with the recording of it as has been inferred by certain uninformed writers.)

The patent was laid before Ferdinand VII, who thereon accorded sanction, and the marriage took place on 15th December, 1817, according to records of the Bonaparte family.

When, thirty-six years later, the daughter of this marriage, Mademoiselle Eugenie de Montijo, was married to Napoleon III, Emperor of France, the stir in Europe and the reaction of the Conheath family thereto is well reflected in a letter of William Escott Kirkpatrick, son of John Kirkpatrick of Conheath, which I show overleaf. He appears to have taken little action in the matter; not even attending the Royal wedding of his first cousin!

An account of the wedding is given in Vol. II of the letters of Queen Victoria 1837-1861, in a letter from Lady Augusta Bruce to the Duchess of Kent dated 31st January, 1853, which concludes:-

"I suppose that a sort of national prejudice made me attribute the grace and dignity of the scene, for what there was of either came from her, to the blood of Kirkpatrick!"

She remembered our old family connections with the Bruces, and a Closeburn pedigree which rivalled that of the Guzmans, in length!

(iii)

The evidence given in the preceding pages satisfied the family and King Ferdinand VII of Spain in 1817, but when in 1853 the marriage of the Empress Eugenie took place, antiquarians sought further information as to her Closeburn Connection.

Thomas Kirkpatrick "of", or "in", Knock, was, (for the purpose for which this patent was obtained), correctly defined as being "paternally descended from the ancient barons of Closeburn"; for he was of a colony of Kirkpatricks resident, from at least 1650, in the neighbourhood of Kirkmichael.

There had been much intermarriage there, and they could only be descendants,either direct from Closeburn, or from it, through the collateral branches of Kirkmichael and Ross, which are dealt with in the family history, difficult to sort out without documentary evidence.

The lands of Knock, Over and Nether Glenkiln, Craigshields, Dalcrum and Auchenskew in the parish of Garrell, Blackcleugh and Lamphite in Glenae, were all close together.

The Ross Kirkpatricks of earlier times had held Knock, but in 1558 the Knock lands had passed from the Kirkpatricks to the Douglases of Drumlanrig.

The Kirkmichael lands as named above, were originally held by Alexander Kirkpatrick of Kirkmichael, a brother of Sir Thomas Kirkpatrick of Closeburn who died in 1502; they both being sons of Sir Roger Kirkpatrick of Closeburn by his wife Lady Margaret Somerville, vide our history. (I shall refer to the Empress' connection with this branch later).

I find now a rather dramatic sequel to the story of the Empress Eugenie's connection with Closeburn.

As William Escott Kirkpatrick wrote in 1853, their marriage did "attract in an unusual degree the attention of all Europe", and the Conheath connection was frequently discussed.

All the time, valuable charters, which would have explained much, were securely locked up and buried in a lawer's strong room- and for 170 years these papers remained apparently unseen and unknown to the family most concerned, until they were produced in 1952!

Also further corroborative evidence, sasine records filed for easy reference, were not then available in Register House, as is the case now.

At that time of limited banking facilities, it was customary to borrow money from neighbours by pledging the family lands as security for such debts, and our forebears appear to have indulged in this practice of executing "bonds". As will be seen, this now affords a useful 'check up' on the lineage of William Kirkpatrick of Conheath; but it needs Closeburn records to link up such evidence.

Dr. Clapperton's evidence takes the lineage from "Thomas Kirkpatrick of Knock" to William of Malaga.

John Kirkpatrick's evidence in 1826, from Hornfleur, confirms this, and continues the story to where the mother of the Empress marries the Comte de Teba.

(iv)

William Kirkpatrick of Conheath's story (1737-1787) has now to be told.

The son of Robert Kirkpatrick of Glenkiln, in Garrell parish, he was nine years old when his father died. As shown earlier, he appears in the first part of his married life to have lived in Garrell parish, moving to Caerlaverock sometime after 1762.

It is not surprising to find that, with his very large family, he found himself by 1773, deeply in debt. In that year he is shown to have been owing the bankers in Ayr £5500, (a large sum at that time), and in the same year he borrowed another £1000 from one, John Harkness of Holstein, on the security of his lands of Over Glenkiln and Blackcleugh, in Garrell, which he had inherited from his father. (Ref. Dumfries sasine entries Nov. 519 and 879.)

Shortly before this, Sir Thomas Kirkpatrick 3rd Baronet of Closeburn died, and was succeeded by his son Sir James 4th Baronet, who, upon his own "resignation" in December 1773, obtained a fresh charter of their Barony dated 11 March, 1774.

In this it is seen that his two brothers, George and William, had been given "superiority" of certain lands. (George of nine, William of four).

This was done, perhaps to provide better supervision over the estate, (for at that time Closeburn lands were badly in need of attention, as described in our history), or, as was often done, such delegation allowed of extra votes for Parliament.

Sir James Kirkpatrick then finding his Kinsman, William Kirkpatrick of Conheath in great financial difficulties, granted him the

174

'life rent' of one of the Closeburn lands- Newton- but he retained in the family, in his own brother William's right, the "superiority" of Newton. This is clear from the following Closeburn charters:-

(a) Closeburn charters Inventory No. 144, stated that "for certain onerous causes and considerations", Sir James Kirkpatrick granted to William Kirkpatrick "his brother german", (real brother), the lands of Newton. This is dated 25th November 1773. Registered Dumfries 14. Ap. 1781. and:

(b) "Disposition by James Kirkpatrick of Closeburn Bart. to William Kirkpatrick of Conheath in life rent, and to Sir James and his heirs in fee, of lands of Newton, being parts of the Barony of Closeburn, excepting the right of property of the lands feued out by Sir James to William Kirkpatrick, "his brother german", dated 11 March 1774. Registered in the particular register of Sasines for Dumfries, 15 March 1784.

The situation at that time is thus clearly seen by charter to be that the real, (german) brother William held the full "superiority" of Newton, while William of Conheath had the benefit of the 'life rent' only of that land.

But, in 1780, Sir James Kirkpatrick found that he would have to sell Closeburn.

In order that the barony might be sold as a whole, his brother William made a "resignation" of the lands of Newton to him as seen in a charter which reads as follows:-

"13 April 1780". "Disposition by William Kirkpatrick in Kirkland (in Closeburn), lawful son of deceased Sir Thomas Kirkpatrick of Closeburn, in favour of Sir James Kirkpatrick of Closeburn, Bart., his brother german, of the lands of Newton". Registered in books of Council and Session 14 April 1781.

There was thus room for confusion locally as between the two Williams- for William of Conheath continued to hold the 'life rent'.

In 1783, Sir James Kirkpatrick sold the Barony, with certain exceptions, to the Rev. Jas. Steuart Menteth.

No doubt the new owner wanted to know the position of this 'life renter' with regard to the Closeburn property of Newton, and this I think accounts for William of Conheath going off and getting a full pedigree and account of his family connections written out by Dr. Clapperton, which proved so useful later.

It is evident that Sir Jas. Steuart Menteth continued the 'life rental' to William of Conheath, for in Closeburn Inventory No. 175, there is a note of the charters handed over to Mr. Baird, (successor of the Menteth's in 1852):-

"Charter by the said Mr. Jas. Steuart Menteth with the consent of the said William Kirkpatrick of Conheath, and William Kirkpatrick brother of the said Sir James confirming the foresaid disposition of the lands of Newton by the said William Kirkpatrick Sir James' brother - to Sir James - Sir James Sasine thereupon."

William of Conheath died in 1787, when, (as seen in a notarial note earlier referred to), the 'life rent' of Newton lapsed. He left most of his debts unpaid and some of his lands in Garrell pledged.

It was in these circumstances that his eldest son, John Kirkpatrick, returned to Scotland from Ostend to settle his father's estate; and found it necessary to establish his position with Closeburn by matriculation at the Lyon King's office, in 1791. The Lyon King could have had no difficulty in finding proofs of the correctness of his claim, with Sir James Kirkpatrick still alive, and Dr. Clapperton's evidence available, and no one could foresee that in 1853 these charters would become of public interest.

The box containing them passed into the hands of Mr. Baird's lawers apparently. He died shortly afterwards, a trust administrating the estate, until the barony was sold to a syndicate, who later partitioned it. This accounts for these important charters escaping notice in 1853 and later. Had they been produced then, much unnecessary speculation as to the ancestry of the Empress would have been avoided. Unhappily too, Charles Kirkpatrick Sharpe died two years before the Empress married, or we should have had her ancestry certified beyond Thomas Kirkpatrick of Knock.

(v)

Evidence now available in Register House from records of sasines establish the relationships determined nearly a hundred and seventy years ago. I think this should therefore be recorded.

Vide Particular Register of Sasines Dumfies:-

On 20th January, 1744 Robert Kirkpatrick "in Craigshields"

bought the whole lands of Over and Nether Glenkiln including Lamphite and Blackcleugh, six merk lands, milns etc., Alexander Dalzell, and thereby became known as "Robert Kirkpatrick of Glenkiln", as named in the patent of arms, son of Thomas Kirkpatrick of Knock.

This charter gave real warrandice and security of these lands and others, in case of eviction thereof, in "all whole the ten merk land of Kirkmichael", etc.

On the same date, the same Robert Kirkpatrick gave a discharge to Alex Dalzell of Glenae of his debt of £700 and rents; held in security - "all and hail the ten merk lands of Kirkmichael, the lands of Pleughlands the 40/- land of Craigshields and Dalcrum, the 40/- land of Holehouse and lands of Glenae". There had earlier formed part of the Barony of Amisfield.

Robert Kirkpatrick of Glenkiln, who married his cousin Henrietta Gillespie, daughter of John Gillespie "in Craigshields", did not live long.

He was said to have been executed for his adherence to Prince Charles Edward, and his tombstone in old Garrell churchyard showed that he died in 1746. His wife died in 1771.

Dr. Clapperton showed his four sons as being Thomas, Robert, William and John, with one daughter Henrietta, married to William Kirkpatrick, merchant and baillie, Dumfries.

1. The eldest son Thomas married Janet Craig, by whom he had five daughters only, and all were living in 1784, (names given). Thomas was infeft in his father's lands in 1749, by precept from Dalzell, and is there mentioned as "in Craigshields". It appears as if Thomas with his young family continued to live there with his widowed mother. His widow appears to have later possessed Craigshields and Dalcrum, and to have married James Swan, merchant of Lockerbie. (Dumfries sasine entry No. 2356).

2. Robert, the second son of Robert Kirkpatrick of Glenkiln, is shown as unmarried, and it is probably he who is shown dying as such, in the Commissarriat of Dumfries in 1860. His eldest brother having died before him.

3. William, the third brother, ("Conheath"), great grandfather of the Empress Eugenie, is seen to have been in great financial trouble and to have pledged certain of his lands inherited from his father Robert

Kirkpatrick of Glenkiln, before he was given a 'life rent' interest in Newton by Sir James Kirkpatrick of Closeburn. (Dumfries sasine entries 519-879, Over Glenkiln and Blackcleugh).

4. The fourth son, John, married Jean Forbes of the Isle of Man. These parents dying, they left an orphan son John, who is shown as "at school in Dumfries", in 1784. Both these Johns are mentioned as son and grandson of Robert Kirkpatrick of Glenkiln in Dumfries sasine entries, (847-848 of 21st May, 1791). Where the grandson John is seen to have assisted his uncle John Kirkpatrick of Conheath to liquidate the family burden of debt, by contributing his portion of the inherited family lands, (two fifths of Nether Glenkiln).

Two sasine enties, subsequent to 1791, also bear on this subject, (No. 1092 of 5th December, 1793 and No. 3207 of 27th May 1814), when James Swan and his son John's relationship and interest in these lands are specified.

There are also Kirkcudbright Sasine records to show that under his marriage contract of 9th April 1789, John Kirkpatrick of Conheath (Culloch), merchant at Ostend, married Janet Stothert; and, having established his position as regards Closeburn and his father's estate by patent in 1791, he then shouldered his father's outstanding debts.

By 1805, he himself had been declared bankrupt and his wife had then to pledge her lands; the widow of John Harkness farmer of Holstein, a former creditor of William Kirkpatrick of Conheath, being "seiged" in part of her Torkatrine lands, in settlement of a bond for £900 previously taken out. (Kirkcudbright sasine entries Nos. 1426-1429-2443-2879-3325). In June 1813, this story finished, when William Escott Kirkpatrick, son of John Kirkpatrick took over the burden of the undischarged debts of £2000 and £1000. (Sasine no. 3324).

It will be seen that the names and relationships of those given earlier in Dr. Clapperton's Conheath pedigree are those shown later in Dumfries and Kirkcudbright sasine records, as pledging their ancestral inherited lands.

None of this family in sacrificing them, could have had any doubt as to what relationship William Kirkpatrick of Conheath bore to Robert Kirkpatrick of Glenkiln!

John Kirkpatrick's evidence of 1826 and that of his sister, Miss Jane Kirkpatrick of Nithbank, shows that William Kirkpatrick of Malaga was their brother.

In the controversy which started, both within and outside the family, in 1853 as to the earlier connections of the Empress, Mr. Campbell Gracie junior, of Dumfries, whose grandmother was a Miss Kirkpatrick, reputedly of Kirkmichael, (or Kelton), prepared two "trees" showing the Conheath conection of the Empress linked to Closeburn through their Kirkmichael branch. These trees were sent, in 1854, through Miss Jane Kirkpatrick of Nithbank to her niece, the Comtesse de Montigo.

Mr. Campbell Gracie found further evidence to support his view, when, in 1860, the Empress visited Scotland as seen overleaf.

The relationships however as between Robert Kirkpatrick of Glenkiln, Thomas Kirkpatrick of Knock and George Kirkpatrick of Knock were then not fully established and circumstances at that time were not favourable to the production of documentary proof.

There are however some indications that a further extension of the lineage through Kirkmichael did exist. It does not seem likely that there will be more definite proof of this obtainable now.

It is interesting to note that, as regards the original lands of the Barons of Kirkmichael.

These passed first into the Charteris family; and then to the Dalzells in 1649.

In the Register of the Great Seal, there is an entry under date 9th June, 1575, Vol. xxxiv-262, that the King confirmed a charter 11th March 1572/3, in favour of Alexander Kirkpatrick of Kirkmichael, by which, with consent of Roger Kirkpatrick of Closeburn and Thomas Kirkpatrick of Alisland, his curators, in implement of a marriage contract dated at Dumfries, 23rd January 1571/2, he granted to Margaret Charteris, then his spouse, lawful daughter of John Charteris of Amisfield, the life rent of the £10 lands of old extent of the town of Kirkmichael, (reserving to himself and his heirs the tower, mansion house and mill thereof.)

Later Agnes Charteris, daughter of Sir John Charteris of Amisfield is seen to have married Thomas Kirkpatrick, Laird of Closeburn, (1628-1648), and they had eleven children.

Appendix VIa

Copy of "Patent"
issued by the office of the Lyon King at Arms, 16th May, 1791.

To all and sundry whom these presents do, or may concern:-

We, John Hooke Campbell, of Bangaston, Esq., Lyon King of Arms,do hereby certify and declare that the ensigns memorial pertaining and belonging to John Kirkpatrick of Culloch, Esq., in the Stewartry of Kirkcudbright and merchant in Ostend, eldest son and heir of William Kirkpatrick, Baron of Conheath, by his lady Mary daughter of John Wilson of Kelton, Esq., which William was third son of Robert Kirkpatrick of Glenkiln, Esq., by Henrietta daughter of John Gillespie of Craigshield, Esq., which Robert was a second son of Thomas Kirkpatrick of Knock, Esq., who was paternally descended (Note: evidence that "Robert of Glenkiln" was equally "paternally descended" from Closeburn) from the ancient and respectable family of the Kirkpatricks, Barons of Closeburn in the county of Dumfries, on whose remote ancestors Ivon de Kirkpatrick obtained a charter of the said Barony of Closeburn under the Great Seal of Scotland in the reign of King Alexander the Second, of a date the fifteenth of August, in the year 1232, whose male descendant and representative as our historians testify, was of eminent service to King Robert the first, in his struggles to obtain the Crown of Scotland anno 1306, and whose later representative, Sir Thomas of Closeburn Knight was, on account of his loyalty and the eminent services to the Crown performed by his family advanced to the dignity of a Baronet of Scotland by patent under the Great Seal of the Kingdom, of the date the twenty sixth of March, 1685, wherein many honourable privileges were conferred on his family by his sovereign, King James the seventh, are matriculated in the public register of the Lyon office, and are blazoned as on the margin, thus:-

viz. Argent, a saltyr azure between three stars, one in the collar point and two in the flanks - gules on a chief of the second, three cushions or - Above the shield is placed a helmet befitting his degree, with a mantling gules, the Doubling argent - On a wreath of his liveries is set for crest, a dexter armed hand holding a dagger in pale distilling drops of blood from its point, all proper - And in an escrole above the crest, this motto, "I

Closeburn

Isle of Wight

SIR THOMAS KIRKPATRICK 1st Bt. Cr. 1685 d. 1703/4.

SIR THOMAS KIRKPATRICK 2nd Bt 1700-1720.

SIR THOMAS KIRKPATRICK 3rd Bt 1720-1771.

SIR JAMES KIRKPATRICK 4th Bt. 1771-1804.

SIR THOMAS KIRKPATRICK 5th Bt 1804-1844.

James, probably 2nd son, born 1668, left Scotland in disapproval of his father's 3rd marriage in 1686, leaving on the wedding day. Married Ann Hoar in 1703, and settled in Isle of Wight 1704.

JAMES 1710 — 1782.

JAMES 1762 — 1847.

Roger, b. 1779, mar Lilias Anderson of Stroquhan, Died 1843.

Joseph K. Isle of Wight 1788 — 1856 (St Cross)

Maria Isabella Kirkpatrick 1st Cousin of * MARIA MANUELA KIRKPATRICK

1. **James. K.** b. 1820. Dy Surg General, Hon East India Coys Service. m. 1854 Margt Jane Proctor d/o Lieut N.P. 21st Lt Dragoons of Kilkenny and Droog Vlei. S.A. died 1890.

Two sons. 2. Robert b. 1821 Solicitor London d. 1856 3. Thomas Capt 26th Madras Inf. b. 1822 d. 1864. Both unmar. D.S.P.

Two daus Jane b. 1823 Mary Lilias 1824-1898 Both unmar.

Roger. K. of Laggan Tees b. 1825 mar Ap 1856, died 6th June 1890.

Isabella Margaret Kirkpatrick of St Cross Isle of Wight.

Rev Roger Sandilands J.P. 1859 – 1943 D.S.P.

John Geo. W.S. Edin 1864 - 1940 D.

Elizabeth Rachel 1854-1941 unmar.

Lilias. 1856 – 1927 mar 1881 Sir P. J Hamilton-Grierson Advocate. 2 sons 2 daus.

Mary Elizabeth Frances 1857-1920 unmar.

Roger. C.B. C.M.G. M.D. Colonel R.A.M.C. 1859 - 1933. unmar D.S.P.

William D.S.O. Major. Ind Army Punjab Frontier Force. 1863-19.. m Lilias Sto.. D.S.P.

between

Conheath

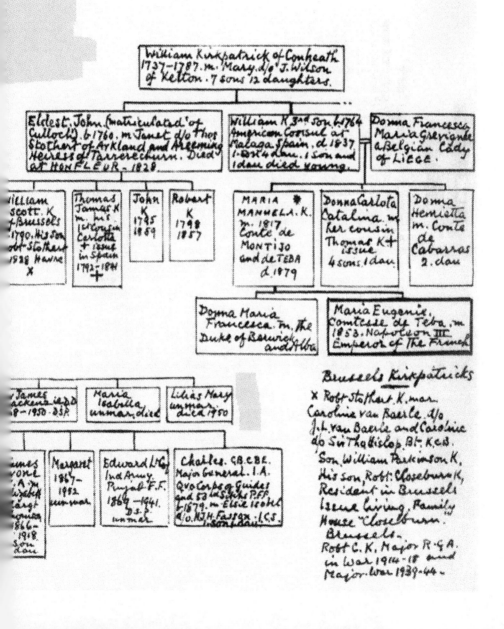

William Kirkpatrick of Conheath 1737-1787. m. Mary, d/o J. Wilson of Kelton. 7 sons 12 daughters.

Eldest, John (matriculated 'of Culloch'), b. 1760. m. Janet, d/o Thos Stothart of Arkland and Mteeming Heiress of Tarrerechurn. Died at Honfleur 1828.

William K. 3rd son, b. 1764. American Consul at Malaga, Spain, d. 1837. 1 son 4 dau. 1 son and 1 dau. died young.

Donna Francesca Maria Grevignée a Belgian Lady of Liège.

William Scott. K. of Brussels 1790. His son Robt Stothart 1838 Hawke X

Thomas James K. m. his 1st cousin Carlotta + issue in Spain 1792-1844 +

John K 1795 1859

Robert K 1799 1857

MARIA MANUELA. K. m. 1817 Conte de MONTIJO and de TEBA d. 1879

Donna Carlota Catalina. m. her cousin Thomas K + issue 4 sons 1 dau.

Donna Henrietta m. Conte de Cabarras 2 dau.

Donna Maria Francesca. m. the Duke of Berwick and Alba

Maria Eugenia, Comtesse de Teba. m. 1853. Napoleon III Emperor of The French.

James Mackenzie K 8 - 1950. D.S.P.

Maria Isabella unmar. died

Lilias Mary unmar. died 1950

James Lyonel A. m Elizabeth Margt Ferguson 1866 - 1918 son dau

Margaret 1867 - 1952 unmar

Edward L/Cy Ind Army Punjab. F.F. 1869 - 1941. D.s.p. unmar

Charles. C.B. C.B.E. Major General. I.A. Qvo Corps of Guides and 53 th Sikhs P.F.F. 1879. m. Elsie Isobel d/o W.H. Fasson. I.C.S. son dau

Brussels Kirkpatricks

X Robt Stothart K. mar. Caroline van Baerle. d/o J.t. van Baerle and Caroline d/o Sir Tho Gislop Bt. K.C.B. Son William Parkinson K. His Son, Robt Closeburn K, Resident in Brussels Issue living. Family House "Closeburn. Brussels. Robt C. K. Major R.G.A. in War 1914-18 and Major. War 1939-44.

mak siccar" - which armorial ensigns above blazoned, we do hereby ratify, confirm and assign to the said JOHN KIRKPATRICK, Esq., and the heirs male of his body, as their proper arms and bearing in all time coming.

In testimony whereof these presents are subscribed by Robert Boswell, Esq., our Deputy, and the Great Seal of our office is appended hereunto.

At Edinburgh, the 16th day of May in the year one thousand and seven hundred and ninety one.

R.O. Boswell.

Lyon Deputy.

On the back is written   Lyon Office.

The written patent is duly ordered in the records of this office by James Cummyng, L.A.C.

Notes:

(1) When William Kirkpatrick of Conheath died in 1787, his eldest son John, then settled as a merchant in Ostend, had to return to Scotland to settle his father's estate, which he found much involved. It became necessary for him to establish his position in Scotland, and his connection with Closeburn. He therefore applied for a grant at the Lyon King's office, and having no holding in this country, he registered under the name of "Culloch", taking this name from his wife's lands near Castle Douglas. He married Janet Stothert daughter of Thos. Stothert of Arkland and Areeming. She inherited Tarscreechan, (modern name Torkatrine), from her grandfather Hugh Aitken; as shown in Kirkcudbright sasine records Nos. 1426-1429; Her marriage contract with John Kirkpatrick was dated April 9th 1789- (sasine entry Kirkcudbright 3325). Tarscreechan (meaning, in Gaelic, "little hill") overlooked the lands of "Little Culloch" and "Meikle Culloch".

(2) The "minor Barons" of Scotland were often styled "Baron", if they were only the owners of a few scattered lands, as was the case with William Kirkpatrick of Conheath.

(3) The historical nature of the wording given in this grant of arms shows it was granted for the purpose of establishing this John Kirkpatrick of Conheath's (Culloch) position as regards the Closeburn baronial family. - (As will be shown this relationship had already been established in 1784, unofficially.)

Later research indicates that there was a closer connection of "Thomas of Knock" with Closeburn than could be then specified.

184

Appendix VIb

The Conheath Connection
according to Dr. Clapperton of Lochmaben, the local antiquarian

"To William Kirkpatrick of Conheath, these few remarks on the surname of Kirkpatrick are dedicated by his most humble servant Robert Clapperton 1784:-"

(1) Gives immediate personal relationships of William of Conheath (A number of those are shown living at the time).

(2) Gives the earliest history of Closeburn extending to its cadet branches Torthorwald and Ross.

"James Kirkpatrick, son of Thomas Kirkpatrick of Knock married in England and had three sons and two daughters, Elizabeth and Anne Kirkpatrick, viz John K., Abraham K., and Robert K., and two daughters, Elizabeth and Anne Kirkpatrick.

Abraham K. had two daughters, one married to Mr. Aiskill, by whom he had a son and two daughters, one of whom married Mr. Craiggs of Togago, the other Mr. Reid of London; and the other daughter married Dr. Sherson, by whom she had a son Abraham K. Sherson.

Elizabeth K. was married to Mr. Escott, by whom she had two sons, viz. John Kirkpatrick Escott, Esq., and William Escott.

Robert Kirkpatrick of Glenkiln, son of said Thomas K. of Knock and brother to James K. before mentioned, married his cousin Henrietta Gillespie daughter of John Gillespie in Craigshields, by whom he had four sons and one daughter viz. Thomas, Robert, William and John K. and Henrietta Kirkpatrick.

1. Thomas married Janet Craig and has five daughters living, Viz. Henrietta, Margaret, Mary, Elizabeth, Jean Kirkpatrick.

2. Robert who is unmarried.

3. William K. who married his cousin Mary Wilson daughter of John Wilson of Kelton by whom he had 19 children, ten of whom are still living, viz:

Mary married to Thos. Wilson, writen in Edinburgh; by whom she has three children, mary, Thomas and James Wilson.

     John K. Merchant at Ostend.

     William K. Merchant at Malaga.

     Thomas K.

     Robert K.

     Alexander K.

     Janet K.

     Jean K.

     Rose K.

     Harriet K.

     Jean and Rosina Unmarried.

     4. John K. the fourth son married Jean Forbes in the Isle of Man, by whom he had one son, John K. now at school in Dumfries. His father and mother died when he was an infant.

     5. Henrietta K. married to William Kirkpatrick, General Merchant in Dumfries, by whom he has now living two sons and three daughters, viz: Charles K. gone to the East Indies, Roger K. bred to the sea, Elizabeth K. married to Major Fead, Royal Artillery, Henrietta K. married to Lieut. John Johnson, younger son of Thornynhat and Agnes Kirkpatrick".

     Note: The above Conheath pedigree (given in 1784) carries down to William Kirkpatrick of Malaga (born 1764).

     Later, his daughter, Maria Manuala married in 1817 the Count de Teba. Their younger daughter was Eugenie, Empress of the French.

Appendix VIc

Extract From a Letter
addressed to Sir Thos. Kirkpatrick, 5th Baronet of Closeburn, by John Kirkpatrick of Conheath, (matriculated 16th May, 1791 as 'of Culloch').

Au Chateau Le Noyer,
près Honfleur,
France.
12th Sept., 1826.

Dear Sir Thomas,

I understand from my sisters, who reside at Nithbank, that you were occupied in framing a genealogical tree of your family, and that you were desirous of knowing from what branch mine sprung, for the accomplishment of your object.

I have taken some pains to examine into this subject, and I beg to enclose a sketch of what I have been able to ascertain relative to it.

Referring to Dr. Clapperton's evidence, he writes:-

"About 1649, my great grandfather, Thomas Kirkpatrick of Knock, was paternally descended from the house of Kirkpatrick of Closeburn.

Thomas of Knock had two sons, James K. his eldest son married in England, had three sons and two daughters. The eldest son Abraham married and had two daughters, one married to Mr. Aiskill, British Consul at Malaga, had one son and two daughters. Elizabeth married H. Craig, Esq., of Tobago and Charlotte to James Reed, Esq., High Sheriff of Essex and Director of the Bank of England, London. Reed has one son and one daughter - the daughter married to - Elvington, Esq., Deputy Governor of the Tower of London.

Elizabeth, daughter of James, married Mr. Scott, by whom she had two sons, John K. Escott and William Escott. J.K. Escott married and has one son, the present Robert K. Escott of Ongar Hill, Chertsey.

Robert Kirkpatrick, of Glenkiln and second son of Thomas Kirkpatrick of Knock, married his cousin Henrietta Gillespie daughter of John of Craigshields, by whom he had four sons and one daughter, viz:

Thomas, Robert, William and John and Henrietta K.

William married his cousin Mary Wilson daughter of John Wilson, Esq., of Kelton Stewartry of Kirkcudbright, by whom he has had 19 children, whereof are now living:

Mary K.
John K.
William K.
Thomas K.
Robert K.
Jane K.
Rosina K.

Mary K. married to Thomas Wilson, Esq., Edinburgh. Has one son and a daughter, Thomas and Jane, married A. Borthwick, Esq., and afterwards Mr. Proudfoot of Moffat, who have issue.

John K. married Janet Stothert daughter of Thos. Stothert of Arkland and Areeming, has four sons and one daughter, viz: William Escott Kirkpatrick, merchant at Havre de Grey married Eliza Parkinson, daughter of Jeremiah Parkinson, Esq., London and have two sons. Thomas James K., Merchant, Montril married his cousin Carlotta K. and has two sons and one daughter.

Maria Isabella Kirkpatrick married Joseph K. junior- Banker, Newport, Isle of Wight.

John Kirkpatrick, Vice Consul at Adra, Spain.

William Kirkpatrick, Merchant, Adra, married C. Grivignee daughter of Henry Grevignee, Merchant, Malaga, Spain - has three daughters:

Marigritta married to the Count Teva (Jeva, I suppose), Granada in Spain.

Henriquetta married to the Count Cabarrus of Malagaaand.

Carlotta married to her cousin Thomas James Kirkpatrick of Montril Spain.

Thomas K. Merchant, Malaga, married Rien, niece of- Rien, Esq., Merchant, Malaga.

Janet K. (dead) married to the Rev. Dr. Scott, Minister of St. Michel's Church, Dumfries.

Jane and Rosina unmarried.

188

Appendix VId

Table

giving the Births and Deaths of the Family of William Kirkpatrick of Conheath's nineteen children.

Miss Jane Kirkpatrick of Nithbank, Dumfries, was the last surviving member of this family and the table is generally attributed to her, as it was amongst other papers belonging to her.

"William Kirkpatrick, son of Robert Kirkpatrick, Esq., of Glenkiln and Henrieta Gillespie of Craigshield (Ahenskew) born in March 1737- died in Conheath December 1787"

Caerlaverock Churchyard.

"Mary Wilson, eldest daughter of John Wilson, Esq., of Kelton and Isabella Fraser- born 1739 married to the aforesaid William Kirkpatrick 22nd December 1755. Died at Conheath 29th June 1785"

Caerlaverock Churchyard.

1. Their first child stillborn, a daughter born in 1757.

Dumfries Churchyard.

2. Mary Kirkpatrick born 5th June 1758.

3. Robert Kirkpatrick born 20th June 1759. Died 1760.

Garrel Churchyard.

4. John Kirkpatrick born 1st August 1760. Died at Honfleur 28th Sept. 1828.

5. Henrietta Kirkpatrick born 11th December 1761. Died 1762.

Garrel Churchyard.

6. Isabella Kirkpatrick born 15th April 1763. Died 1781.

Caerlaverock Churchyard.

7. William Kirkpatrick born 24th May 1764. Died 1837

In Spain.

8. Janet Kirkpatrick born 22nd June 1765. Died 1817.

9. Thomas Kirkpatrick born 25th July 1766. Died In Spain.

10. Jane Forbes Kirkpatrick born 18th Sept. 1767.

Died 21st Dec. 1854.

11. A daugher stillborn March 1769.

Caerlaverock Churchyard.

12. Rose Kirkpatrick born 12th April 1770. Died April 1833.

13. Harriet Kirkpatrick born 3rd June 1772. Died. In Spain.

14. A stillborn son November 1773.

Caerlaverock Churchyard.

15. Robert Young Kirkpatrick born 24th Nov. 1774. Died in London.

16. A daughter stillborn 1775.

Caerlaverock Churchyard.

17. Alexander Kirkpatrick born 1777. Died 1777.

Caerlaverock Churchyard.

18. Alexander Kirkpatrick born 1780. Died 11th Aug. 1814 at Wilmington, South Carolina.

19. Elizabeth Kirkpatrick born 1781. Died 1782.

Caerlaverock Churchyard.

NOTE. Glenkiln, Knock, Ahenskew, Craigshields, are all within a mile or two of each other in the Glenkiln area of the parish of Garrel, just north of Kirkmichael.

Judging by record above, in his early married life (till 1762), William lived in Garrel parish and moved thereafter to Caerlaverock (on the Solway), where he and his wife were buried.

Appendix VIe

Extract from a letter
of William Escott Kirkpatrick (Conheath branch) to his cousin in Scotland,
reference "the intended alliance" of the Emperor Napoleon III.

Dated Brussels,
28th Jan. 1853.

"There were so many generous accounts in the English papers, that I had some thoughts of troubling you to get inserted a statement of the family of Countess Montijo, which I had prepared.

However, in the article of the Times of Monday last, upon the marriage of the Emperor, the short notice of the Kirkpatricks is fair enough; but there was no occasion to add that the Scottish heralds set to work with such diligence that a suitable pedigree was produced, for I find that the date of the patent granted[1] to my father, by the Herald's Office was 16th May 1791 , which was before my uncle William Kirkpatrick Esq., of Malaga was married, and established his descent[2] from the Closeburn branch; of course before his daughter, who is now Countess Montijo was born".

As this marriage is attracting, in an unusual degree, the attention of all Europe, our name is brought very prominently before the Public".

X   X   X
W.C. KIRKPATRICK.

Notes:
1. Patent granted to "John of Conheath" who, at that time took out arms to establish his own connection with the main line of Closeburn under the name of "John of Culloch" He took the name "Culloch" from his wife's property in Kirkcudbright. Settled as a merchant in Ostend, he matriculated under a name in this country. His wife was Janet Stothert, heiress of Tarscreechan, (modern Torkatrine), overlooking the lands of Little and Meikle Culloch - vide sasine records for Kirkcudbright.

Marriage contract 9th April 1789.) son and heir of William Kirkpatrick of Conheath.)

2. This was done in 1817 when the marriage of William of Malaga's daughter, Countess Montijo, was being arranged for. Certificate of family and parentage being secured from the Lyon King of Arms Office in Edinburgh. (Referred to in letters of the Countess). This certificate appears to have been Patent of 1791 referred to above). Vide The Scottish Antiquary-1898-99, Vol. 13-14 page 159 News Note, it was Charles Kirkpatrick Sharpe who obtained the certificate and "sent pedigree", which is the family tradition.

Appendix VI f

Copy of Extracts
from a letter to the Editor of the Dumfries and Galloway Standard,

Dated Dumfries, 15th December, 1860.

"Dear Sir,
The Court Journal, the Glasgow Herald and other papers, have lately given very inaccurate statements regarding the descent of her Imperial Majesty, the Empress Eugenie."

"I therefore trouble you with a sketch of Her Majesty's descent as shown upon the genealogical tree of Her Majesty's family, compiled by me, a copy of which I had the honour of presenting to Her Majesty during her recent visit to Scotland, and which Her Majesty was graciously pleased to accept. On the accuracy of the following you may rely."

"Alexander Kirkpatrick, first Baron of the Barony of Kirkmichael, in Dumfriesshire, was the second son of Roger Kirkpatrick, Baron of Closeburn and Margaret, daughter of Thomas, first Lord Somerville, by Janet, daughter of Alexander, Lord Darnley. The Barony of Kirkmichael, Alexander Kirkpatrick got as a reward for the capture of James, ninth Earl Douglas, at the Battle of Burnswark, A.D. 1484."

[... ...]

"The barony remained in the hands of Alexander till 1622, when part of it was sold by the then Baron, William, to Sir Charteris."

"William had two sons; and died 9th June 1686. He and his eldest son "George of Knock" lie interred in Garrell Churchyard, Kirkmichael."

"Robert, his second son, of and in Glenkiln, married Henrietta Gillespie of Craigshields. He had four sons and one daughter."

"His third son was William Kirkpatrick, Esq. of Conheath, near Dumfries, and Over and Nether Glenkiln and Lambfoot, Kirkmichael." (NOTE: William "of Conheath", born 1737 died 1787 at Conheath.

193

Buried in Vault Caerlaverock).

"He married Mary Kelton in Galloway. Issue nineteen children. His sixth child was William Kirkpatrick, merchant and American Consul at Malaga, who married Fanny (Correct name Francisca Maria Grovignee of Liego), daughter of Baron Grivignee, of Malaga: issue three daughters: Charlotte (Correct name Carlotta Catalina) married her cousin Thomas Kirkpatrick (Correct name Thomas James Kirkpatrick), son of John Kirkpatrick, mechant of Ostend (Correct designation - John, Second son and fourth child.), by Janet Stotherd of Arkland and Areeming: Harriet married the Count de Cabarras; and the eldest, Mary Kirkpatrick (Correct name Maria Manuela Kirkpatrick.) married the Count of Montijo, a Grandee of Spain of the first rank - issue two daughters: the eldest married the Duke of Berwick and Alba and died this year: the second is the beautiful and amiable Eugenie, Empress of the French. Robert, the eighth child, became a merchant in London and died there. No issue. Thomas died in Malaga, no issue. Alexander died in New York, no issue. These are all the sons who reached manhood."

[... ...]

J. Campbell Gracie

(Note: Mr J. Campbell Gracie had apparently a close family connection. According to records of the Dumfries & Galloway Standard, Mr. J. Campbell Grace's wife was "niece of William Kirkpatrick of Kelton". (This should be "Conheath". He married Mary Wilson of Kelton). Mr Gracie would thus have had access to the very complete genealogy of William Kirkpatrick of Conheath given by Dr. Clapperton in 1784, which shows his father as being Robert Kirkpatrick of Glenkiln. Proofs of this are found in sasine records of Dumfries and Kirkcudbright; (later referred to).

Appendix VI g

The Irish Kirkpatricks' History
dealing with the Kirkmichael connection

The Irish Kirkpatrick's "Chronicles of the Kirkpatricks", published in 1897, can be quoted as regards the connection of the Empess Eugenie, as extending the genealogy further back from the Conheath connection of the Empress.

It records that "William Kirkpatrick 'the last Lord of Kirkmichael' had two sons, George of Knock (the elder) and Robert of Glenkiln.

Both properties were part of Kirkmichael estates in the parish of Garrell".

William Kirkpatrick died on 9th June 1686 and is buried in Garrel Churchyard, where it is said his tombstone was cleared from overgrowing grass by Mr. Campbell Gracie of Dumfries in 1860, a well-known antiquarian and geneologist. Mr. Gracie stated that George Kirkpatrick of Knock, after visiting Ireland in 1690, served in the army and left with the rank of Major. He settled down at Knock, where Mr. Campbell Gracie remarks "he took an active interest in the affairs of his church at Garrell".

"He is buried in the same grave as his father and beside his brother Robert of Glenkiln (died 1746)." In 1861 the tombstone was in good preservation and the inscription read:

Here lies the corps of William Kirkpatrick,

Who departed this life 9th June, 1686.

(Here the coat of arms is engraved in high relief).

His eldest son George of Knock, who

departed this life 1738 - aged 67 years

Note 1: Garrell has long been included in the parish of Kirkmichael - since the 17th Century. Garrell Church, a small plain stone and lime building, is in ruins - just a few feet of the walls (in height) remain.

Note 2: The Kirkmichael branch of the Closeburn family is given in Burke, page 1146, down to William of Kirkmichael, died 1686.

Note 3: Robert of Glenkiln's grave is reported by J.G. Kirkpatrick to show his name and death as 1746. Inspected probably in the first quarter of 20th century. By then, the report stated "Close beside it is another stone, older, but from design not older than the previous generation, on which the name Kirkpatrick is decipherable, but the rest illegible. There is a shield with supporters but the arms are obliterated."

Note 4: The fact that both Campbell Gracie and J.G. Kirkpatrick, at widely separated intervals of time, have testified that on this "Kirkpatrick" tombstone a coat of arms was engraved, plainly indicates that this was the grave of a "cadet" of the family of Closeburn. It could not possibly be that of any other of that name, not entitled to these arms (as has been suggested by one writer). "George of Knock" must needs be a very close relation to have been buried in the same grave.

Appendix VII

In the Days of "John Company"
(The Honorable East India Company's Service)

In the middle of the 18th century, certain members of a branch of the Closeburn family rendered distinguished service in India. A Colonel James Kirkpatrick, an officer of the East India Company's Madras service, is first mentioned as "an experienced commander of Horse" and as having married Katherine, daughter of Andrew Munro at Madras in 1762. He commanded the forces in Sumatra in 1777, and died as a Major General; (the highest rank to which an officer in "The Company's" service could rise), in his 89th year, in 1818, at his seat "Holldale", Kent.

He had three sons - William, described as "the Orientalist", George, who was in the civil service in Bombay, and James Achilles, whose career is told below.

The eldest, William, very soon distinguished himself by his political service.

In 1793, the Court of Nepaul, (the land of the Gurkhas), alarmed by an invasion from China, had implored assistance from the Bengal government. "No Englishman had hitherto passed beyond the range of lofty mountains which separats the secluded valley of Nepaul from the north east parts of Bengal."

The Bengal government sent Colonel William Kirkpatrick (assisted by three other officers and a surgeon) as envoy to the court.

His very full report on that country, later published by the Board of Directors, shows that he traversed that then unknown country very widely. (A copy of this report can be seen in the Scottish National Library, Edinburgh, and, I fancy, in India House, together with his other Oriental works).

He next rendered distinguished service under Lord Wellesley when he went out to India as Governor in 1798.

In a despatch dated 10th January, 1802, Lord Wellesley wrote of him:- "I fortunately found him at the Cape, on my way to India, and I have no hesitation in declaring that to him I am indebted for the seasonable information which enabled me to extinguish the French influence in the Deccan, and to frustrate the vindictive projects of Tippoo Sultaun."

He filled the offices of Resident at the Court of Scindiah and at Hyderabad and was Secretary to the Military Department of the Government. He was forced by ill health to retire to England at the early age of forty seven.

Lord Wellesley, in his despatch, wrote that he had served his country with the greatest honour and ability and wrote:- "Lieut. Colonel Kirkpatrick's skill in the Oriental languages, and his extensive acquaintance with the manners, customs and laws of India are not equalled by any person whom I have met in this country."

His perfect knowledge of all native courts, of their policy, prejudices and interests, as well as of all the leading political characters among the inhabitants of India, is unrivalled in the civil or military service; and his integrity and honour are as universally acknowledged and respected, as his eminent talents, extraordinary learning and politiacal experience."

Lord Wellesley offered in the handsomest terms to apply on his behalf for English honours, which, however, he courteously declined. He died a Major General in 1812, in his 58th year, leaving four daughters.

William's youngest brother, James Achilles, was acting as Assistant Resident at Hyderabad when William was forced by ill health to leave India, and thus the change of British interests at the court of the Nizam of Hyderabad was made over to James Achilles Kirkpatrick. In an article, Mr. J.J. Cotton, I.C.S., has written, many years ago: "It was during the latter's nine years incumbency of this office that he had the duty of negotiating three important treaties, by the most famous of which a British subsidiary force was to take the place of Raymond's French contingent. When, at the eleventh hour Ali Khan wavered on being brought face to face with such a renunciation, Lord Wellesley's agent proved himself equal to the occasion.

In person, Kirkpatrick ordered the advance of Colonel Roberts and his troops, whereupon 14,000 Sepoys and 124 officers under Perron surrendered their arms without a struggle. The Governor General rewarded the Resident by making him his Honorary Aide-de-Camp, a remarkable distinction at that time, for he was the first person on whom the honour was bestowed. Robert Horne, the portrait painter, has, incidentally, brought into one of his state pictures a reference to this diplomatic triumph. His somewhat uninspiring portrate of the Marquess Wellesley which hangs next to Dance's half-length of Clive, in the Council Chamber at Calcutta, represents the great proConsul resting his hand on a parchment scroll inscribed 'Subsidiary Treaty, Hyderabad 1798.'

The Governor General had indeed every reason to be greatful to his Lieutenant. He was voted an annuity of £5,000 for a term of twenty years by the Court of Directors, and the payment was ordered to date from 1st September, 1798, the day on which the treaty was concluded with the Soubahdar of the Deccan."

I have not been able to trace the Closeburn connection of these kinsmen of ours; but I think the first Colonel James Kirkpatrick, who was born in 1729, seems to fit in as a son of the James, son of the 1st Baronet, who, in 1686 quitted Scotland and founded the Isle of Wight branch; as much of the above detail comes from Richard Godman in "Kirkpatrick of Closeburn" and the Isle of Wight pedigree shows that the original James had a son of the same name.

I find that James Achilles died a Lieut. Colonel in Calcutta in 1805, leaving one son, William, who died in 1828, and a daughter, Catherine Aurora, married to Captain James Winslow Phillips, 7th Hussars.

This Catherine Aurora, seen to have been the daughter of James Achilles Kirkpatrick, figures in an old newspaper cutting wich I found in India many years ago under the heading: "Kitty Kirkpatrick." "An Anglo Indian Romance." This cutting gives a few extracts from an interesting article by Mr. J.J. Cotton I.C.S. in the last Calcutta Review". No dates! No ending! The more tantalizing as the last page of the story is missing!

The first "extract" stated that "Kitty" born in 1764, is one of the most literary of Anglo Indian celebrities: she was the original, (so far as there was an original), of Blumine in Carlyle's "Sartor Resartus".

James Achilles Kirkpatrick was known to have made a romantic marriage at the court of the Nizam of Hyderabad. The news cutting gave this account of it:- "The courtship of Kirkpatrick by the Indian Begum reproduces, with additions and variations, much of the sentiment of this north country ballad. "(not given!).

"Such was the thoroughness with which the Resident threw himself into his Asiatic surroundings that he altogether dropped his English name in his dealings with the Court. In the vernacular correspondence he is known only as Hushmat Jung, "the Magnificent in battle". His inamorata was Khair-un-Nissa, Begam, by interpretation, "Excellent among women." Whatever may have been the appropriateness of the high sounding title, in Kirkpatrick's case, it was certainly no misnomer in that of the lady!

She was of purest Persian descent, while claiming relationship with the Prophet himself. Her grandfather, Akil-un-Dowlah, was the 'bakshi', or paymaster to the English subsidiary force.

The wooing was effected in truly Oriental fashion.

Kirkpatrick was sitting alone one evening when, to his astonishment, he was visited by one of those old women who play the part of matchmakers in Eastern society.

From her he learnt of the passion of Khair-un-Nissa, who had fallen desperately in love with him at first sight, as she watched him through the purdah, during an entertainment in her grandfather's house. The Englishman at first repelled the advances made to him; but the Princess would brook no denial.

After repeated but unavailing overtures through her emissary, the girl at last resolved to take the matter into her own hands. A veiled figure was ushered by night into the Residency and pleaded her suit so passionately that Kirkpatrick's heart was melted. He must, indeed, have been more than man to hold out any longer. His own account of the fiery ordeal of that nocturnal interview is given in a letter to his brother, William."

(And here Mr. Cotton's romantic story breaks down, for the sequel must have been on another page; which, alas, is missing!!)

But he did marry the Begum, and it is an amusing story of the old days of "John, Companee Bahadur"!

Appendix VIII

Addendum, 1954

When my attention was drawn to the articles on the early history of the Closeburn family, to which I have alluded in the foreword, I was determined to trace the source of the statements made therein.

These statements about the family were buttressed by a large number of assumptions and assertions, which, if true, would present a picture of deception on such an extensive scale, that I cannot credit this, when the Closeburn evidence is examined. This evidence I have been able to collect and collate largely because I have had access to family papers previously held by various members of the family now deceased, and also from more recent information.

Had the so-called "senior" line of Kirkpatricks in Annandale "died out" after some centuries and the Closeburn Kirkpatricks in Nithsdale done what they are alleged to have done, i.e. adopted as their own the traditions and throughout Dumfriesshire and would not have passed unnoted until, in the twentieth century, this story was served up as a fresh tale and a new pedigree was produced for the Closeburn family. The Annandale folk would certainly have then had a good deal to say about it!

In the article to which I refer, there are many references to Bain and to "Closeburn writs".

The latter, only discovered in 1952, do not relate further back then the 16th Century, so they do not bear upon the ancient history.

Early traditions are the memories preserved and handed down by generations who knew little of, and cared less for, the art of writing. The monks of those days in their monasteries were the scribes, some of whom later are named as amongst our earliest historians.

As regards these: Dr. A.M. Mackenzie points out that no contemporary Scottish chronicle has survived dealing with the initial period of the Scottish War of Independence, and that the one authoritative writer of that period of Scottish history was Hemingburgh, an Englishman, an Austin Canon of Guisborn in Yorkshire.

The first authoritative Scottish historians of that time came a generation later i.e. Fordun and Barbour. Wynton, who wrote c. 1380, is commended as especially reliable and accurate with regard to events near his life time.

All three local, and modern, historians, McDowell, Ramage and Clapperton, narrate the Closeburn story.

When, towards the end of 1953, I received an invitation to address the Dumfriesshire and Galloway Antiquarian Society with regard to my family, I carried out much further research, in order to be able to reply to the last article published in that journal.

In one paper I could not possibly deal with more than a few of the points raised, but in the paper which I read to the society, which appears overleaf as Appendix VIII, I show what I believe was the root cause of the misleading statements in recent times about Closeburn.

It is inevitable that much of Appendix VIII is a repetition of the history already told in these pages. I offer no apology for that. I feel that only by presenting this paper in its entirety can it be seen how it was that the erroneous statements about the Closeburn family appear in the Report of the Historical MSS Commission for Scotland, which can be seen to have resulted in many misleading developments and conclusions.

Earlier in this book I wrote that I hoped to include here some of Charles Kirkpatrick Sharpe's personal letters which might be of interest. I have so far exceeded the patience of my readers already, that such were better omitted.

We have only one fixed date by which I can attempt to reconcile the dates of our early ancestors with the information we have regarding them.

King Robert the Bruce died in 1329 at the age of fifty five.

Here is a table making a guess at birth dates, which appear to correspond with available information:

Table:

	Approximate dates of birth.	Age at 1306.	Relevant dates.
Stephen K.	c. 1248?	58	Kelso Charter 1278. Pennersax Charter c. 1319/1320.
King Robert Bruce.	1274	32	Died 7th June, 1329.
Roger K.	c.1277?	29	One of Peace Commissioners 1314 and 1320.
Duncan K.	c1279?	27	Laird of Torthorwald. Supported Sir William Wallace in battle 1297.
Thomas K.	c. 1301?	5	Received Charter Bridburgh 1319. Witness 1355.
Winifred K.	c. 1326?	-	
Thomas K.	c. 1360?	-	Ayr Charter 1409. Conservator for peace 1438.
Roger K.	c. 1380?	-	Succeeded about 1438. Commissioner of West Borders 1455.

Appendix IX

Paper read to the Dumfriesshire and Galloway Antiquarian Society
on 18th December, 1953, by Major General C. Kirkpatrick, C.B., C.B.E.,
entitled 'Records of the Closeburn Kirkpatricks.'

First I want to say how much I appreciate being asked to speak about my family here. I am sure no Closeburn Kirkpatrick has ever addressed this society before. It is a privilege I much appreciate.

Now to introduce myself. I am the great grandson of Sir James Kirkpatrick, the 4th Baronet of Closeburn. My brother Major William Kirkpatrick took out a patent of arms at the Lyon Kings Office in 1937 as his direct descendant, as legal proof of our connection with the main branch of Closeburn. My grand uncle Sir Thomas 5th Baronet, was Sheriff of Dumfries for 33 years and when these two ancestors of mine died here, most generous tributes were paid in Dumfries to their high principles and unflinching integrity in their public and private duties. Charles Kirkpatrick Sharpe was a great grandson of the 2nd Baronet and his sister Jane was married to the sheriff, Sir Thomas.

Each of these men have contributed vital important evidence to the history of our family, especially Charles Kirkpatrick Sharpe, who has been most unjustly criticised by certain people. I would find it extremely difficult to disbelieve what they have testified to on any important issue and I find proof of the accuracy of their evidence. I have no need for a fresh pedigree.

As the last surviving Closeburn Kirkpatrick of my generation, I have felt it a duty to pass on to my posterity the records of our past as I know them to be and to try and clear up the hideous mess that has been made of our family history.

Now a book I have been writing for many months for a limited circulation only, has been forestalled by the publication in the July number of this journal by an article entitled the Early Kirkpatricks. My reduplicated typescript work must however stand as written and I hope it will not be long before I can present the Ewart library with a copy of it.

You can only read our story properly there, so please reserve judgement.

As a Closeburn Kirkpatrick in complete disagreement with much that has been written of recent years of our early history I have got to go very fast and briefly to get even a little of what I want to say into my allotted hour. For the last 70 years Closeburn history has been grievously misrepresented especially since 1925, when the unfruitful excavations of Auchencas Castle were reported in this journal, for it was this which produced Sir Roger Kirkpatrick of Auchencas out of his historical obscurity, in Moffat.

So to come straight to the root of the matter. All Closeburn pedigrees are primarily based on Nisbet, the greatest heraldic historian of his century, who wrote 250 years ago. He lived from 1675 to 1725 and he published his classic work the System of Heraldry in 1722 for which he prepared Heraldic plates of Principal Scottish families between 1696 and 1702. Expence of production prevented these being published then, but in 1892 Sir Francis Grant and Andrew Ross produced them as Nisbets heraldic plates.

On Nisbet's death, a disaster occurred. The first edition of his System of Heraldry was injured by a fraudulent reproduction of it several times repeated in 1742 and later, published by a literary forger, Fleming. This was not discovered till years afterwards. Seven pages of the preface to Grant's Heraldic plates are devoted to exposing these forgeries of 1742, and the definite warning is given that the mutilated transcriptions printed thereafter, especially those in the marshalling of arms and cadency chapters, (where individual distinguishing marks are given) may therefore be disregarded. The caution was given that reference to Nisbet as an authority thereon can only be made to the earliest editions of 1722.

You will hardly have failed to notice that in the July Journal, Nisbet is very adversely criticised because of extracts quoted from an 1816 edition of the system of Heraldry.

With Nisbet I must link the name of the late Francis Grant K.C.V.O., who for 45 years was Lyon Clerk, keeper of the Records of Scotland and Lyon King of Arms, for he was joint editor of the Heraldic Plates, in which the above warning was given. He wrote the pedigree of the Kirkpatricks of Closeburn, largely of course from Nisbets history of our family written 250 years ago.

For us, Nisbets evidence is of great value because,

(1) He wrote it before the disastrous fire of Closeburn in 1748, testifying to what he saw there.

(2) He was the only authentic writer, who wrote within that period of 46 years when all records of the Lyon Kings Office were temporarily lost when, without these records, it was found necessary to order a registration of arms in 1672, when a proper check of earlier records could not possibly have been made. Nisbet visited the principal Scottish families and saw their records, starting about 1692.

Replying to an enquiry of mine regarding Nisbet, the late Sir Francis Grant wrote to me 16 months ago as follows:- "The large book I showed you with the Closeburn arms, was Sir David Lindsay of the Mount Lord Lyon's Register of 1542. This is the oldest register of arms in Scotland now existing, and it is predecessor of the present registers. This gives the Closeburn arms as re-registered in 1673".

He went on "The old records of the Lyon office previous to 1650 were carried off by Sir James Balfour, Lord Lyon, to his Castle of Denmylne in Fife, where he died in 1656. In 1660 no one seems to have known of this, and it was stated they were probably carried off by Cromwell". (It was for fear of this that Sir James Balfour hid them). "In 1661 when certain other records were being returned to Scotland, a large number, (85 hogsheads of them) were lost by the vessel carrying them being sunk. The records were meanwhile slumbering at Delmylne till 1696 (when they were recovered and amongst them was Sir David Lindsay's Register of 1542, now in the National Library.)

The present public register of all arms and bearings in Scotland was founded by act of Parliament in 1672" (that is before the earlier 1542 Register was retrieved in 1696). But Nisbet was writing by then, interviewing what he calls the principal families and personally noting their records. Fifty pages of Nisbet's Heraldic plates tell his story, and Sir James Fergusson writes of him in his "Lowland Lairds", which you should read.

Now Dr. Maitland Thomas, a charter experts report on the public records of Scotland states that the sole existing great Seal record of Robert the Bruce is apparently of the year 1321. The rest are missing and that during the war of Independance few records can have been kept. Those in charge of records in 1676, he writes, left them on the floor of Register House to be damaged by a flooded water pipe. Tradititionally, quite a lot more were destroyed by fire also, about 1670. (Seton's Heraldry p. 71).

So Nisbet, on the old Scottish families, is of the greatest value, always provided you quote him correctly! Modern produced evidence of the early days needs to be adequately proved; so do assertions and assumptions.

Now the Historic Manuscripts Commission for Scotland published its report on Dumfriesshire Vol. 15 in 1881, and with that report I must connect the name of Sir William Frazer, who has been so followed and quoted with regard to the Early Kirkpatricks by Mr. Reid. Sir Francis Grant did not accept this report on Closeburn.

In the Historic Commission's report, the following introductory remarks were made about the Closeburn Kirkpatricks. "The Kirkpatrick traditions have connected this family with Nithsdale at an earlier date than is warranted by charter evidence". The report then added "all the Closeburn charters were lost in the fire of 1748".

With these words, the traditions and 300 years of the earlier accepted history of our family were wiped off the slate and obliterated from official record. Grievous harm was done by these two erroneous statements which have misled many people and made others suspicious of the truthfulness of our records. No Closeburn Kirkpatrick was in any position to combat such a verdict of the Historic Commission for Scotland in 1881. We knew all charters had not been burnt, but that some most important ones had been saved from the fire from which Charles K. Sharpe had later made lithograph copies, as recorded for posterity.

But how to prove their accuracy seemed impossible then. Charles Kirkpatrick Sharpe was a brilliantly talented antiquarian and an artist. His beautiful etchings, which he himself reproduced, were published, in a volume in 1869 after his death. In this it is stated that he began making reproductions of them in copper-plate in 1813. His Mss. History is a guide to earlier authoritative evidence. It is so very fully referenced, that I do not actually need to quote from his text the history of the Early Kirkpatricks. I beg you to make a very special note of this.

In the case of the lithograph charters, in every case he has stated in whose possession the originals were at the time of writing. Ten of them are noted as being in possession of the 5th Baronet, the sheriff, on whose death in 1844 the Dumfries Courier wrote that he was in very truth a man in whom there was no guile. Straight forward honesty was legibly written in the features of his countenance. Was such a man likely to connive with C.K.S. in fabricating a family history, and faking the records of the sheriff's office?

Proofs of my ancester's truthfulness however were left for later generations to find and this only came in spring 1952, when the whole situation was changed; because two boxes of Closeburn charters, dating back to 16th century only, were surprisingly deposited in Register House by lawyers who must have acted for the Menteths who bought Closeburn in 1783 - and these unknown to anyone, (C.K.S. included), had been lost to knowledge until 1952. That alone was clear proof that one vital statement of Historic Commission, the story that all charters were lost, was not only wrong, but most misleading for anyone outside the family.

And the second proof came that same spring, when I discovered the original 1811 Mss. History of C.K.S. in possesssion of a Sharpe descendant in England - and no single person has had a chance of studying it since, as I have been working on it, and checking it myself.

To return to the Historic Commission; on further investigation I saw that the first land grant under the head of Closeburn was dated 21st November, 1423. These charters of 1232 - 1264 - 1278 - 1319 - all known to us, are entirely omitted in this account of Closeburn, by the Historic Commission, under the heading of Closeburn.

The report continues. "In the memorable encounter between Robert Bruce and the Red John Comyn, Regent of Scotland, which took place on 4th February 1305, in the Greyfriars Church at Dumfries, Sir Thomas Kirkpatrick played such a prominent part, that it has ever since been a matter of family and national history". All national histories I have read refer to a Roger Kirkpatrick, not a Thomas; and Roger is the family tradition.

The one Sir Thomas Kirkpatrick of Closeburn whom Fraser mentioned in 300 years was discovered by him acting as a witness to his cousin Roger of Torthorwald in 1355; but, although he is Sir Thomas Kirkpatrick of Closeburn, Fraser does not show him under Closeburn. I calculate this man was just about 5 or 6 years old in February 1306 when he is accused of being in Greyfriars.

But Nisbet in 1722 showed this Thomas to be the eldest son of Roger mak sicker of Closeburn who got a charter of Bridburgh from King

Robert Bruce in 1319 for his father's and his own special services to the King - and Bridburgh was thereafter a property of the Closeburn family through the centuries. Mak sicker's second son, Roger of Nyddisdale and Caerlaverock, is well established by much earlier evidence, I'll tell you about.

I next found out on the best authority that the reporter to the Historic Commission who was mainly responsible for producing the report was a Mr. William Fraser, who was Deputy Keeper of the Records for several years, and I must here quote Sir James Balfour Paul, an ex Lyon King of Arms, who wrote "Before sitting down to write a family history it is of course necessary to know something about the family whose history you are going to write". There is no evidence to show that Fraser knew anything about the Krkpatricks beyond what he saw in Annandale charters, which alone he had on his desk. (The content of these charters is not of course questioned).

Fraser had an urge to write family histories, but Sir James Balfour Paul, referring to what he called "Fraser's Cycle of family histories" remarked that "they were not free from occasional error". Dr. George Burnett the Lyon King of his time went much further, for he actually published a book criticising Fraser's work. Fraser's "Red Book of Menteth" (two thick volumes) was criticised by Burnett for its inaccuracies in "The Red Book of Menteth reviewed".

I have the authority of a third ex King of Arms, the late Sir Francis Grant, K.C.V.O., that he had frequently found Sir William Fraser inaccurate, and he gave me that in writing after I had had a talk with him. In a letter he referred me to Scots Peerage where, he wrote, I would find many corrections to Fraser's pedigrees by the Curator of the Historical department who was Fraser's chief assistant - so I have no respect at all for Fraser's comments as regards my family, especially as elsewhere he referenced our 1409 charter while omitting it under the Closeburn heading.

There is a very full history of Upper Nithsdale "Drumlanrig and the Douglases" written by Ramage about 1875. He had free access to the Drumlanrig charters and in his preface he wrote that he had made a pretty minute examination of the inventory and that he had not failed to examine all the chartularies of the monasteries which contained references to the parishes of Closeburn and Dalgarnock, wherein Ramage finds charter evidence of the old Closeburn barons, confirming the charter reported by Dr. Clapperton in 1784, where Ivon is first mentioned, regarding the Torduff fishings in 1141.

Ramage next states that all the Drumlanrig charters were being sent to Mr. William Fraser at Register House for study. Clearly Fraser did not trouble about the Closeburn baronets, who long before 1881 had left the district. He was content to believe that Closeburn was sunk without trace, and paid no attention to Ramage's book, where a full acount of Closeburn was given. Nor did he pay any attention to Nisbet who wrote in 1722 of what he had seen at Closeburn before the fire.

Now there never could have been any charter of Closeburn land in Drumlanrig. Such charters would have been with the Barons of Closeburn until many of their records were burnt, for Closeburn was established in 1232 and Sir William Douglas obtained Drumlanrig in 1356.

Ramage shows the Closeburn lands were on the East bank, and the Douglas lands on the West bank of the Nith, which later extended across into Annandale and Torthorwald, where the Carliels succeeded the old Kirkpatricks in Southern Annandale. So with Carliele writs in one hand, and the Annandale Kirkpatrick writs in the other, Fraser sat down to write about Closeburn.

The Annandale charters given in this report show those Kirkpatricks, mostly Rogers, as witnesses to grants of land to other people in Annandale. No grant of land to any Annandale Kirkpatrick is seen in Kirkpatrick Juxta. Closeburn is dated 1232. There was no baronial family of the name Kirkpatrick in Dumfriesshire other than Closeburn at that time - and there is no doubt Kirkpatricks were settled both in Annandale and Nithsdale long before the Bruces came from Yorkshire, and I am sure they bred many children - not only one Ivon or Roger, very common names in our family.

I find that, contrary to tradition and the evidence of accepted authorities, Fraser's story has now been developed so that the old history of the Closeburn barons in the war of Independance has been twisted out of recognition by assertions that Roger Mac sicker, Thomas of Bridburgh, Roger of Nyddesdale and Caerlaverock, Humphrey Kirkpatrick of Torthorwald, Roger the special delegate in 1357, and his hostage son, were all of the Annandale fraternity. There is good evidence to the contrary, I can tell you.

Bain also in 1881 produced his "collection of documents for Scotland" - an index or summary of all the known papers. It is a fair inference that Fraser and Bain worked hand in hand. Bain is responsible for an entry regarding that treacherous knave Sir Roger Kirkpatrick of Auchencas we read of who seems to lived from 1305 to 1332, in English pay and borrowed money from them in 1306. But references to him quoted, give no indication that he was ever near Greyfriars. There can also be little doubt that the conception that there was a senior branch of Kirkpatricks existent in Annandale arose from the faulty usage of these Annandale writs; combined with what Charles K. Sharpe once termed "Imaginative research".

To turn to Charles Kirkpatrick Sharpe. I was surprised to find in the introduction to "the Early Kirkpatricks", Campbell Gracie's name mixed up with Sharpe's Mss., and mine, in this statement:- "In Sharpe's lifetime, Campbell Gracie made a pedigree chart from Sharpe's Mss., a copy of which he presented to Empress Eugenie in 1860 - a copy of this is in the Dumfries Museum". Now that same statement I heard here last year - where is the proof of this assertion?

I have seen the chart in the Dumfries Museum. It is the same as others issued by Gracie of date 1854 and later, and it shows the Empress married! Well, she married in 1853 and Charles Kirkpatrick Sharpe died in 1851. He knew nothing of the Empress Eugenie. Gracie's chart of the Early Kirkpatricks differs considerably from Charles K. Sharpe's written pedigree as I have it. There is no chart in the Mss. History. In Gracie's tree, Caerlaverock Roger is wrongly shown as succeeding to Closeburn, thus misleading others.

Thereafter, as you read, Gracie's copied chart was blamed for many modern writers being put wrong, including the editors of Nisbet's Heraldic Plates, Sir Francis Grant. I find no basis for this serious allegation. Actually, if you will look at page 129 of this journal, you will see that Mr. Provost states on authority, that Mr. Gracie was asked by Mr. Sharpe of Hoddom to trace the connecting link to Closeburn and he was given access to the late Kirkpatrick Sharpe's papers to assist him to do so. That is supported by other evidence - actually, Miss Jane Kirkpatrick of Nithsbank, Dumfries, the sole surviving daughter of William of Conheath, helped Gracie to prepare his charts in 1854. She kept the Conheath family records. Gracie must stand on his own feet. (Annandale Herald 7th June, 1873).

And now I come to the worst misrepresentation of all in the July Journal, where Nisbet is quoted as having seen a charter of King Alexander II in the hands of a bogus Sir Patrick Kirkpatrick. A warning is given that the affirmations of Nisbet must be regarded with the utmost caution. Later in this article, you are told that the seal of Sir Roger Kirkpatrick of Closeburn of 1435, which Nisbet testifies to having seen, is equally to be accepted with the utmost caution. It is added that no other reference to this Roger has been found. These are most damaging statements. I have just told you Nisbet's story and you can wipe Sir Patrick Kirkpatrick's name off the slate, because the writer has taken his story vide his footnote, from the marshalling chapter of the 1816 Edition of System of Heraldry specifically debarred from quotation by Sir Francis Grant, himself a great heraldic authority. I trust that these most damaging remarks on my family will be retracted in the transactions of this society.

I must read to you the established 1722 edition of Nisbet from which our early pedigree is taken. Before I do so, I must explain that in the old Latin charter, the letters J and I look very similar and Dr. Claperton in 1784 states he found the first names, Ivon, Yvon, "perhaps the same as we now pronounce Ewen" - (and Ian is the Scottish name for John) - so I find Nisbet writes John for Ivon - referring to the 1232 charter - (you can see what I mean when you look at it.)

This is Nisbet 1722. Arms of Kirkpatrick of Closeburn in the shire of Nithsdale - Argent a saltier - and chief, azure, the last charged with 3 cushions or - crest, a hand holding a dagged in pale, distilling drops of blood, with the motto "I make sure". Supporters two lions guardant.

Remarks: This principle family has been in use to carry supporters since the year 1435, as by the evidents and seals which I have seen by the favour of the late Sir Thomas Kirkpatrick of Closeburn, a few of which I shall mention. John Kirkpatrick of Closeburn obtains a charter of confirmation of the lands of Kilosbern, (which belonged formerly to his ancestors), from King Alexander II.

Roger Kirkpatrick successor to the aforesaid John, whom Buchanan calls Rogerus a Cella Patricii was among the first of those worthies that stood up for the interests of King Robert the Bruce as he was returning from smiting Red John Comyn in the church of Dumfries. This

Roger went into the church expressing these words "I'll make sicker" - sure - and there gave Comyn several stabs with a dagger, for which the family has used the dagger for crest and for motto, "I make sure".

Nisbet goes on:- (here please remember Fraser's "Thomas mak succar"). Sir Thomas Kirkpatrick succeeded his father Roger in the Barony of Closeburn, who for his father's and his own special services to his king and country got the lands of Redburgh (Bridburgh) in the sheriffdom of Dumfries as the charter of King Robert the Bruce bears, dated at Lochmaben 4th June 14th year of his reign (Brideburgh remained in Closeburn hands for centuries thereafter).

Sir Thomas was succeeded by Winfredus de Kirkpatrick who got the lands of Torthorwald. (Charles Kirkpatrick Sharpe here makes a cousin get it) and Nisbet goes on to say:- "His son or grandson Sir Thomas Kirkpatrick of Closeburn made a resignation of the barony of Closeburn and Bridburgh into the hands of Robert Duke of Albany, Earl of Fife, and Governor of Scotland, for a new charter of Tailzie to himself and his heirs male, in which there are several substitutions in favour of his brothers and nephews too long here to be mentioned". Charles Kirkpatrick Sharpe gives these in full and this is a matter of great importance as showing the succession here, in 1409, under the Great Seal.

Nisbet continues:- "He was succeeded by his brother Roger Kirkpatrick, who was one of the gentlemen of inquest serving Wm. Lord. Somerville, heir to his father Thomas Lord Somerville, before Sir Henry Freston of Craigmillar, sheriff Principal and Provost of Edinburgh the 10th June, 1435. To this writ of service, which I have seen in the custody of Somerville of Drum, Roger Kirkpatrick of Closeburn's seal is appended, upon which are the aforementioned armorial figures. (as before).

Nisbet quoted this service record from the Mss. History of the Somerville family. In it, the eldest daughter of 1st Lord Somerville is shown marrying in 1427, Hay of Yester, the youngest Margaret marrying this Roger, Laird of Closeburn. They are called "gentlemen of eminent qualitie, chief of their names and families. (Closeburn and Restalrig)".

Nisbet no doubt copied the date 1435 from the Somerville M.S. history of 1679 which he saw in Drum, from which this entry is taken; but Charles Kirkpatrick Sharpe (presumably after checking the Edinburgh public record), notes the date in his history as 1445 - clearly someone made a slip of the pen.

214

But despite this clear evidence of evidence of succession your journal declares that Roger did not succeed, but that Sir Thomas had three sons and to daughters. This Sir Thomas died d.s.p. and the two daughters shown as Elizabeth and Margaret were not his offspring. In consequence that pedigree becomes chaotic.

Poor John 1st Lord Carlyle is thus shown to have had, for his undouted mother, Elizabeth Kirkpatrick of Torthorwald, and for his wife, Elizabeth Kirkpatrick of Closeburn, with a very ancient sister-in-law Margaret Kirkpatrick of Closeburn, who, by Vatican records, was the widow of Patricius de Moraira in 1394, a date 38 years before her very young elder sister's indenture of marriage was signed!

I cannot credit that! Nor need you, if you look up Ramage and see some one has made a mistake again. This time of a hundred years! But historians do make slips of the pen; quite often I find, and I prefer the Closeburn record about this, our pedigree is quite different to the one in the journal here.

This Thomas died without children. He had one illegitimate son only called George.

I've read you what Nisbet had to say, about our motto 250 years ago, and many jokes have been passed about it and Charles Kirkpatrick Sharpe's eccentricities in the Edinburgh Clubs. I feel sure you have heard it suggested that Charles Kirkpatrick Sharpe turned "I make sure" into the Lowland Scots form "I mak siccar". Quite the wrong way round of course: and I find Sir Herbert Maxwell quoted as writing that "Roger probably spoke Norman French when he killed the Comyn. Certainly not "Lowland Scots".

Now the big Oxford dictionary gives no less than 5 meanings to the word "sicker", and it is shown to have been in common use in very early days - Chaucer used the term in 1384. Dr. Agnes Mackenzie, the Scottish historian of international repute, has pointed out that sicker was a word of Danish origin, probably more frequently used in Scotland. Barbour, born in 1320, used it in his book The Bruce. Brunner's Chronicles in 1330 gave Edward "sikkered him wele". In the time of James II 1450 "the Kings peace was proclaimed over all the country under which all men might travel sikkerly without paying for protection." The terms was used from King to commoner. There is a ring of truth about our old tradition; and how badly truth, it is seen, can be contorted.

Nisbet covers 170 years of our early pedigree in the direct line, so we can pass to Roger of Nyddesdale and Caerlaverock; and in the journal, more than half Wynton's story about him is omitted. Had it been quoted in full, you could have no possible doubt that Hoge of Kirkpatrick Nyddesdale and Hoge who was murdered in Caerlaverock were one and the same person.

Lord Hailes quotes Fordun with regard to him - you are told Fordun makes no mention of a Kirkpatrick and that the first mention of a Roger was made 200 years after Greyfriars. This assertion is not correct. Fordun had a continuator or disciple in Walter Bower, or Browen, just as Sir Wm. Fraser has a continuator in this generation. Fordun left many notes to Bower who incorporated them in their joint work Scotichronicum - which is very often referred to as Fordun.

Dr. Agnes Mure Mackenzie has a lot to say about this. She quotes a later text of Bower as giving "rather a detailed description of Lindsay cutting the throat of the peacefully sleeping Kirkpatrick, and later, (with reference back to a very detailed account of the death of Comyn) Bower adds "the said James and Roger were first born, or heirs, of those who took part with Robert Bruce in the killing of the Red Comyn in the Friars Kirk at Dumfries" - She then completes the full version of Wynton, which was omitted in the journal, and translates Wynton's story as below of Hoge Kirkpatrick of Nyddesdale:-

Hoge (Roger) Kirkpatrick held all Nithsdale to Scottish Allegiance from the time when the Castle of Dalswinton was taken and razed to the ground. After that, he took Caerlaverock. Later in the same year Hoge Kirkpatrick was slain by Jakkis James Lindsay in Caerlaverock etc. etc. Dr. Mackenzie remarks "The use of Hoge instead of the full Roger is interesting. It means he caught the popular imagination".

There is no evidence at all that Roger Kirkpatrick of Torthorwald, a sheriff of Dumfries, had anything to do with the Niddesdale Caerlaverock operations, or that he had his throat cut there, (a pure guess). Moreover it was Sir Roger Kirkpatrick of Nyddesdale and Caerlaverock who sat in Parliament of 1357 negotiating regarding the ransom of David II. Later, Sir Roger was special delegate to England.

His young son Umfray was handed over to the English as hostage. This hostage could not possibly have been Humphrey Kirkpatrick of Torthorwald of 1321, for Rymer specifically states that the hostages handed over in 1357 were twenty youths of quality. This man was certainly not a youth, and if he really was the son of Auchencas as we are told he was, he could have had no "status" at all; - son of a treacherous murder, so 'twas said. I think it was our Sir Roger's crest that was a wolf's head on a helmet. He is not to be confused with Roger "Mak siccar", as previously explained.

So now we have the two sons of mak sicker fixed. Thomas the elder and heir, by Nisbet's evidence and charter - Roger of Nyddesdale and Caerlaverock by Wynton and Bower. In the oldest family chart, which appears to have been drawn out prior to 1720, Roger mak sicker and Duncan, who married Isobel daughter of Sir David Torthorwald, are shown as sons of Stephen (1278).

So what of Mak siccar? Firstly, a strong tradition. "The Rev. M. Black in his history of Penpont wrote, about 1647, that after Greyfriars, it was said that Roger Kirkpatrick of Closeburn hid the Bruce in the thick woods at Cairney Croft near Closeburn and in a poor man's cottage called Brownrigg, who thereafter got a grant of pasturage from the King. Place names nearby such as King's Well - Bruce's Well - King's Quarry - Rob's Corse - Kingsland Burn, are quoted as lending weight to this tradition.

In February 1307 when Bruce lands in Carrick with a few knights and 180 followers, McDowell mentions in History of Dumfries that Kirkpatrick of Closeburn was one of them. I explain this in my history - Lanercrost Chronicles give the clue to this McDowell tradition.

After Bannockburn, Sir Roger Kirkpatrick, then knighted, was sent by the King as one of four Commissioners to treat for peace with Edward II at Berwick. That is Scottish history. The safe conducts for passage of these knights written in old French are given by Rymer and are quoted in my history dated 18th September 1314. At this time Sir Roger of Auchencas, sitting in Bruce's Castle at Lochmaben in English pay, packed up and made his "get away" as fast as he could - so well, that he disappeared from view for some 20 years. Again in 1320 Sir Roger of Closeburn was employed on a similar mission, and the safe conducts for that are again given in old French by Rymer.

You may gather that it was not only because of the fire of Closeburn in 1748, that I take its early history from public records, which incidentally gain support from Charles K. Sharpe's lithograph charters. So I now want to speak about these. First, about the original charter.

We have a small piece of moorland still in my family of the old Barony called Thriepmuir. In 1773 Charles Duke of Queensberry laid claim to it. My great grandfather Sir James the 4th Baronet, contested this claim which was settled by arbitration before Mr. James Ewart of Mullock. It is written that it was believed that Thriepmuir was very particularly described in some of the old charters of Closeburn which it would therefore be desirable to see. The original charter was produced. I have an extract of the decreet arbitrae, signed on every page by the then sheriff clerk of Dumfries, James Dickson.

The case was settled in favour of my great grandfather 4th Baronet, on 24th July 1773. Mr. James Ewart's judgement being "that having heard all evidences, together with a plan or eyesketch of said Thriepmuir and charter granted by King Alexander II upon the 15th day of August and 18th year of his reign 1232 he declared that the Duke of Queensberry "had no right or interest in the said Thriepmuir".

Grose in 1797 testified that this charter was in Sir James' possession. Charles K. Sharpe saw it in the hands of Sir Thomas 5th Baronet, and made his lithographed copy from it.

I've brought you here a photograph of the 1232 lithograph which we have. The seal of Alexander II is very clear, seen to show the front and also the reverse of the seal. A portion of the seal must have been missing, but sufficient is there to recognise it as that illustrated in Seton's Scottish Heraldry as one of the earliest Scottish Royal Seals. This charter is recorded in Register House. On the left the front of the seal portrays the King on horseback with sword drawn and shield. On the right the King is seated on his throne with the orb in his hand.

I have another copy of the charter, a photograph, where the single medallion seal shows the front of the seal only as depicted in the journal. The seal is a black blot in which the figure of Alexander II can be traced only by one who knows the charter I have here, or has seen the original of this photograph.

It seems to me extraordinary that the writer of this article has omitted all reference to the photograph of the charter he prints, and does not explain where he got it from, or the blot of black on the seal. I'll explain that Yellow and Brown colour of seals do not easily photograph without special precautions, as a photographic plate is not sensitive to those colours, and the result is it comes out black. I've had a similar

218

experience with another charter I had photographed.

I have two important comments to make regarding a paper which I heard read here last year entitled "Who was mak siccar". An account of it was published in the Dumfries and Galloway Standard on 16th May 1952. My first comment is this - Charles K. Sharpe wrote as follows about the Greyfriars incident. In two volumes of his published personal corespondence, he stated "The fixing of the stab upon Closeburn is merely through tradition, authorized strongly by the crest and motto of the family;" "unanimous tradition gives Roger of Closeburn the honour of stabbing a half dead regent".

Elsewhere in acknowedgement of a gift of a Comyn relic for his museum, Sharpe replied:- "it interests me the more that I have the shame of being descended from father to son from that bloody minded person who finished off the work which King Robert had bungled!" That shows that Sharpe wrote of what he sincerely believed - expressed in his usual sardonic language.

My second comment is that Charles Kirkpatrick Sharpe was most unjustly, one might almost say unthinkingly pilloried in that paper. You will read that he is accused of producing a coat of arms unrecorded and unknown to the Lyon's office with no less than 16 quarterings to accompany the chart he sent to his kinsman William Kirkpatrick of Malaga, when the latter's daughter, the mother of the Empress Eugenie, was to marry the Conte de Teba and Montijo.

This preposterous story of 16 quarterings is only a repetition of a joke circulating in the Edinburgh clubs in Sharpe's time. Antiquarian Notes of 1898-99 when referring to it, added this contradiction, (which I notice is omitted in this paper!) "We learn on authority, that Mr. Sharpe's relatives have never heard of his doing this, nor do any of his papers now existing support this tale. What he did do, was to send a pedigree showing the Spanish Kirkpatricks descent from the main stem".

All that he had to do was to walk round to the Lyon King's office and get a copy certified of the Conheaths patent of arms of the 16th May 1791. That is neither unrecorded nor unknown. I have a certified copy of that patent here now, extracted from the public register of arms in 1902, signed by Sir Francis Grant, then Keeper of the Records; and I had a copy sent me by the present Lyon King. Signs armorial are shown thereon, and they are those of a cadet of the line of Closeburn.

The foundation for this charter was the very clear evidence of Dr. Clapperton in 1784. This has the sasine entries of the two counties of that time to support it. Also other evidence written then; not the least being a note by my great grandfather which to me indeed seems conclusive. I can have no doubt of the accuracy of this carefully worded patent, nor in my opinion could Charles Kirkpatrick Sharpe have doubted this when he examined it.

William of Malaga in writing to him in 1817 no doubt mentioned that Sharpe should find his own eldest brother John of Conheath's patent of arms, (taken out many years before, to show his connection with Closeburn), in the Lyon's office. I must ask you now to remember that in 1784 Charles Kirkpatrick Sharpe was 3 years old and in 1791, ten years old. At that age, he could neither have fabricated, nor forged this evidence, which I have cheched by sasine records. This point is so important just now, that I have put the dates and ages on the board for you to see.

Our early history is well established by monastic records. The first witness on Ivone's 1232 charter was William de Bondington Bishop of Glasgow. That very year, Ivone bestowed upon the Kelso abbacy, the ancient chapel of Kilosbern, traditionally connected with the early Christian churches of St. Patrick. This grant was confirmed by the Bishop of Glasgow, and is recorded in Kelso chartulary (No. 278).

Ivone's son Adam and grandson Stephen are both recorded in Kelso chartulary No. 342; and Fraser missed it all! I've no time to tell you more about this, but you will find full details in Ramage.

I must again quote Nisbet about this Stephen. He wrote, "Stephen Kirkpatrick is the ancestor of a very ancient family, the Kirkpatricks of Closeburn in Nithsdale. They have very good vouchers for their antiquity. There is an exact and complete series of this family from this time down to Sir Thomas Kirkpatrick of Closeburn Baronet". (and I have got this pedigree as Charles Kirkpatrick Sharpe wrote it, nearly 100 years after Nisbet, with a very few minor changes).

Stephen's two sons according to our history and Dr. Clapperton's excellent treatise, written in 1784, were Roger Mak sicker and Duncan, who married Isabel daughter and heiress of David Torthorwald, thus obtaining the lands of Torthorwald.

Records about Sir Wm. Wallace are very scanty, but Henry the minstrel, wrote of the traditions, the folk lore and the fighting of those times in his Books of Wallace. In them, the deads of Sir John Graham and Kirkpatrick the Lord of Torthorwald are very fully extolled - Kirkpatrick, frequently mentioned, is referred to as the "cusin dear" of Wallace, and his relationship to Sir Reginald Crawford whose daughter was the mother of Wallace, is indicated. This book (quoted here on page 45), should be compared with McDowell pages 60, 61.

"Henry the minstrel" was no historian, but as McDowell writes in his history, Wynton, Fordun, Heminburgh and Henry the minstrel, (the latter not always to be implicitly trusted), are the chief authorities relied upon by modern writers, for these early incidents in Wallace's career, and Kirkpatrick's work was "nobil fer to ken". Sir David Torthorwald is recorded as being paid fees by the Chamberlain of Scotland in 1287. "Blind Harry's" stories of Wallace are airily dismissed in the journal as pure nonsense!

Dr. Clapperton, an antiquarian of Lochmaben, who is reported to have had access to many charter chests, especially that of the Carliels of Torthorwald, wrote in his Anecdotes of the Kirkpatricks in 1784. Duncan, brother to Roger and son to Stephen Kirkpatrick of Closeburn, married Isabel, daughter and heiress of Sir David Torthorwald, who is seen as witness to a donation of money in the records of the Chartulary of Abbeyholm about 1289".

"Upon Duncan and his spouse Isabel's resignation, King Robert Bruce grants them a charter of the lands of Torthorwald dated 10th August. Their son Umfrey gets another charter of the same lands from the same King, dated 16th July, the 16th of his reign, which was in the year 1322, vide writs of Carliel. The first charter is not recorded. Probably lost with many others of the old Scottish records. Of this distant period there can be no certainty, but a vividly told account of how and where this Lord of Torthorwald assisted Wallace in battle remains as a tradition, to be read in the Books of Wallace, which I quote in my book.

You can see in the Journal of 1925-26 how the idea of a so-called extinct senior branch of Kirkpatricks arose from the writings of Fraser and Bain.

It is to be realized that Fraser, imagininng that a single original Ivo, without a surname or date came with Bruce from Yorkshire, determined to locate him in Kirkpatrick Juxta, without any evidence whatsoever, charter or otherwise to show this. A much more probable place was Kirkpatrick

Fleming, where a man by the name Ivo de Kirkpatrick in those days got a grant of land near by, at Pennersax. And when the crumbled ruins of Auchencas were excavated in 1924, there was no evidence found there either to determine who were its earliest inhabitants.

So, you can read in the journal of that date that, until the 15th century, history is, with one solitary exception, silent about Auchencas castle, in the parish of Kirkpatrick Juxta. The solitary exception was that a Sir Roger Kirkpatrick of Auchencas, one day on December, 1306, borrowed money from the English governor of Annandale according to Bain, at Lochmaben.

It was written "This sole surviving reference, (to Auchencas), raises at once the interesting question of the origin of the Kirkpatrick family" - because of course, Fraser had previously swept the board clean of Closeburn Kirkpatricks with their claims to antiquity.

Thus the story developed that it was certain the first Ivo, an Anglo Norman knight, could not have built Auchencas, but, if a guess might be hazared Sir Humphrey de Kirkpatrick built it; and his descendent who lived there in 1306, Sir Roger Kirkpatrick, gave the final stab to the Comyn. This man was said to have been in English pay in September 1305, and a favourite with Edward I.

Was it likely that he would kill a nominee of Edward's for the Scottish throne? - and, now we are told this Roger can no longer be identified as the assassin of Comyn, and it is suggested that his son, also by name Roger, conveniently knighted, killed Comyn.

There are thus two contradictory stories. In the 1925 account Sir Roger of Auchencas was said to be a young man as the dead implies, and alive in 1357. He was in garrison at Lochmaben in 1313 in English pay (Bain quoted). Thereafter Sir Roger and his wife, together with Humphrey Kirkpatrick of Torthorwald said to be his son, and his wife fled to England in 1332 (Bain quoted).

Today the story is that Sir Roger, an aged man in 1313, was too old to murder anyone in 1306, but that his son, Roger this time, disregarding the cautioning of his old father, must be suspected of the crime.

Today it is said that after 1313 nothing more was ever heard of this Sir Roger. He did not fly to England. Humphrey, son by the first story, with Roger, son by the second story, fled together in 1332. The assumption is then made that both of these were released and took up residence in Torthorwald, although by English records nothing further was ever heard of the fugitives.

What proof is there that these were his sons? There must not be confused with two brothers Humphrey and Roger Kirkpatrick who by charter, are seen to have lived in 1218, 100 years before. These it was written, may have been sons of "Ivo", when the apt remark was made, "too often paternity must be assumed". My remark is too many and too often assumptions have been made about by family in this journal; and assertions.

What proof is there that Auchencas in N.W. Annandale and had any connection with Torthorwald, or indeed that Ivo had a relation with either? How is Humphrey of Torthorwald shown to be the son Annandale, of Auchencas?

I have already shown that this Humphrey 1321 could not possibly have been one of the youths who Rymer states had to be delivered to the English in 1357, and who was the son and heir of Sir Roger Kirkpatrick the plenipotentiary who sat in Parliament to determine the fate of these hostages, their sons and heirs, in September 1357.

Why should Bruce have rewarded this Humphrey for his father's services as suggested? What had his father done? He had not even killed the dying Comyn! He had held Lochmaben Castle in English pay against Bruce.

A Sir Roger Kirkpatrick of Auchencas and Humphrey Kirkpatrick no doubt did fly to England in 1332, when war broke out afresh. Those who had interests in England did so; like the Carlyles and Comyns - and moreover some fought against their own brother Scots. Stories built up on one reference to Auchencas carry no conviction.

The tale ends "The story presents the historian with some difficulties." It does! But the story as told by Closeburn does not. There is good reason to think that Humphrey Kirkpatrick of 1321 got the lands of Torthorwald for the services his father Duncan Lord of Torthorwald rendered to Sir William Wallace in 1297 and that Stephen and Thomas Kirkpatrick of Closeburn got their reward at the same time from Robert the Bruce for services rendered to him in the war of Independance, as listed in Robert I's recorded charters.

Now as regards our traditional origins. Theological authorities and most antiquarians agree that the name Kirkpatrick or Kilpatrick was originally a place name, associated with the various early Celtic churches founded in the 5th century by St. Patrick in the south of Scotland, from the Clyde to the Solway firth. The celtic "Kil" first meant a missioner's cell, then a chapel, increasing later to a small community; and the term Cella Patricii was applied to the religious communities thus formed by St. Patrick. So we have Kil-osbern. Cosmo Innes quotes a very early charter which was signed by the abbots of Melrose, Kelso and Osbert. The Gaelic Gil or Gillie meaning servant came to be used for the missioner or priest, especially in Galloway - Gilpatrick.

The Kil was said to have begun to change to Kirk sometime after the 8th or 9th centuries, when the original church of St. Ninian because subordinate to York and English officials. The derivation of Kirk is from the Greek Kyriakon meaning "of the lord" - "The Lord's" (Kirk) - of St. Patrick. It was the Scots-Irish immigration through Galloway which established itself on the left bank of the Nith after the Romans left, as mentioned in McDowell's History of Dumfries, that leads us also to believe that the family origin was there. Tradition says that the ancestor of the Barons of Closeburn possessed land in Nithsdale in the year 800, but the first of the principal family as styled by Nisbet, was Ivone Kirkpatrick, who lived before 1141.

Buchanan is quoted as stating that Malcolm III, soon after his accession in 1056, ordained at a Parliament in Forfar that the Scots should follow the custom of other nations, and take their names from their lands. Fraser, obsessed with his Annandale records, writes of one original Ivo, who got the fishing rights of Blawode. This charter shows neither surname nor date. Fraser surmised Ivo lived about 1190. "All the Kirkpatrick" he said "claimed this Ivo as their ancestor", which is quite incorrect.

Fraser wrote "Ivo", but the Latin text of this charter given in his own Commission Report, spells this name Iuoni. Nevertheless, this Ivo became Ivo de Kirkpatrick, who got a grant in Pennersax, not Kirkpatrick Juxta. As I will show later, the prefix 'de' to the surname was used by the nobility then, whether of Anglo Norman extraction or not.

It was next stated that Ivo must have got a part of Kirkpatrick Juxta given him. No proof of this, or charter is shown, nor is a place mentioned, to support this statement. This was Fraser's big error, and it has caused much trouble. It was stated that the family thereafter was known as Kirkpatrick of Kirkpatrick, or "of that ilk". I don't believe that for a moment; especially as the statistical account of Dumfriesshire shows that Kirkpatrick Juxta, was, in old days, called "Kilpatrick". Does "of that ilk"anywhere appear in a Latin charter?

So we find 'de Kirkpatricks' labelled "of that ilk", and "of Kirkpatrick", who did not belong to Kirkpatrick Juxta at all, and much confusion has been caused thereby. It helped to create the story of Auchencas. Our first Closeburn charter shows an Ivon or Yvon as living before 1141, the first record of our family on paper. He appears as a witness to a charter of Robert Brus the elder or first Lord of Annandale and his wife Eufemia, heiress of Annan, granted the fishings of Torduff to the monks of Abbeyholm.

This charter, given in Latin, as quoted in my book, was extracted from the Register of Holmcultram Abbey by Dr. Clapperton. It is also referred to by Ramage. But it is not mentioned by Fraser. This Ivon has neither surname nor date, but this Robert Brus died in 1141. These grants of fishing rights on the Solway to Ivone which have no surname date of place of residence attached to them, do not seem to me anything one can dogmatise about. They verge upon the traditional. There were at least four Kirkpatrick, or Kilpatrick communities in Dumfriesshire alone at that time.

Now about the Kirkpatrick seals. Many early documents were burnt in the fire so there are few seals. I take exception to the way these seals have been presented in the journal. So much is omitted, which should have been explained.

The first two are Annandale seals. The one with three shields, attributed to Sir Roger Kirkpatrick, is ahown in Bain and elsewhere as that of Sir Roger Kirkpatrick of Auchencas. The second is that of John Kirkpatrick of Torfinnan. Both of these men fought for the English at Falkirk. They had nothing to do with Closeburn.

I next find it written that "To a document dated 26th September 1357, the seal of Sir Roger de Kirkpatrick "of that ilk" is appended". This mysterious document can be none other than the record quoted by Rymer of the proceedings of Parliament which met in Edinburgh on that date, to confirm the terms of ransom for the release of David II. Rymer gives the names of those signing and affixing seals, here are some of their names:- Listen carefully to them. Jacobus de Lindsay, David de Graeme, Johannes de Maxwell, Rogerus de Kirkpatrick, Patricii de Ramsay -"Milites - Knights". No, "of that ilk" there! but all good Scottish knights, with the prefix 'de' to their surnames and after their christian names, as was the custom then.

This Roger cannot be thus made into a resident of Kirkpatrick Juxta! He was Sir Roger Kirkpatrick of Nyddesdale and Caerlaverock those crest must have been the wolf's head of 1357, for it was his young son who was the hostage. Later Sir Rogerus de Kirkpatrick, "Domicellus" appears, in the Latin, as appointed to see that the terms of the treaty were observed. Dated 26th October, 1357. "Domicellus" signifies the son of a baron. (which we know he was). Ref. Lord - Wilkins L.L. Anglo Sax. P. 208.

I've told you about the coat of arms of 1435, where that Roger of Closeburn was clearly identified by Lord Somerville and Nisbet. Now, about the seal with a difference. Had the contents of this charter been disclosed even in outline, you would have realized why there was a difference. It was not for the reason suggested, I'm sure.

'Charter to Padzane' does not explain the contents, where at great length, the charter relates that owing to the wrongful alienation of certain Closeburn lands without the licence or concent of the King or his predecessors, these lands had been temporarily taken over by the Crown in James IV's time, (between 1488 and 1513, Flodden). Because of this, much readjustment of former writs became necessary. It appears that during that period and early in 16th century, during the wardship of a minor, Thomas by name, (not Henry), a dishonest guardian John Kirkpatrick of Alisland and a Henry Kirkpatrick, who had a long life of undetected crime, obtained illegal possession of Closeburn lands.

They were twice proceeded against by the Crown, but escaped punishment, despite protest by the Bishop of Glasgow. Padzane was a very minor victim of the fraud. You can read a partial account of this on pages 86 to 88 of this journal. The charter reveals that the lands of Auchenleck and Newton pertained to the father of the Sir Thomas Kirkpatrick of Closeburn referred to, prior to 1488, (as indeed they did, according to the charter of 1424, copy of which we have); and this takes us back nearly to 1409, when you will remember there was no break in legal succession. A charter of Robertmure during the minority, which we have bears on this matter too.

Things were not straightened out till 1585, when an

"Inquisition" was held at Dumfries. Fifteen leading gentlemen of the Country, empanelled under the Deputy Sheriff, declared, on oath, that Thomas Kirkpatrick of Closeburn of 1585 was the lawful and nearest heir of his great grandfather Sir Thomas Kirkpatrick who died in 1502. That is a most important document as proving the unbroken legal succession of Closeburn over that century, its continuity with the past, despite the Seal which has a difference. I reject the imputation given on page 109 of the journal. In Sir Thom. Kirkpatrick of Closeburn's Ayr Charter of 1409, David Kirkpatrick, as his cousin German, appears last on the Tailzie of Succession. He did not succeed to Closeburn.

I prefer the family pedigree as determined by these fifteen gentlemen, to anyone given me by any later historian. How can anyone in 1953 presume to determine close family relationships over far distant centuries?

In 1545, the cheif of Closeburn could muster 400 men, Kirkmichael Kirkpatrick 220 and the Ross Kirkpatrick 165 men, and, of these, I count at least one in ten as being either a Thomas or a Roger Kirkpatrick. Many eldest sons of Closeburn were called Thomas. The 5th Bt., the Sheriff, was the 12th Thomas in 22 names. But no record anywhere has ever put six Thomas's in succession from Stephen, as given in this journal.

So, I find this suppositious pedigree does not bear examination. It contains obvious and fundamental inaccuracies, only some of which I have hadtime to point out.

You have I hope noticed that I have quoted the Closeburn story from old established authorities. First from Wynton, who became Prior of Inchcolm about 1395, which would give him a birth date between 1340-1365. His Chronicle stops at 1406. My authority is at variance with the date given in the journal, 1420-1424.

Walter Bower was born in 1385, died 1449. Maurice Buchanan was 15th century. Nisbet 1722. Rymer, recorder of official documents. Ridpath, Lord Hailes, and, in more modern times, Dr. Agnes Muir Mackenzie and Sir Francis Grant who verified the Closeburn history before he published it and had access to family records. Early authorities are not quoted nor proofs given to support many of the assumptions regarding the Early Kirkpatricks made in the journal.

References are made to the opinions of Bain and Fraser, very

227

modern writers; and there, Closeburn history is dismissed in a few inaccurate words. My book will show a much fuller account of our story, and the pedigree of the family I have here, extracted from Charles Kirkpatrick Sharp's text of 1811 and completed to date, will go into the book to support the history. It is a story of service to King and country, through the centuries - of bold knights and fair ladies; and I am here tonight to testify to the honour of my ancestors, and to support the traditions that I find existed in this county, of the Kirkpatricks of Closeburn.

Index

A

Abbeyholm 21, 37, 47, 221, 225
Ahenskew 189, 190
Aldgirth 85
Alisland 14, 87, 90, 92-95, 133, 135, 145, 146, 163-166, 179, 226
Alva 14, 135
Annan 20, 22, 25, 37, 90, 119, 123, 225
Annandale 9, 17, 19, 20, 22, 24, 25, 37-39, 41, 54, 60, 67, 73, 80, 90-92, 99, 121, 125, 126, 143, 146, 163, 201, 210-213, 222-225
Annisfield 83, 96
Apine 99, 146
Applegirth 92
Areeming 184, 188, 194
Arkland 184, 188, 194
Auchencairn 53
Auchencas 31, 121, 126, 206, 212, 217, 222, 223, 225
Auchengeith 53
Auchinleck 39, 88, 93, 165
Ayr 14, 49, 62, 77, 99, 100, 144, 174, 203, 227

B

Bangaston 181
Bannockburn 5, 47, 55, 59, 77, 124, 144, 217
Bengal 197
Blackcleugh 173, 174, 177, 178
Blawode 26, 37, 224
Bridburgh 13, 14, 41, 59, 60, 62, 63, 67, 75, 82, 85, 93, 94, 117, 144, 203, 210, 211, 214
Brussels 169, 191
Burn[s]wark 82, 144, 165, 193

C

Caerlaverock 5, 62, 64, 67, 69-72, 144, 174, 189, 190, 194, 210-212,
    216, 217, 226
Capenoch 31, 108, 109, 114, 134, 136, 137, 138, 140, 147
Carco 85
Carrick 38, 43, 53, 54, 161, 217
Castlemilk 49, 94, 120
Clackmannan 43
Clanry 88
Clarilaw 21
Cleveland 39
Cokpule 85
Combquinton 117
Conheath 7, 12, 40, 149, 152, 163, 166, 169-195, 212, 213
Craigdarrock 133
Craigmillar 80, 214
Craigshield 181, 189
Craigshields 173, 176, 177, 185, 187, 190, 193
Crogo 85
Culloch 170, 178, 181, 184, 191

D

Dalcrum 173, 177
Dalgarnock 21, 24, 75, 78, 91, 93, 95, 113, 129, 211
Dalgonar 91, 140
Dalswinton 62, 144, 216
Denmylne 159, 207
Dolphinton 140
Dornock 49
Douglas 16, 42, 48, 55, 73, 76-84, 91, 94, 96, 107, 114, 126, 131, 135,
    137, 144, 146, 165, 184, 193, 211
Drooge Vlei 11
Drum 14, 166, 214
Drumlanrig 26, 29, 38, 42, 48, 63, 65, 77, 78, 94, 95, 99, 100, 115,
    119, 126, 146, 163, 167, 173, 210, 211

Drumm 159
Dryff 47
Dumbarton 19
Dumfries 17, 26-29, 42, 43, 49, 52-55, 57, 59, 60, 64, 70-72, 83-86
88-92, 96, 99-102, 106, 111, 113, 115, 116, 121, 126, 127, 131,
134, 135, 138-141, 144-147, 163, 164, 166, 170, 174, 175, 177,
178, 179, 181, 186, 188, 189, 193-195, 205, 209, 212, 214,
216-219, 224, 227
Dundreth 117
Dunskellie 94
Dupplin 47, 144
Durrisdeer 62, 67, 144

E

Edinburgh 15, 27, 35, 39, 60, 69, 71, 76, 80, 82-84, 86, 88, 90-92,
94, 108, 111, 129, 140, 149, 150, 152, 184, 185, 188, 192, 197,
214, 215, 219, 225
Eglinton 14
Eister 37
Elieston 99

F

Falkirk 17, 30, 225
Finlayston 82
Flodden 84, 226
Forfar 21, 224
France 6, 12, 95, 135, 154, 169, 172, 187
Friermynnyn 88

G

Galloway 6, 19, 20, 24, 38, 43, 47, 51, 55, 94, 143, 194, 202, 205,
219, 224
Garley 88
Garrel 163, 189, 190, 195
Garrell 119, 173, 174, 176, 177, 193, 195

Gartsherrie 115, 137
Garvillgill 118
Gillipatrick 20
Glenae 173, 177
Glencairne 92, 93, 105, 131
Glencorse 53
Gleneagles 92, 93, 145
Glengarrock 39
Glengip 118
Glenkiln 173, 174, 177-179, 181, 185, 187, 189, 190, 193-195
Gospatrick 20
Guisborn 22, 201

H

Halidayhill 85
Harlwood 88
Hoddam, Hoddom 14, 135, 147, 212
Holehouse 177
Holmcultram 25, 37, 47, 225
Honfleur 170, 187, 189
Hyderabad 198, 199

IJ

Isle of Wight 12
Jerusalem 78

K

Kelso 14, 21, 23, 41, 43, 95, 143, 203, 220, 224
Kelsoburn 21
Kelton 166, 171, 179, 181, 185, 188, 189, 194
Kenton 101, 102
Kenya 11
Kilkenny 11
Kilpatrick 19, 20, 24, 73, 224, 225
Kinmount 49, 122
Kirkcudbright 134, 178, 181, 184, 188, 191, 194

Kirkmichael 24, 39, 80, 83, 90, 91, 92, 98, 119, 144, 163, 165, 166,
        173, 177, 179, 190, 193, 195, 196, 227
Knock 163, 166, 173,-196

L

Lag 84, 85, 87, 90-92, 94, 100, 121
Lagganlees 133, 149
Lamington 99, 146
Lammerton 14
Lamphite 173, 177
Lennox 14, 40, 43, 55
Liberie 85, 164
Lincleuden 85
Lochmaben 28, 45, 52, 59, 60, 82, 145, 185, 214, 217, 221-223
Lockleven 68
London 17, 48, 69, 118, 152, 185, 187, 188, 190, 194
Longueville 52

M

Malaga 171, 172, 174, 178, 186-188, 191, 194, 219, 220
Mar 14, 94, 135, 145, 146
Melrose 23, 79, 164, 165, 224
Middlebie 38, 78
Montijo 12, 169, 171, 172, 191, 192, 194, 219
Morton 20, 93
Mosskesson 47
Mount 129, 157, 207
Muckleknox 96
Mullock 29, 218
Murdiston 133

N

Nepaul 197
Newcastle 68, 69, 72, 124

Newerk 82
Newtoun 85, 88, 89
Nith 20, 41, 48, 211, 224
Nithbank 166, 170, 178, 179, 187, 189
Nithsdale 9, 14, 19, 20, 24, 26, 37- 42, 54, 62, 67, 68, 71, 78, 90, 92,
    94, 99, 124, 131, 134, 146, 163, 165, 201, 208, 210, 211, 213,
    216, 220, 224

O

Ostend 171, 176, 178, 181, 184, 186, 191, 194
Otterburn 121

P

Palestine 78
Pennersax 75, 77, 78, 91, 124, 203, 222, 224
Pennirsax 38, 54, 77, 78
Penpont 23, 53, 73, 76, 134, 217
Pleughlands 177
Poldovy 39
Poldunelarg 39
Polidivan 39
Potuisse 39
Punjab 150, 151

R

Raploch 133
Redkirk 19
Riddingwod 85
Roinnpatrick 19
Ross 5, 13, 28, 47-49, 63, 90, 107, 117-120, 125, 126, 144, 161, 163,
    173, 185, 206, 227

S

Sanquhar, [Sanchar, Sanquahr] 20, 42, 86, 88, 94, 163
Sauchieburn 84
Schawis 88

234

Solway 19, 25, 84, 87, 89, 145, 165, 190, 224, 225
South Africa 11
Spangok 88
Speddek 85
St. Cross 12
Stanehous 85
Stirling 84, 94, 100, 109, 115, 134, 152
Stroquham 11
Sumatra 197
Sundrum 82

T

Tarscreechan 184, 191
Teba 12, 78, 79, 170, 171, 174, 186, 219
Templands 41
Terregles 94
Thorbeck 38
Thornynhat 186
Thriepmuir 29, 31, 106, 114, 137-139, 218
Tilliquhillo, 96
Torduff 20, 25, 37, 143, 211, 225
Torkatrine 178, 184, 191
Torphichan 146
Tortherwald 24
Tourraine 77
Trochquhane 84, 85
Troghrig 85

W

Wamphray 117, 118
Whithorn 19, 24
Wigtown 51, 96
Williambie 38

CPSIA information can be obtained at www.ICGtesting.com
Printed in the USA
LVOW10*2041270515

440114LV00014B/477/P